D0934380

ARMS OF LITTLE VALUE

ARMS OF LITTLE VALUE

The Challenge of Insurgency and Global Instability in the Twenty-First Century

G.L. LAMBORN

CASEMATE
Philadelphia & Oxford

All statements of fact, opinion, or analysis expressed are those of the author and do not reflect the official positions or views of the CIA or any other U.S. Government agency. Nothing in the contents should be construed as asserting or implying U.S. Government authentication of information or Agency endorsement of the author's views. The material has been reviewed by the CIA to prevent the disclosure of classified information.

Published in the United States of America and Great Britain in 2012 by
CASEMATE PUBLISHERS
908 Darby Road, Havertown, PA 19083
and
10 Hythe Bridge Street, Oxford, OX1 2EW

ISBN 978-1-61200-104-3
Digital Edition: ISBN 978-1-61200-116-6

Cataloging-in-publication data is available from the Library of Congress and the British Library.

10 9 8 7 6 5 4 3 2 1

Printed and bound in the United States of America.

For a complete list of Casemate titles please contact:

CASEMATE PUBLISHERS (US)
Telephone (610) 853-9131, Fax (610) 853-9146
E-mail: casemate@casematepublishing.com

CASEMATE PUBLISHERS (UK)
Telephone (01865) 241249, Fax (01865) 794449
E-mail: casemate-uk@casematepublishing.co.uk

CONTENTS

ACKNOWLEDGMENTS

The author wishes to offer his grateful thanks to the following individuals for their help, expert advice, encouragement, and professional fellowship over the years. Several of these individuals offered timely, insightful comments on this work while it was still in draft. All contributed over the years to the author's understanding of insurgency and political warfare, and the vital connection between our forces overseas and our policy community here in Washington, D.C.

Doctor John J. LeBeau, George C. Marshall Center; Dr. Arturo G. Munoz, RAND Corporation; Col. Grant Newsham, USMC; Dr. John Nagl, Center for a New American Security; Dr. David Kilcullen, CAERUS; Dr. Marvin Weinbaum, Middle East Institute; Dr. T.X. Hammes, National Defense University; and Dr. Michael Shurkin, RAND Corporation.

Thanks also go to Ron Hammond, RA International Corporation; Col. Jeff Haynes, USMC (Ret.), Global-21 Strategic Solutions; Maj. David M. Lamborn, United States Army; Capt. Matt Pottinger, USMC, Council on Foreign Relations; Ms. Aurora D'Amico, U.S. Department of Education; and Wallace G. Klein, World War II veteran and my honored former teacher.

Special thanks also are due to Ms. Cassandra Sheehan for her tireless help with the text, especially with regard to the charts, footnotes and bibliography, to E.J. McCarthy, the author's agent, who kept the author's spirits up when he had almost thrown in the towel, and to Mr. Richard Kane of Casemate Publishers, who graciously accepted this work, did a superlative job editing the text, and creatively challenged the author at every stage. Author also wishes to thank many others who, though not named, at various times in the author's past have been of assistance. All are deeply appreciated.

The observations and opinions in this work are solely those of the author and do not represent the views of any U.S. Government department or agency, nor any private corporation or group. The author takes full responsibility for any errors of fact.

DEDICATION

This book is dedicated to the memory of 1st Lt. Todd W. Weaver, 101st Airborne Division, a graduate of the College of William and Mary, and to all other American soldiers and marines who lost their lives in Afghanistan, Iraq, and other "low intensity" conflicts. Todd graduated summa cum laude in government from William and Mary, was inducted into Phi Beta Kappa, and graduated from that institution's senior ROTC program. On 9 September 2010, while leading his platoon in Kandahar province, Afghanistan, Todd was killed, the victim of an improvised explosive device (IED). He is mourned by his family and missed by us all.

It is also dedicated to the American policy community in the hope that our policymakers will exercise more thought and less haste when considering U.S. military involvement in politically unstable countries. As many regions become increasingly unstable, and the likelihood of violent upheaval in certain areas grows ever more likely, American policymakers will have to exercise great wisdom, restraint, and farsighted judgment before committing young Americans to battle. No American soldier, sailor, airman, or marine should have to die because the Washington policy community's political thinking was flawed or its military strategy was inappropriate to the situation.

If wisdom eventually prevails in our formulation of policy toward politically unstable lands, Todd, you and your brothers will not have died in vain.

FOREWORD

Arms of Little Value appears at an opportune moment. Retired U.S. Army Colonel Larry Lamborn's latest book serves as a very useful frame of reference for interpreting the basic shift in strategic thinking currently being implemented by the White House and the Pentagon. Afghanistan is the centerpiece of the new strategy. As has been widely publicized, conventional forces are withdrawing and the process of transition is under way calling for Afghan Security Forces to take responsibility for the conduct of the war by 2014. Although there has been much public hand-wringing about withdrawing U.S. combat forces "before the job is done," Lamborn views the situation differently, offering the following observation:

> The greater the *cultural distance* between the local population and that of an intervening force, the greater will be the strength of its rejection. It follows that forces deployed to intervene to counter an insurgency should ideally be *home-grown*, of the same culture as the people involved in the conflict. There may well be a negative reaction by the people to intervention, but it should be of less intensity if those who are assigned that task are of "the same blood and belonging." Afghan forces, when properly trained and disciplined for counterinsurgency work, should be more effective with other Afghans than are American or European soldiers.

Regarding the debate over the optimal number of troops needed for an effective "surge," Lamborn, in typical iconoclastic fashion, dismisses force ratios and population ratios as largely irrelevant: "The master insurgent, Mao Tse-tung, remarked that: 'Numbers by themselves confer no particular advantage,' " given the fundamentally political and psychological nature of insurgency.

In announcing the time frame for withdrawal of conventional forces from Afghanistan, American officials have also stated that a much smaller contingent of U.S. military trainers, advisors and special operations forces (SOF) intend to fulfill a stay-behind role, assuming an appropriate agreement is reached with the Afghan government. The SOF function usually is described as counterterrorism, focusing on door-kicking raids at night to capture or kill targeted individuals wherever they are hiding. Putting aside the controversy in Afghanistan over these commando tactics, I would argue that the complementary counterinsurgency SOF mission to organize and support the village stability operations/Afghan local police (VSO/ALP) program is more consequential.

Accepting Lamborn's contention that "insurgency stands Clausewitz on his head in that its centerpiece is the capture of the nation's people politically and psychologically," and that both insurgency and counterinsurgency should be conceived as armed politics, it is critical to involve the rural Afghan population in the campaign against the Taliban. Regardless of its shortcomings, VSO is the type of paradigm-changing initiative needed to defeat the insurgency, particularly as there is increasing concern among foreign observers and Afghans alike that the large conventional army and police that the United States and NATO have created will deteriorate once foreign funding, logistical support, and close air support have been withdrawn. As American and European politicians seek to stave off financial crises in their own countries, calling into question long-term commitments to continue pumping billions of dollars into Afghanistan, a new refrain is heard among analysts: We have built an Afghan army that Afghanistan cannot afford. Creating a counterinsurgency capability that Afghanistan could afford and sustain on its own would have been a better strategy. That path not taken is what *Arms of Little Value* is about.

In promoting his views on effective counterinsurgency, Lamborn touches on an underlying issue that transcends COIN pros and cons: how to best exercise American power abroad in a manner that is more effective and less costly in terms of treasure and blood than overreliance on outright military force. Part of the pleasure of reading *Arms of Little Value* is the irreverence with which it dismisses the conventional bureaucratic thinking of the Washington establishment on this issue. "Instead of understanding, we spout jargon. Instead of clear thinking, we employ catch phrases and acronyms. Instead of sound strategy, we act in spasms of uncoordinated activity. Instead of thoughtful policy aimed at shaping the future, we have knee-jerk reactions to the crisis of the moment." Seeking to shake readers' assumptions, Lamborn's approach may seem counterintuitive. *Arms of Little Value* seeks to promote a change in mentality, a new way of looking at the recurring problem of insurgency and counterinsurgency in disparate regions of the world where the United States has a national security interest.

At the same time, his book falls within a long-established tradition of eclectic historiography in which a broad array of social science and humanities disciplines are brought to bear in explaining historical events.

Lamborn argues that the fundamental mistake of the United States has been to deal with insurgency essentially as a military conflict, despite repeated declarations about the need to win hearts and minds:

> Acting together the U.S. Army and Marine Corps have created and published *Counterinsurgency* (FM 3-24). We have a handful of brilliant scholars such as Dr. [John] Nagl and a few others to thank for the field manual. But the existence of the FM does not by any means indicate that the army has had a Damascus Road-like doctrinal conversion. Many generals wedded to the old doctrine of firepower, massive force, and high technology still think these are the essential keys to victory in any war.

Arms of Little Value posits that "insurgency has its roots deep in the grievances of the people as a whole. It is a social war with religious, racial, class, and economic aspects." Accordingly, multiple historical examples are summarized, including the American Revolution against the British, in which a militarily superior force ultimately lost to the insurgents because it did not understand or address the grievances of the people.

I also see in *Arms of Little Value,* a connecting thread to a great tradition in world literature going back to Thucydides: the soldier-scholar. As a combat veteran of the Vietnam War and a participant in counterinsurgency campaigns in various parts of the world since then, Lamborn falls within this literary tradition. Throughout history there have been perceptive military writers who have sought to analyze and describe warfare in terms of its political, social and economic context. For example, the eye-witness account of the conquest of Mexico by Bernal Diaz del Castillo gives considerable emphasis to the religion, customs and politics of the native Indians. At every step of the way on the march to the Aztec capital, Castillo describes how Hernan Cortes debriefed local chiefs thoroughly, seeking cultural intelligence to better understand the strengths and weaknesses of the people he intended to conquer.

In contrast to that sixteenth century example of human terrain mapping, Lamborn writes:

> We may pause to ask ourselves how well we knew Vietnam, or Somalia, or Iraq, or Afghanistan before sending in our armies? Certainly we had maps and perhaps some overhead photography (for what those are worth in an insurgency), but did we have even so much as a clue about the political and cultural aspects of these lands, to say nothing of the nature of our potential enemies or the terrain, their home turf ? Or, did we merely plunge into these lands, supremely confident that our military might, technological advantages and American ingenuity were sufficient to guarantee victory?

Commenting on his own experiences in Vietnam, he adds, "Certainly those of us who became new second lieutenants in the 1960s were steeped during our cadetship in the great campaigns of Grant, Pershing, and Patton against their uniformed foes. We were given virtually no training worthy of the name in either the theory or practice of the strange kind of war we faced in Vietnam." Reflecting on that experience, Lamborn became convinced that to defeat the insurgent it is necessary to understand him and, therefore, it is necessary to understand the environment that produces him: "How, then, is it remotely possible for these pundits to discuss 'counterinsurgency' in a thoughtful manner if they cannot comprehend the highly complex roots of an insurgency they profess to be countering?"

To get at the complex roots of insurgency *Arms of Little Value* delves not only into revolutionary ideology, but also material factors such as overpopulation, birth rates, literacy rates, income disparities and unemployment, education, hunger, poor health systems and even inequitable water distribution. "Insurgencies are thought to be diseases," Lamborn writes, but "they are not. Rather, insurgencies are merely the outward manifestations of deeper illnesses." In seeking to uncover the deeper illnesses promoting insurgency, *Arms of Little Value* mirrors the approach that outstanding revolutionary leaders have taken:

> A good example of this thinking is seen in Mao's writings of the 1920s and 1930s in which he spends a great deal of time discussing political and economic conditions as opposed to strictly military tactics. As is well known, China suffered from gross inequity in land holdings, which was one of the key political problems Mao believed to be at the root of the country's ills. . . . By carefully examining each district's situation, Mao and his colleagues became more familiar with the economics and politics affecting the people living in those localities than were the appointed government officials sent out from Nanking. With Mao having greater knowledge of the land question, he was in a better position than were government officials to make political use of it.

It is important to point out that Lamborn avoids making facile correlations between poverty and insurgency, or injustice and insurgency. On the contrary, the poorest, most oppressed populations often do not revolt. It is the perception of disparity that seems to be the common denominator; with the corollary that enough people need to believe that their situation can improve through decisive action. This has been described by some theorists as the "rising tide of expectations" and helps explain why insurgencies can break out in countries where social and economic conditions are actually improving. Copious evidence exists that rapid modernization and economic growth do destabilize traditionalist societies.

Afghanistan is a current case in point. The billions of dollars that have poured into that impoverished country over the past decade through an uncoordinated array of foreign government and non-government donors have magnified income disparities, fueled corruption on an unprecedented scale and exacerbated social conflicts. Yet, going in, the assumption among U.S. military and civilian planners was the opposite, that economic development would produce stability. To strengthen the new regime, massive amounts of money were spent, whereas the approach suggested by Lamborn would have urged caution about overturning the existing system without first understanding it, or having a clear idea of what would replace it.

Although *Arms of Little Value* does not focus on the current state of the U.S. counterinsurgency campaign in Afghanistan, the lessons from the past that it provides are highly relevant. As a general principle, "the United States must never agree to work with any regime anywhere at any time that adamantly refuses to put its own house in order." The issue of reform is paramount:

> The problem that has vexed a string of U.S. administrations of both political persuasions was how to encourage certain client regimes that are battling active insurgencies to undertake serious programs of political, economic, social, and military reform. Despite heavy diplomatic pressure and huge amounts of aid, some client regimes—the former government in South Vietnam is a good example—seemed impervious to real change.

Despite the overriding need to implement long-term reforms that bring about genuine social change, "a workable system of incentives and disincentives that produce the desired changes in clients . . . has not yet been devised." This complicates addressing the central question of insurgency defined as a clear choice between the promises of the government versus those of the insurgency, and actual deeds.

At a time when concepts of nation-building and active promotion of social progress abroad again seem to have fallen into disfavor among policymakers, Lamborn argues the contrary. "We can and should be taking a greater interest in the needs of broad masses of people who . . . are now well aware of the social ills they suffer and are actively seeking means to redress their grievances." Rejecting alliances with "rapacious and despotic" local rulers, *Arms of Little Value* states that "the people and government of the United States must always be on the side of the people, not necessarily on the side of rulers . . . American policymakers would do well to promote economic and social measures aimed at slowly, but steadily raising the socioeconomic standards of people in Third World lands. The people living in these lands must know . . . that we Americans are their allies."

How to let these foreign populations know that Americans are on their side raises the issue of what has been variously defined as strategic communication, public diplomacy, information operations and psychological operations. Lamborn laments that American capabilities in that field have deteriorated badly. His closing argument is compelling:

> If the agony we experienced in Iraq and Afghanistan—due to our inability to grasp the nature and scope of those wars—has taught us nothing else, it should have taught us to pay attention to the aspirations of the local people and thereby avoid inflicting pain on ourselves and others. It should have taught us that insurgents fight on their terms, not on ours. Above all, it should have taught us to formulate a thoughtful policy and then develop an *integrated civil-military strategy* appropriate to that policy.

A final note on that comment is the quote from Cicero inspiring the book's title: "For arms are of little value in the field unless there is wise counsel at home."

Arturo G. Muñoz, Ph.D.,
RAND Corporation, Arlington, VA,
March 20, 2012

EXPLANATORY NOTE

TERMINOLOGY

In this short work, there will be three frequently used terms that, for many, often carry somewhat nebulous meanings. Before we plunge into the substance of our discussion, we first should clarify what it is we mean when we use those terms.

The three terms are *political mobilization, morale, and moral.*

Political mobilization—central to an insurgency—derives from the verb *to mobilize* which, according to the American Heritage College Dictionary means *to assemble or coordinate for a purpose* and *capable of movement.* Mao Tse-tung, a master of the art who considered political mobilization vital to success, described the process as not only explaining one's purpose and goals to the people, but linking their interests to one's political program, then organizing and motivating the people to achieve those ends.

We might then define political mobilization as the *process of organizing and motivating people to attain clearly defined goals that serve their perceived interests.*

The terms "morale" and "moral" are closely related, deriving from the same root word.

Morale—a key element of success in battle—is formally defined as being the *state of spirit as exhibited by confidence, cheerfulness, discipline, and willingness to perform assigned tasks.* By contrast, a breakdown in morale entails loss of confidence, despair, indiscipline, and unwillingness to perform assigned tasks. We may infer that inspiring leadership, clarity of purpose, and certainty of success contribute to high morale.

Moral has several dictionary meanings, among which are the usual ideas of right conduct in human interactions. However, a less frequently used dictionary definition is: *having psychological rather than physical or tangible effects.* One of Napoleon's more famous maxims is: *The moral is to the physical as three is to one.* By this Napoleon meant that while physical effects of warfare were important, what really mattered to the soldier in the field was his psychological reaction to battle. It follows that if a soldier's morale is high, his psychological state will be positive and enable him to accomplish his mission.

WIKITANIA

As the reader progresses through the text, he or she will eventually discover the Republic of Wikitania, a politically unstable state somewhere in the so-called Third World whose leadership is questionable, whose people are restive, and whose economy is vulnerable to internal and international threats. Wikitania may resemble one or another Real World countries with which the reader is familiar, but it is doubtful that the Wikitanian regime will lodge a diplomatic protest over what bad things we may say about them.

PREFACE

A year and more has passed since the tragic death in Afghanistan of U.S. Army 1st Lieutenant Todd Weaver, to whom this work is dedicated. Since the fall of 2010, when this book was written, the world has witnessed the overthrow of four authoritarian regimes (Ivory Coast, Tunisia, Egypt, Libya), the independence of South Sudan, and deepening crises in Yemen and Syria. The war in Afghanistan continues with little improvement in the administration of justice or governance in that unhappy land, and it now appears that Pakistan's internal situation is becoming critical. Many of the world's less-publicized insurgencies continue on much as before. Conditions in the *other half* have not changed for the better.

The world greeted with enthusiasm what is called "the Arab Spring," likely a journalistic reflection of "the Prague Spring" of 1968. As with the Prague Spring, which threatened the stability of Communist rule in eastern Europe a generation ago and raised so many similar hopes, we should be cautious about the Arab Spring we have just witnessed. Apart from the dismissal of an Old Guard of rulers in Cairo, Abidjan, Tripoli and Tunis, have there been any real changes in the underlying socio-economic factors that brought about these upheavals? Is the condition of the people in Egypt or Libya any different today than it was one year ago? If little has fundamentally changed in state or society, it is possible that, as in Prague a generation ago, we may at some point witness attempts by military forces or parties of zealots to restore authoritarian regimes to power. Certainly the possibility of renewed upheaval remains.

President Saleh in Yemen and Bashar Assad in Syria are now the focal points for popular uprisings, either of the snap insurrection type or more likely by means of protracted armed revolution. In both Syria and Yemen we see the possible defection to the rebels of elements of the armed forces. If this trend continues, we could see the fighting spread, just as it did in Gadhafi's Libya. And, like Gadhafi's forty-year long regime, the father and son Assad dictatorship may be in peril. Saleh, with thirty-three years in power, is vulnerable if his remaining base of support evaporates. But what then for Syria or Yemen?

Despite excellent news coverage of these important developments, one wonders how well the American public or the American policy community comprehends the changes taking place. If Americans think of foreign developments at all, they tend to the extremes of unwarranted optimism, as in the case of the Prague Spring, or total pessimism. Seldom do we reflect critically about foreign events based upon a healthy Missouri skepticism: "show me." Change is afoot, to be sure. But what is its direction and pace?

Unbearable political and social conditions around the world are growing worse, and it is highly likely that we will witness other "Springs." They may be in the Arab world, but countries in South Asia, Africa, and other regions also suffer from the social-economic conditions that foster instability. My strong suspicion is that Americans in general remain barely aware of the tumultuous events taking place in distant lands and lack both the foreign-area knowledge and political skills to deal with more Springs.

As the twenty-first century opens, the United States possesses unparalleled power: military, political, economic, cultural, and ideological. The question before the American public, its political leadership, and its civilian and military services, is how wisely that power will be used. What are our aims and our methods? Are we capable of longer-term strategic thinking or will an in-box, short-term mentality prevail? Will we use our military forces more wisely? How can America's cultural and ideological influence be put to positive use in a dynamic world? Have we the patience and knowledge needed to adjust intelligently to the changes now underway or yet to come?

G. L. Lamborn
April 2012

OVERVIEW: 

ARE WISE COUNSELS POSSIBLE IN INSURGENCIES?

For arms are of little value in the field unless there is wise counsel at home.—Cicero

The punishment of wise men who refuse to take part in the affairs of government is to live under the government of unwise men.—Plato

In the coming century the security challenge for the United States will not originate from space-based lasers or high technology weapons, but from the crowded streets and marketplaces of Africa, Asia, and Latin America. While our policymakers and military planners fix their gaze on hyper-costly, space-age technology that can be applied to advanced weaponry, the most serious near-term threat to America's people, institutions and interests comes from overtaxed and undernourished people, fetid slums, high birthrates in squalid tenements, peasants living in unimaginable poverty, and callous exploitation. It will come from unfulfilled expectations and unrealized hopes, from ignorance manipulated by cynical zealots, from decades old resentments and hatreds, and from a growing desire by many people to change the world.

Despite unprecedented wealth and power enjoyed by the world's leading countries such as the Group of Twenty,[1] the fact remains that nearly three quarters of the world's population must survive on perhaps one quar-

[1] Formerly known as the "Group of Eight," this larger group was formed in Berlin in 1999.

ter of the world's available resources. Worse than this lopsided disparity is the possibility that the gap may be widening between the rich and powerful West, and its East Asian allies, and the "Rest of the World," as some corporations and even government bureaucracies call it.

Perhaps for millions of "At the Mall" Americans who know little world geography and even less history, and who could not distinguish Brazil from Brunei on a map, the festering security problem is invisible.

After all, if you can't see something, it doesn't exist. Right?

And yet, whether these "At the Mall" Americans realize it or not, they are joined at the hip with the lives and destinies of peoples half a world away. This is because people living in Asian slums or African shantytowns may now be at the societal "breaking point." Rapidly expanding populations are overtaking limited food supplies, persistent disease is destroying families and sapping intellectual and physical capacity, illiteracy keeps people dependent on their masters and vulnerable to manipulation, and, impelled by gnawing hunger, the daily search for food keeps millions of people in fear and desperation. It should therefore come as no surprise, even to those sojourning at the Mall, that desperate people are highly susceptible to ideologies offering solutions to end their misery and degradation. Leaders who set themselves up by promising to change lives for the better will be followed. As noted by the sixteenth century Dutch scholar Erasmus: "In the land of the blind, the man with one eye is king."

Insurgency is one potent option for change in politically unstable lands. Despite much airtime and printer's ink spent discussing insurgency, the American defense establishment and the policy community still wander in the dark about what it is and how best to deal with it. Many policymakers and generals are like the legendary blind men trying to describe an elephant. Each has part of the truth, but only a part. As a whole, however, the elephant of insurgency remains a mystery. Instead of understanding, we spout jargon. Instead of clear thinking, we employ catch phrases and acronyms. Instead of sound strategy, we act in spasms of uncoordinated activity. Instead of thoughtful policy aimed at shaping the future, we have knee-jerk reactions to the crisis of the moment. We prove Swedish chan-

---

Because China and India, with their immense populations, are included in the Group of Twenty, they skew the population numbers. However, inasmuch as millions in both countries live in poverty, the fact remains that three quarters of humanity must survive on one quarter of the world's total resources.

cellor Axel Oxenstierna's words to his son in 1648: "Do you not know, my son, with how little wisdom the world is governed?"

While it is true that the ideas of a number of great strategists have been advanced to explain instability and insurgency—and some of these theories do apply in part—no Western strategic thinker has yet succeeded in defining insurgency in strategic terms. Perhaps it cannot be done. But it is counterproductive for policymakers and generals to apply the wrong strategic ideas when dealing with an insurgency. Even worse is for them to have no discernable strategy at all.

The Fashion of the Day at the Pentagon is to discuss COIN. For those of us who speak English rather than Pentagonese, this means counterinsurgency. It is instructive, however, that the great majority of writers on the subject of COIN do not understand the "IN" in COIN. How, then, is it remotely possible for these pundits to discuss "counterinsurgency" in a thoughtful manner if they cannot comprehend the highly complex roots of an insurgency they profess to be countering? Pentagon pamphlets and PowerPoint presentations proliferate on COIN. And yet, the causes and nature of insurgency *per se* are seldom mentioned.

It is also instructive that little is taught either in public schools or universities about the nature of the Third World. Yes, some excellent programs exist at a number of our top universities. But how many students enroll in programs that require study of non-European languages or Third World politics? Relatively few. For this reason, we have a very thin "bench" of foreign area experts to staff critical positions in our government and military. Neither is it disclosing a great secret that the American public as a whole is woefully ignorant of lands and peoples beyond our shores—save, perhaps, Cancun and Baja California. Moreover, when thinking of foreign affairs the American voter appears stimulated more by preconceived notions and hazy misperceptions, often fired by some politician's praise or denunciation, than by patient research and careful thought.

Many years ago, the cartoon character Pogo, lamentably now almost forgotten, stated a truth that should be taken to heart by every policymaker: *"Think ahead to put trouble behind."* How often do we as a people, and the government, which is supposedly ours to direct, take thoughtful steps to prevent or pre-empt the violence and destruction of an insurgency or revolution by helping mitigate or eliminate the causes of the upheaval?

How often have we as a people, or our representative government, come up with imaginative programs that guide otherwise vulnerable Third World regimes toward responsible government that truly is *of the people, by the people, and for the people?*

I believe that America is presently in a unique position—unique in history as well as in the present political world—to shape the future of humanity. I say that because we are still capable of influencing events in far off lands in a positive way through sober analysis and thoughtful policies. We are still in position to put ourselves on the side of the people, and not on the side of cozy protection rackets pretending to be governments. Through the ideals expressed by the Founding Fathers, we are still capable of projecting an attainable vision of a just society based on respect, governed by law, moderate in politics, unstinting in generosity, and unfailing in optimism.

What is missing in the present day is wisdom. This is not to say that it has vanished in our country. It is still there. But I am afraid that it is often in hiding. What frequently appears in wisdom's place is a clever counterfeit that promises "quick and easy solutions" that quite often prove neither quick nor easy. There is a tendency toward short-term thinking—politicians (and unfortunately the American public as well) wanting results *now*! This is like planting a seedling and expecting a sixty-foot shade tree the very next day. Instant gratification, or promises of same, is a sure indicator not of wisdom, but of its opposite. There are always people who want something for nothing. I would hope that the reader immediately sees that neither is this path based on wisdom. Then, there are the hucksters in politics, in business, and in civil society who prefer mouthing slogans that sound attractive but are empty of substance. These are the men who lead us down dark paths. As Sir Francis Bacon once remarked: "Nothing doth more hurt in a state than that cunning men pass for wise."

With this brief note as a preface, let us survey the world we live in, the nature of the deep problems our fellow beings confront on a daily basis, the reality of insurgency and its causes, how conventional strategic ideas do and do not fit the challenge, our American (un)preparedness for dealing with insurgencies, and our need for wisdom—not merely in our top elected leaders and military figures, but throughout American society.

CHAPTER 1

HOW THE OTHER HALF LIVES

The sixteenth century French literary genius Francois Rabelais observed "that it is very true which is commonly said, that the one half of the world knoweth not how the other half liveth."[1]

Although this witticism is most often repeated in jest, for the great majority of Americans, unfortunately including a surprising number of policymakers and professional military members, the statement is quite true. We really do not know the realities of daily life for virtually half of the world's population.

A WORLD OF PAINFUL CHANGE

The political world has grown increasingly complex over the past hundred years, especially following the retreat of European colonialism in the 1960s and 1970s. In bygone days, when the maps of Africa and Asia were painted in red to identify British territories, purple for French colonies, green for Portuguese, and so on, understanding the politics of the so-called Third World was fairly simple. Colonial administrations sat on top of their colonies, and no intercolonial struggles between European powers had taken place since the World War I ouster of the Germans from their colonies in Africa and Asia.[2] Capitals in Europe decided politics in the colonies.

---

[1] Rabelais, Book 1, p. 32

[2] That is, since 1918 no European invasions took place in one another's colonies, with the special and limited exception of the territories controlled by the pro-fascist Vichy French

But the departure of the Europeans from Asia and Africa in the three decades after 1945 unleashed strong internal pressures in their former colonies that had been partially or wholly suppressed until independence. Ethnic politics emerged in many areas; nationalist or Marxist politics in others; militarism in some; irredentist ambitions in yet others. "State" structures, or at least the post-colonial administrative structures, tended to bend or sag in some newly independent countries. In others, such as the Belgian Congo or the Portuguese colonies in Africa that inherited little or no indigenous political expertise, the administrative structures set up by the Europeans disappeared entirely.

Especially since the collapse of the great European empires that covered a period of thirty years following World War II, we have seen the emergence of tough military dictatorships in places like Myanmar (Burma) and Nigeria, Marxist or quasi-Marxist regimes in the successor states of French Indochina and Portuguese Africa, Islamist governments in some African and Asian lands, and a bewildering array of hybrid regimes from Marrakesh to Manila. Even the successor republics of the former Soviet Union have evolved from their authoritarian Communist roots into many shades of still authoritarian political models, each of which is in some way influenced by its distinct cultural heritage. Kyrgyzstan obviously is not Armenia, and neither resembles Moldova.[3]

---

regime during World War II. These territories were French North Africa, French West Africa, Syria, Madagascar, and French Indochina. The Anglo-German war in German East Africa [Deutsch Ostafrika] during World War I is well worth studying as an example of the difficulty of conducting conventional operations against a small, but determined irregular force led by talented officers. Paul von Lettow-Vorbeck, the brilliant German commander, was never cornered or captured by the British force of 125,000 and only agreed to an armistice on 25 November 1918 when advised that the war in Europe had ended two weeks earlier. Lettow-Vorbeck operated with no help whatsoever from Germany, with a tiny cadre of German officers and native *askari* soldiers, and used only what supplies he could find along the way or capture from his enemies.

[3] The break-up in 1991 of the Union of Soviet Socialist Republics into some fifteen independent countries—successor states—may be said to be the collapse of the final European "colonial empire." The USSR had inherited most of the territory acquired by the Tsars from the 1600s to the 1890s. Not least, all six former Soviet satrapies in eastern Europe also became independent of their former Russian masters. The People's Republic of China is something of an "empire" as it rules the non-Chinese territories of Tibet, Xinjiang (Chinese Turkestan), and Inner Mongolia, and exerts some influence over North Korea.

In addition to pent up nationalist, ethnic, or religious forces in the successor states of the European empires, since about 1970 the world has seen the emergence on three continents of significant non-state actors with political agendas. Because non-state entities do not fit the mold of modern European diplomatic practice established by the Treaty of Vienna of 1815, these groups are effectively outside conventional diplomacy. Many non-state actors have ideologies of various sorts and are motivated in some cases by visionary or transcendental beliefs. Some of these entities are transnational and seek to influence the politics of entire regions, and several such groups are highly capable of spreading their ideology across languages and cultures, thereby extending their power. Dr. John J. LeBeau, a professor at the George C. Marshall Institute, and a specialist on terrorism, observed that some insurgencies are trans-national:

> Indeed, a case can be made that a number of these insurgencies do not see themselves as discrete armed movements operating against a single nation-state or regime to right local grievances and install alternate policies, but rather as part of a broadly international, religiously-based war against those they identify as anti-Islamic. The sheer number of these Koranically-inspired groups suggests that they are likely to dominate the insurgent stage for the next several years and possibly decades.[4]

And yet, apart from daily coverage of Afghanistan and up until recently Iraq, the American public, including our professional military, is generally unaware of what major forces are shaping and reshaping the Third World. These include rapid and in some cases fundamental social change, urbanization at an accelerating pace, population growth that for many lands is exponential, mixed progress in education and economic development, soil exhaustion, the telecommunications revolution, and much else. In some regions the changes are taking place so rapidly, and with so much dislocation of long-established social and economic patterns, that it is creating serious instability.

Instability fosters social disorder and political violence. These in turn open the door to zealotry and hatred, often exploited by transnational

---

[4] LeBeau, *The Quarterly Journal*, pp. 157–158.

groups. While an insurgency may flare up and then appear to quietly peter out, we should be aware that so long as the underlying social and political conditions are unchanged, the potential for renewed violence remains. Where smoldering embers exist a fire is always possible.

Let's take a quick walk around the planet to see what's going on.

ASIA

Starting with Asia we note that the continent's two largest countries, both in terms of population and territory as well as the world's second and twelfth largest economies, respectively, are the People's Republic of China and the Republic of India.[5] Both of these countries, despite their relative prosperity, have ongoing insurgencies. The Chinese grappled with a fifteen-year ethnically based insurgency in Tibet and, although quiescent for the moment, a resurgence of separatist violence in Tibet at some point cannot be ruled out. In China's far western Xinjiang province, the Uighurs—an Islamic people of Turkic origin—have opened a low level war against Han Chinese rule, perhaps with some quiet help from their Turkic kinsmen in Central Asia.[6]

India has for years battled the Naxalites, a Marxist group operating in Bengal and other parts of northern India. A recent press report indicates that the Naxalites now operate in sixteen of India's states. India also faces continuing resistance from Kashmiri separatist groups that may receive covert backing from Pakistani elements. In addition to these internal challenges, India must also keep a concerned watch on the stability of its neighbors: Bangladesh, formerly East Pakistan, and Nepal. To the south is Sri Lanka, formerly Ceylon, which only recently concluded a successful counterinsurgency campaign against the Tamil Tiger movement whose insurgency lasted thirty years.

So much has been written about unhappy Afghanistan that we need not say more here. With only a brief respite between 1996 and 2001, Afghanistan has been at war for over thirty years. Pakistan, however, also

[5] China and India are both members of the "Group of Twenty" despite widespread poverty in each country.

[6] The People's Republic of China was itself born of a violent insurgency that extended from 1927 to 1949 and, in a sense, from a century of "humiliations" beginning with the Opium War of 1839–1842.

suffers from ongoing and incipient insurgencies that, if not checked, could become threats to the secular regime in Islamabad. The mineral rich Baluchistan province has had a sputtering ethnically-based insurgency. A witches' brew of fanatical Islamist insurgent groups hold sway in Pakistan's frontier area with Afghanistan and even control or influence districts just north of the capital city, Islamabad.[7]

Neither is formerly Soviet Central Asia immune from insurgency. Kyrgyzstan has seen politically inspired violence that is likely to recur in the future. Both Tajikistan and Uzbekistan also have incipient or active insurgencies. The Islamic Movement of Uzbekistan (IMU), though presently more active in Afghanistan and western Pakistan, could return to the mountainous eastern part of its native land. The IMU would seek to replace the secular, post-Communist regime in Tashkent with an Islamist government.

Indonesia had its share of troubles with Timor-Leste, commonly known as East Timor, the former Portuguese colony that it forcibly absorbed in 1975. Inhabitants of Timor-Leste, many of whom are Catholic and Portuguese-speaking, refused to be absorbed into the predominantly Muslim, Bahasa-speaking Indonesian republic. After a bloody insurgency and international intervention on its behalf, Timor-Leste gained its independence from Indonesia in May 2002.

Elsewhere in Indonesia, Islamist extremism and agitation could, at some point, transform instability into a true insurgency in Java, Sumatra, and other main islands. Organizations such as Jemaah Islamiyeh have carried out attacks aimed at foreign tourists and native Christians. This group desires that an Islamic state take power in Indonesia.

French Indochina (Vietnam, Laos, and Cambodia) has seen nearly constant upheaval since the end of World War II in 1945. The tough military regime in Yanggon (Rangoon) appears to have suppressed the ethnic rebels in northern Myanmar (Burma) for now. As a betting man, I believe we will see the reappearance in some form of these tribal resistance fighters. The separatist insurgency in southern Thailand between ethnically Malay Muslims and their Thai Buddhist overseers has been expertly described by David Kilcullen in his excellent book, *The Accidental Guerrilla*.

---

[7] The seven "agencies" of the Federally Administered Tribal Areas [FATA] and the districts of Buner and Swat are home to some of the world's most dangerous insurgent movements.

Western Asia also has its share of insurgencies. The Iraqi insurgency, caused in significant part by ill-considered political moves following the defeat of Saddam Hussein's Baathist regime by the American-led coalition forces, has been well documented. Also, we should not fail to note that Israel had its hands full in occupied Lebanon with insurgent groups like Hizbollah. In Israel itself, the Palestinian Intifada has been a significant challenge to Israeli predominance. T.X. Hammes has covered this political challenge in great detail in his well-researched book, *The Sling and the Stone.*[8]

Robert D. Kaplan, presently a Senior Fellow with the Center for a New American Security, forecasts fundamental change in the Arab world in coming decades:

> Much of the Arab world, however, will undergo alteration, as Islam spreads across artificial frontiers, fueled by mass migrations into the cities and a soaring birth rate of more than 3.2 percent. Seventy percent of the Arab population has been born since 1970—youths with little historical memory of anti-colonial independence struggles, post-colonial attempts at nation-building, or any of the Arab-Israeli wars. The most distant recollection of these youths will be the West's humiliation of colonially invented Iraq in 1991. Today seventeen out of twenty-two Arab states have a declining national product; in the next twenty years, at current growth rates, the population of many Arab countries will double. These states, like most African ones, will be ungovernable through conventional secular ideologies.[9]

In this context it should also be noted that millions of young males throughout the Muslim world are coming of working age in countries where the economies are stagnant, governmental administrative ineptitude and nepotism are commonplace, and corruption is widespread. Many young men cannot find jobs, cannot marry, and cannot establish "normal" lives. They are therefore easy prey for firebrands with extremist messages.

---

[8] Dr. Hammes, a retired Marine Corps colonel, also has very solid chapters on other upheavals which he describes as "Fourth Generational War." Author commends Dr. Hammes' book to all military officers.

[9] Kaplan, p. 70

Although Oman's successful counterinsurgency against Dhofari rebels aided from Aden is now a quarter century in the past, there is continued instability in the southern part of the Arabian Peninsula. Recent press reports indicate an incipient insurgency in Yemen. Whether or not a renewal of violence in Yemen and Aden will affect the stability of the Sultanate of Oman or the Kingdom of Saudi Arabia is an open question.

Yet another sputtering West Asian insurgency that is likely to persist for decades, like a skin disease, is the ethnic struggle of the Kurds against all three of their rulers: Turkey, Iraq, and Iran. Although the Turks could claim victory in their battle with the PKK (Kurdistan Workers' Party) insurgents, especially with the capture of PKK leader Abdullah Ocalan, thousands of Kurdish people still live in Turkey and feel themselves second- or third-class citizens, and view their language and culture as threatened. Kurdish relations with governments in Baghdad and Tehran have not been the best, and Kurdish memory of past genocide under Saddam Hussein is still fresh. Making matters all the more difficult is the dispute over who owns the rights to Kirkuk oil deposits—fully 40 percent of Iraq's total oil reserves are found in Kurdistan.[10]

AFRICA

Moving on to Africa we see nearly the entire continent grappling with insurgencies, or at least the political and social instability that leads to incipient insurgency.

Eastern Africa has witnessed insurgencies in Sudan, Uganda, and our old favorite, Somalia. Sudan is divided between a Muslim north and a Christian south. The spoils of war include control over oil resources in southern Sudan. Complicating matters is the continuing turbulence in the Darfur region of western Sudan, a rich recruiting ground for extremist Islamist groups. Shaky ceasefires exist in southern and western Sudan, but the permanence of these agreements is open to question.[11] Tribally based

---

[10] PKK = Partiya Karkeren Kurdistan or "Kurdistan Workers' Party." It is a quasi-Marxist movement whose goal is the creation of an independent Kurdish republic.

[11] An Agence France Presse (AFP) report of 24 September 2010 titled "South Sudan agrees to ceasefire with rebel fighter" notes: "South Sudan is still recovering from decades of war with the North, during which about two million people were killed in a conflict fueled by religion, ethnicity, ideology and oil."

insurgents, some of whom profess a bizarre Christian ideology, afflict Uganda. Somalia, with virtually no central government, is beset by a potpourri of warlords, criminal elements, tribal militias, and armed groups, such as al-Shabaab, that are aligned with al-Qaida.[12]

Central and southern Africa has witnessed insurgencies of various stripes in Mozambique and Angola, both former Portuguese colonies, in Zimbabwe (the former Rhodesia), South Africa itself, and Namibia. Although most of this region is quiescent, political instability in Zimbabwe, disputed elections, as well as beatings and murders of opposition members by the Mugabe regime, provide ripe conditions for insurgency there. The former Belgian Congo, once upon a time Zaire and now the Democratic Republic of Congo, is legendary for insurgencies and rebels of every color of the political rainbow. Rebel Laurent Kabila, the would-be savior of the Congo, ousted longtime dictator of Zaire Mobutu Sese-Seko and then promptly established his own tyranny. It is hardly surprising, therefore, that new rebels have appeared in Kabila's wake and have taken over half of the country.

Angola and Mozambique are especially interesting cases in that their anticolonial insurgencies against the Portuguese led to victory in 1975 and then promptly to a falling-out between the insurgent groups themselves. FRELIMO and RENAMO squared off in Mozambique. The FNLA, UNITA, and the MPLA battled each other in Angola. It appears that matters have been settled in both countries, though with continuing tribal issues, but this is not a certain prediction. Moreover, Angola faces the small but dangerous challenge of FLEC to its oil rich exclave of Cabinda. Stay tuned.[13]

---

[12] Mention must be made of the tribal Mau-Mau insurgency in British Kenya in the 1950s.

[13] FRELIMO: Frente de Libertacao de Mocambique or Liberation Front of Mozambique. Founded as a Marxist-Leninist party, after its victory FRELIMO became the majority party in the state.

RENAMO: Resistencia Nacional Mocambicana or Mozambican National Resistence, a conservative political organization that attempted to oust the Marxist rulers of Mozambique through guerrilla warfare.

FLEC: Frente para a Libertacao do Enclave de Cabinda or Front for the Liberation of the Enclave of Cabinda which is now splintered into three factions. It threatens oil facilities in Cabinda.

FNLA: Frente Nacional do Libertacao de Angola or National Liberation Front of Angola, a nationalist movement formerly under Holden Roberto.

MPLA: Movimento Popular de Libertacao de Angola-Partido do Trabalho or Popular Movement for the Liberation of Angola-Party of Labor, a Marxist-Leninist group organized around 1961 to overthrow Portuguese colonial rule. It was formerly headed

West Africa is a basket case of instability. From Nigeria to Mauretania, essentially the old colonial empires of British West Africa and French West Africa, instability and insurgency are to be found in Ivory Coast, Sierra Leone, Senegal, Guinea-Bissau, Cape Verde, and Nigeria itself. PAIGC was the anticolonial movement that freed Guinea-Bissau and Cape Verde from the Portuguese. In modified form, PAIGC continues to rule Guinea-Bissau.[14] Nigeria has been called "the crippled giant" because of its great oil wealth and human potential that has been tragically crippled by ethnic strife, military dictatorship, and corruption of biblical proportions.[15] The attempted secession of Ibo-dominated Biafra in 1966 led to nearly four years of bloody civil war. As this is written, groups of insurgents threaten Nigeria's oil resources in the Niger Delta. Northern Nigeria (the pre-British Emirate of Sokoto) could fall victim to Islamist agitation. Instability in Cote d'Ivoire (Ivory Coast) resulted in violence and a change of regimes. Even American sponsored Liberia, established in the nineteenth century as a haven for freed American slaves, bathed itself in blood as a series of armed groups vied for power in Monrovia.

The Maghreb, formerly French North Africa, also is no stranger to revolutionary violence. The French war in Algeria (1954–1962) is studied as a classic insurgency and was the main source of influential French army officer and theorist David Galula's experience in counterinsurgency. It should come as no surprise that Algeria has experienced other insurgencies following its independence and will undoubtedly witness further upheavals in the future. Morocco has battled with the separatist Polisario Front for more than a decade in the insurgents' fight for the independence of Western Sahara. Unrest in Tunisia resulted in the overthrow and exile of

---

by Agostinho Neto. Under Eduardo dos Santos it fought UNITA until 2002. The Soviet Union and Cuba provided advisors, troops, and military aid.

UNITA: Uniao Nacional para a Independencia Total de Angola or National Union for the Total Independence of Angola, founded in 1966 by Jonas Savimbi and led by him until his death in 2002. During the Cold War, UNITA received political backing and material assistance from the United States and South Africa to counter Soviet and Cuban aid to the MPLA.

[14] PAIGC: Partido Africano da Independencia da Guine e Cabo Verde or African Party for the Independence of Guinea (Bissau) and Cape Verde. This movement began as a peaceful protest against Portuguese colonial rule, but armed itself as Portuguese reluctance to grant independence became apparent. PAIGC no longer rules in Cape Verde, but is the governing party in Guinea-Bissau.

[15] Title of a book by Eghosa E. Osaghae, *The Crippled Giant: Nigeria Since Independence*. The book, an excellent political history, details the bloody history of Nigeria since its 1962 independence.

President Zine El Abidine Ben Ali, who had ruled the country since 1987.

While the Arab Spring did not bring armed insurgency to Egypt, the political polarization in that land between secular rulers and ultra-religionists, between wealthy haves in a sea of have-nots, and between educated social elites and the ignorant lower classes could well lead to an insurgency at some point in the future. All the ingredients appear to be present for a full-blown insurgency; all that is needed is a charismatic cook and an attractive political recipe. The Muslim Brotherhood, which has been behind a number of terrorist attacks, including lethal attacks on European tourists, could provide both the menu and the chef.

LATIN AMERICA

We turn next to the Western Hemisphere and find violent insurgencies in Peru and Colombia, and a nascent insurgency in Mexico. Each of the ongoing insurgencies has joined hands with criminal groups that finance and arm rebel units. Peru was under the impression that it had defeated Sendero Luminoso[16] by capturing its chief, Abimael Guzman, aka Presidente Gonzalo. However, because no action was taken to correct underlying sociopolitical conditions, the insurgency has reappeared. Colombia continues to battle the FARC, which to a considerable extent now runs a protection racket for that country's cocaine traffickers.[17] Brazil's sprawling *favelas* may also harbor the ingredients of terrorism and instability.

The cartels operating in Mexico are as yet merely criminal syndicates. It is only a matter of time, however, before some of these syndicates develop a political wing and a supporting politico-military program intended to protect their trafficking. The Zetas, a kind of for-hire paramilitary group, may already be evidence of this trend.

We Americans would do well to acknowledge the cold fact that violent gang wars south of our border directly result from widespread cocaine use north of the border. Were it not for billions of *American* dollars spent on

---

[16] The Shining Path, a quasi-Maoist insurgent group drawing heavily on support from Quechua Indians.

[17] FARC: Fuerzas Armadas Revolucionarias de Colombia, or the Revolutionary Armed Forces of Colombia, established in 1964 as the armed element of the Colombian Communist Party. Today the FARC serves mainly as rent-a-guards for cocaine labs. They are still Marxist insurgents, however.

purchasing illegal drugs it is unlikely that the cartels would fight so savagely to preserve their operations. It appears that the United States has something of a double standard when it sends advisors, helicopters, and other material assistance to Mexican law enforcement officers to suppress the drug trade while giving light or even suspended sentences to American drug users, especially when they are well-known celebrities or public figures, the very people directly responsible for thousands of Mexican deaths.[18]

In Mexico as in South America, if the narcotics trade is allowed to flourish, vast amounts of money will be available to fuel political and social instability, transforming historically close allies into failed states.[19]

There were also three now-concluded insurgencies that greatly affected U.S. security policy in the last four decades of the twentieth century: Cuba, Nicaragua, and El Salvador. (We will examine Nicaragua and El Salvador in some detail in a later chapter.) Fidel Castro came to power after a relatively brief insurgency (1955–1958) that ousted dictator Fulgencio Batista.

In South America urban insurgencies raged in the 1970s in Argentina and Uruguay, leading to bloody work by secret police. Last, but not least, Argentine Ernesto "Che" Guevara vainly sought to arouse Bolivian peasants to revolt prior to his untimely demise in 1967. "Che" overlooked the fact that the Bolivian government had carried out a land reform only fifteen years earlier. In any case, as an Argentine, most of the Bolivian peasants viewed Che as an undesirable foreigner.

EUROPE

As we close our quick tour of world insurgency, let us end with a glimpse at Europe. Europe, you ask? Yes, even Europe has had its share of insurgencies. We know about the historical models from Spain and Austria during Napoleon's time. But modern Europe has faced any number of "people's wars" in the Balkans: Bosnia, Croatia, and separatist Kosovo. In the Caucasus, the Republic of Georgia faced insurgents in the breakaway

---

[18] Mexican President Felipe Calderon stated that in 2010, more than ten thousand Mexicans, including eighty law-enforcement officers, died in drug-related combat in northern Mexico. We must also take note of many thousands of Colombians who died as a result of narco-trafficking protected by insurgent groups.

[19] Having a second "Somalia" on our southern border would gravely harm U.S. security.

regions of Abkhazia and Ossetia, and Russia has had a very tough time with the Chechens and other rebels in Daghestan. Ethnic and religious factors color many of these bloody conflicts, but economic factors also fuel the insurgencies.

We also tend to forget four other classic European insurgencies: Basque separatists, the Irish Republican Army (especially its swift campaign of 1919–1921), the Greek civil war of 1946–1949 featuring Communist guerrillas, and General George Grivas's successful nationalist insurgency against British rule in Cyprus (1955–1959).

The point of this whirlwind tour of the contemporary global political scene is to make plain its complexity and the growing influence of culture, ethnicity, ideology, and belief systems. Contributing to insurgency are factors such as the breakdown of tribal societies, the expansion of semi-urban populations, economic dysfunction, desperation over shortages of land and food, and many other challenges to the world's evolving political structure. I do not pretend that this quick tour around the globe is either as complete as a political analyst would like it to be, or as detailed as a military historian would prefer. It is merely outlined for the reader, as a fellow practitioner, to help understand the broad global nature of insurgency. I hope you will research some of these insurgencies, whether historical, such as the French wars in Algeria and Indochina, or ongoing, such as those in Colombia and Pakistan.

Sadly, much of this "down in the weeds" warfare has gone virtually unnoticed by the average American. True, scholars and specialists do track many of these insurgencies, and a few policy analysts speculate on their consequences, but as a matter of policy formulation by administrations of both persuasions, and military preparedness on the part of the Defense Department, the great majority of social and political upheavals and transformations taking place in Africa and Asia might as well be invisible. Since these festering problems are generally unnoticed, when they do eventually surface as political and then military problems for the United States, they invariably take us by surprise. Shame on us.

Who among us in the year 2000 foresaw that we would be militarily engaged just a few years later in violent insurgencies in faraway Iraq and Afghanistan? And so, we were caught completely unprepared. We knew relatively little about either country. We had few linguists, few area experts, and few experienced intelligence officers familiar with the land, the people, the politics, or the culture. And yet, the point can be made that we might have been training our intelligence and Psyop personnel, and a cadre of military advisors, so that they would have had at least a basic level of expertise if and when the need should arise. We didn't.

Can we predict, as we sit here, where American military and civilian power will be called upon to serve ten years from now? We probably cannot.

Even so, it *is* possible to study critical regions where instability and social dysfunction indicate that civil disorder is likely to arise threatening our own national interests.

We've just identified any number of problems all over the world. Are all problems of high policy interest to the United States? Of course not. But some of them definitely are of interest now or may be in the foreseeable future. These key areas deserve intensive study *now*. We should be thinking ahead and preparing now so we might avoid catastrophe later.

In a later chapter we will discuss steps we can take to prepare ourselves today for the wars we may have to face in the future. For the moment, let's turn our attention to some of the socio-economic factors that can lead to the breakdown of civil order and onset of armed conflict.

INCOME

If you divide the world by gross domestic product(GDP), or better by purchasing power parity (PPP)[20] it becomes immediately apparent that, with few exceptions, the roster of countries making up the Lower Half of the global socio-economic scale includes nearly all of Africa, the majority of Asian countries, including China and India, the heartland of South America, including Brazil, Peru and Colombia, as well as most Central American and Caribbean countries.

By contrast, the Upper Half of the global scale consists of almost all of Europe, less two or three Balkan countries, North America, Australia and

[20] Gross Domestic Product (GDP) is the total value of a country's goods and services. Purchasing Power Parity (PPP) is a measure of the relative cost of goods or services compared with a value of 100 based on the U.S. dollar. That is, a U.S. dollar spent in Dacca or Lima will buy more goods and services than the same dollar spent in New York City or Stockholm. Both GDP and PPP can be used broadly to measure and compare Standard of Living between countries.

New Zealand, and the Asian countries of Japan, South Korea, Malaysia and Singapore, Turkey, and the Gulf States and Saudi Arabia.[21] With a few exceptions, this stark division also marks those countries having higher literacy rates, greater average longevity, better housing and health services, more secure food supplies, functioning public services, and responsible local and national governments. The Lower Half lacks all or most of these benefits.

Given the socio-economic data presented above, we might jump to the conclusion that if a country is poor, it will be vulnerable to insurgency, whereas if a country is well off, it will not. Well, that is not necessarily so.

Although it is true that insurgencies tend to appear more frequently in poorer lands than in wealthier ones, socio-economic factors in isolation can be misleading. There are other key factors such as religious and ethnic differences, the uneven distribution of political power and administrative services between various groups, high birthrates, and even the relative lack of food that enter the equation. And the key economic factor is not so much the GDP or PPP of a country, *but gross imbalances in the distribution of wealth* that can trigger uprisings. Countries having tiny, but obscenely wealthy elites and masses of hungry, poor people, may find themselves vulnerable to insurgency even if they rank in the Upper Half. This mass-elite gap becomes even more compelling if it is reinforced by ethnic or religious differences, an in group and an out group, and attempts by the regime in power to repress the out group.

Consider the example of Turkey, which has battled PKK insurgents for two decades even though, as a whole, Turkey ranks in the Upper Half socio-economically. While uneven distribution of political power and imbalances in income contributed to insurgency, the root cause clearly was the ethnically oriented clash between Turks and Kurds. Kurds as a group are on the lower rungs of the socio-economic ladder. Moreover, the Turkish government and Turks generally tend to deprecate Kurdish language and culture.

The Sultanate of Oman is another country that is well off economically, but faced an insurgency in its southern Dhofar region from 1962 to 1975. Until 1970, the Omani government, which is an absolute monarchy,

---

[21] Source of economic data: CIA, *The World Factbook*, 2009.

exploited Dhofar economically and treated the inhabitants harshly. Discontent was initially based upon tribal politics, but after the 1967 independence of Aden, Marxist sources provided external assistance to the rebels.[22]

We often forget that the intermittent contest between the predominantly Catholic IRA and the predominantly Protestant pro-British Ulster Unionists in Northern Ireland constitutes an insurgency, and it is taking place in the United Kingdom, a country that is not only a member of the European Union, but has the world's sixth largest economy. Admittedly, the U.K. is an anomaly in our generalizations, but even though it does not fit the pattern, it cannot be ignored.

Poverty alone is not the cause of insurgency. Often the poorest of the poor do not rise against their governments. Perhaps the reason that popular uprisings are less likely in some desperately poor countries is due to the fact that, although the great majority of the people live in abject misery, almost everyone is in the same situation and everyone lacks equally. And it is not to say that upheaval cannot occur. But desperately poor societies generally are less politically aware than are those that may be a notch or two higher on the social development scale.

Countries most vulnerable to some sort of upheaval may, therefore, be those which are *advancing economically and socially, but at a disjointed pace.* Disparities in income and status may appear between certain groups gaining new wealth that other, disadvantaged groups believe was stolen from them.[23] Certain cliques or political families may come to dominate the political life of a country to the exclusion of others. As the economy

---

[22] The British-Omani counterinsurgency program is a model that should be studied by all practitioners.

[23] Colonel Newsham, a Marine Corps senior intelligence officer, cites the case of the late shah's attempts at modernization in Iran as creating just these cleavages between the clerics and traditional merchants on the one hand and the modern technocrats and westernized elites on the other. Author notes that rapid, uneven development may in fact bring about instability as a socio-economic gap opens or widens between those who benefit from growth and those who do not. Colonel Newsham also states that in white-dominated South Africa, where he had studied, the native elites, though benefiting materially from the roads, mines, schooling, electricity, etc., "were angered by the fact they were inevitably [treated as] 'second class citizens'—no matter how close they got to the colonialists and their society." (Personal letter to author.)

improves, and as people become politically aware, they tend to expect more services and better administration of justice from the government. But if popular hopes are disappointed and the people perceive that their government is inept, corrupt, or both, the result can be widespread and protracted violence. Possibly the most important factor in growing instability is a general *perception of injustice*, fostered by the people's ever wider access to mass media, especially television and radio.

LITERACY

United Nations data on global literacy shows a predictable pattern.[24] The developed countries, consisting of nearly all European and North American countries, the Upper Half of the GDP scale, rank in the top sixty countries globally. Greece, the country in sixtieth place, claims a 97.1 percent literacy rate. Portugal, the least literate European nation, claims 94.9 percent literacy and comes in at seventy-second place globally.

Latin America and Asia have slightly lower rates of literacy than do Europe and North America. With two notable exceptions, Cuba and Guyana both at claimed rates of 99 percent, Latin American countries fall between Argentina, Chile, and Costa Rica at the higher end of the spectrum, 97.6 to 95.9 percent respectively, and the bottom dwellers, Nicaragua, Guatemala, and Haiti, ranging from 78 percent down to 62 percent respectively. Two countries with active insurgencies, Colombia and Peru, have literacy levels at 92.7 percent and 89.6 percent respectively. Mexico, with an incipient insurgency linked to narcotics smuggling, is comparable to Colombia at 92.8 percent literacy. However, there is a disparity in literacy between the *criollos*, persons of European or part-European heritage, and *indigenas*, people of indigenous descent.

With the exception of claimed 99 percent plus literacy rates for all but one of the former republics of Soviet Central Asia, and similar numbers for Japan and the two Koreas, Asian literacy rates resemble those of Latin America. Mongolia, Brunei, and Hong Kong claim rates of 97.3 percent,

---

[24] The following four paragraphs concerning rates of adult literacy are based on data compiled by the United Nations and its agencies through 2007. Not all countries were listed, most notably Afghanistan and Iraq. Author intentionally ignored British Caribbean islands and certain other very minor states such as Malta, Seychelles, Mauritius, and Equatorial Guinea that are listed in the U.N.'s literacy survey.

94.9 percent, and 94.6 percent literacy. At the bottom end of the scale for which there is official U.N. data are Pakistan, Bangladesh, and Bhutan, which range downward from 54.2 percent to 52.8 percent literacy. Afghanistan's literacy rate is believed even lower, though no United Nations data is available for that country. At 66.0 percent India holds place 149 while the People's Republic of China, claiming 93.3 percent literacy, is number 83. We may infer that literacy is higher among majority ethnic groups and lower in the minorities.

Unsurprisingly, the world's lowest average literacy rates are to be found in Africa. South Africa and Namibia top the African list at 88.0 percent each. The literacy rates for the other forty-seven African countries on the U.N.'s list range downward to Niger at 28.7 percent and Mali at 26.2 percent. Indeed, the thirteen countries with the lowest ratings in the world are African nations, with Niger and Mali being at the very bottom. Two countries with active insurgencies, the Democratic Republic of Congo, which claims 67.2 percent literacy, holds place 147 and Sudan, claiming 60.9 percent literacy, is number 155. Somalia was not listed.

What the practitioner should take away from this quick glimpse at world literacy rates is that the great majority of insurgencies do not take place at either end of the spectrum. We are not likely to see incipient or active insurgencies in Estonia or Mali. Rather, with a few special exceptions such as Tajikistan, claimed to be 99.6 percent literate, and Sierra Leone (38.1 percent), most insurgencies except those in Africa take place in lands with literacy from around 80 percent to 94 percent.

I believe the foregoing and admittedly rough data is significant because it amply shows the key role of media and communication, alongside other factors, in spurring insurgent movements. Illiterate people, those who cannot be reached by the printed word, can be mobilized, but only by the spoken word. Radio and television are certainly valuable in doing this as is personal, direct communication. But if people are too poor to buy radios, it follows that political mobilization of large numbers of people either by the regime or an insurgent movement will be difficult indeed.

Conversely, people who have regular access to various types of media tend to be more easily organized and directed politically. Moreover, they are far more aware of societal ills such as disparities in wealth, landholding, political power, and so forth. While electronic media can be effective for mobilizing public opinion, especially through the shock power of images and spoken words, people who can read are also susceptible to influences in newspapers, books, and periodicals. While I offer this as my strong suspicion, I caveat this as being only speculation that bears serious academic study.

Perhaps the greatest potential for insurgency exists in those countries having literacy rates higher than 60 percent, but also having glaring disparities in living standards and the internal distribution of wealth. There is also the need for an educated revolutionary elite of some kind to call the general public's attention to perceived social evils in need of correction through political means. A revolutionary elite is not necessarily Marxist-Leninist or any other specific ideology; it can be nationalist or even reactionary. It is a leadership group that presents a credible alternative to the existing regime, and promises solutions to the perceived ills. Where there are few if any educated persons development of a revolutionary leadership is unlikely.

HUNGER

Another key factor in understanding how the other half lives directly correlates with national income and individual purchasing power: it is hunger.

On 14 October 2009 the United Nations Food and Agriculture Organization (FAO) released an estimate indicating that globally more than a billion people are malnourished, almost one hundred and fifty million people more than its 2006 estimate. The FAO believes that this increase in hunger is due to three factors:

- Neglect of agriculture relevant to very poor people by governments and international agencies;
- The current worldwide economic crisis; and
- The significant increase of food prices in the last several years which has been devastating to those with only a few dollars a day to spend.[25]

[25] See the World Hunger Education Service website at http://www.worldhunger.org/articles/Learn/world%20hunger%20facts%202002.htm, which synthesizes FAO data. These estimates are only that: estimates. Many countries lack data or refuse to provide meaningful data on hunger, as it is a politically sensitive subject for some governments.

It should come as no surprise that, by far, hunger mainly affects people in Asia and Africa. The FAO estimates that 265 million people in Sub-Saharan Africa and 642 million people living in Asia lack daily minimal nutritional intake. Latin America and the Caribbean area account for 53 million malnourished people, with the Middle East and North Africa adding 42 million more who are below the daily minimum line. The developed countries, Europe and North America plus countries like Japan and Australia, combined had only 15 million persons classified as malnourished.

Hunger means vulnerability. People in need of food are many times more susceptible to disease than those who are well-fed. Taking this a step further, hunger also means that life expectancy is shorter and deaths due to malnutrition ever-present. Mohandas Gandhi once noted: "There are people in the world so hungry that God cannot appear to them except in the form of bread."

The World Hunger Education Service observed that while "poverty is the principal cause of hunger," it is equally true that "hunger is also a cause of poverty."[26] Malnourished people are not capable of sustained, productive work and sometimes undernourishment can lead to mental impairment, as well. It follows that if people are physically incapable of earning their daily bread, economic stagnation will be endemic and hunger will devastate the population. This vicious cycle is nearly unbreakable.

Above all hunger means desperation. People who face gnawing hunger will consider any measure to get food. They will follow anyone who promises them relief.

We would do well to remember that many revolutions began, at least in part, because of hunger. For example, on 8 March 1917 masses of starving women in St. Petersburg, Russia, attacked the granaries in desperate search of food. This act triggered a series of events leading directly to the forced abdication of Tsar Nicholas II and the formation of the Kerensky government, and indirectly to the Bolshevik Revolution that November.[27] Food shortages in Nationalist China, Batista's Cuba, and Somoza's Nicaragua also had serious political consequences for those regimes beset by insurgent movements.

---

[26] op. cit. FAO data interpreted by the World Hunger Education Service.

[27] 8 March 1917 was commemorated by the Bolshevik regime as International Women's Day. Although during Soviet times it was a Socialist event connected with the Revolution, IWD has lost its political flavor but is still celebrated in dozens of countries.

Here again, as with many other socio-economic factors, hunger by itself is not the cause of insurgency. People can be desperately hungry, but may still not take up arms against the regime simply because of hunger. However, when it is clear that vast disparities exist between haves and have nots, and especially when masses of people come to believe that these inequalities are the result of small groups seeking to make inordinate profits at the expense of the people, the possibility of upheaval exists.

POPULATION[28]

A final socio-economic factor that we will consider as we try to learn how the other half lives is birthrate and population density. Again, taken alone, this factor is not indicative of the likelihood of political instability or insurgency. But considered alongside many other factors, high birthrates and growing density of a nation's population is an indicator.

We should not be surprised that birthrates are almost inversely correlated with literacy and income. Of the twenty-five highest birthrates in the world all but two, Afghanistan and Yemen, are found in Africa. In the cases of thinly populated countries, such as Mali and Niger, high birthrates may be considered statistical flukes. But in others, such as, Ethiopia, the Democratic Republic of Congo, and Zambia, not to mention Yemen and Afghanistan, a high birthrate is a matter of great concern.

The reasons should be obvious. First, a high birthrate implies a greater need for food; food that may already be in short supply will become even more scarce in the event of prolonged drought, flooding, locusts, and so on. Naturally, housing along with food will become problematic. Second, a high birth rate has the potential for creating a very high degree of unemployment or underemployment. Already weak economies will be strained or broken by a surfeit of people who have no means of contributing meaningfully to production. Nevertheless, by definition all are consumers. This portends the possibility of crime and other antisocial activities as the only means of obtaining even a meager subsistence income. And third, high birthrates suggest the possibility that large numbers of children will be unable to attend school, thereby remaining unable to read or write. This

[28] The U.N. Population Division projects that world population will reach 7 billion during 2011.

dooms millions of children economically as they will be unable to find employment outside a bare subsistence economy.

Of the fifty highest birthrates in the world, we continue to see a large number of African countries including Nigeria, Kenya, Tanzania, Sudan, Zimbabwe, and Ghana, all lands of some importance to the global community. Muslim states in the top fifty include the Gaza Strip, Oman, Iraq and Saudi Arabia. Pakistan is not far behind at number fifty-four, and with a current population estimated at 180 million, its high birth rate is fraught with political and economic danger.

In the next fifty countries, which have somewhat lower birthrates than are typical in Africa, we find more Asian and Latin American countries. The Philippines is sixty-first and El Salvador sixty-fifth. Bolivia, Kyrgyzstan, Nepal, Nicaragua, India, Egypt, Morocco, Venezuela, South Africa, Mexico, Colombia, and Peru are all within this group.

Above the hundredth place there are more Latin American and Asian countries, such as, Indonesia, Turkey, Brazil, Argentina, Algeria, Kazakhstan, Tunisia, and Chile. These are also countries that are to be found somewhere in the middle of the global socio-economic roster of nations.

Interestingly, the first European nation to appear on the list is Ireland at number 135 and with the highest birthrate on that continent, followed by China, the United States, Australia and New Zealand, and then a roll call of the other European states.

For the record, at the bottom of the list, with the world's lowest birthrates, which are barely keeping pace with their death rates, are Germany, Italy, and Japan. Of course, on the positive side of the ledger, I suppose we should take comfort that low birthrates in Germany, Italy, and Japan indicate we will not have to worry about a new Tripartite Pact being signed anytime soon.[29]

BUT WAIT, THERE'S MORE!

We have made a quick around-the-world tour of potential trouble spots, and the many and varied conditions that cause or aggravate those troubles.

---

[29] A humorous reference to the September 1940 pact that created the Axis. At that time, Germany, Italy, and Japan—all with increasing populations—pursued expansionist policies at their neighbors' expense.

Admittedly we've only skimmed the surface; there is much more to the story.

The American public and the Capitol Hill crowd recognize many of the socio-political ills we've mentioned as leading to political violence. They are also more or less concerned with environmental problems such as desertification, clear-cutting of rain forests, soil depletion, chemical pollution, and others. Neither the American people nor the Congress, however, connect the problem of political violence with despoliation of the environment. It appears that neither the public at large nor their legislators have grasped the fact that the growing problems of political instability and environmental degradation are in fact closely intertwined.

Perhaps the key issue for the coming century is that of water. To quote Will Rogers a bit out of context, "they ain't makin' it no more." The truth is that fresh water resources, already scarce in many parts of the world, are diminishing. Water already is a major issue in much of Africa, especially the Sahel, that part of Africa immediately south of the Sahara. There the desert is steadily expanding southward, encroaching on cropland and placing ever greater pressure on expanding populations. Water is a major political issue between Iran and Afghanistan and between Pakistan and India. As the world climate changes and grows warmer, less snow falls on the Hindu Kush and Himalayas. Annual snowfall provides the water that all four countries depend upon for spring crops. Central Asia, parts of China, and even parts of the Western Hemisphere face a growing shortage of water. Lack of this basic resource affects agriculture, industry, public health, and sanitation. Ultimately, scarcity of water could lead to social breakdown and conflict.[30]

Soil depletion, due to over-farming or poor farming techniques in some cases, and to wind erosion and ruin by salt in others, is another problem. Poor farming or irrigation methods set the stage for loss of cropland, or for the gradual decline of agricultural output. In parts of Central Asia and Africa salt is clearly visible in fields that once produced crops. These lands now stand useless. But despite having less arable land and a drop in crop production, populations continue to grow.

Environmentalists do not usually think about the wanton destruction

---

[30] The April 2010 issue of *National Geographic Magazine* was devoted entirely to "Water: Our Thirsty World." Author highly recommends reading this entire issue cover to cover.

of rain forest in terms of national security. And yet, there is a strong connection. While proponents of this destruction say that more cropland is needed to feed growing populations, the cost of this new land is loss of water-retaining forest. Like a kaleidoscope, the change in this piece of an integrated design affects the design as a whole. Soil and water resources are being depleted at an accelerating rate. Destruction of rain forest is pronounced in Africa and South America, and to an extent, even in Southeast Asia. Certain Philippine islands (notably Luzon) and Indonesia (especially Borneo) have been denuded of rain forest and protective cover and thus rendered vulnerable to severe erosion and loss of habitat.

Chemical pollution has political impact as well. European and North American countries recognize the threat of pollution to living conditions and have taken steps to bring this pernicious challenge under control. Sadly, while the Upper Half struggles to bring pollution under control, in the Lower Half the problem is unchecked and probably is growing worse. Kazakhstan is notorious for horrific problems left behind by Soviet nuclear programs. Industrial waste and smokestack effluents befoul China's air and water. Most of Africa along with parts of the Middle East has fallen victim to many kinds of pollution. The price paid for pollution is sharply increased sickness and birth defects, and the probability of lower life expectancy. Again, there is an implication here for political instability.

On this unhappy note, it is time to turn our attention toward other matters. I hope that this section has "set the stage" for our later discussion of the challenges we face abroad and the desperate need for wise counsels here at home. It is how the other half lives.

ROOTS IN DIFFERENT SOIL

Let us leave off with surveys and statistics at this point. Those are for political scientists, demographers, sociologists and others to mull over in detail, but not for us. It is enough for practitioners to understand that the way the other half lives relates directly to the way they act in a political sense. And the way they act in a political sense directly impacts on how we must act and react. It is politics after all, that gives rise to warfare (or so said experts like Clausewitz, Mao, Churchill, and many others).

What I suggest we take away from this peek at how the other half lives is the fact that insurgency has its roots in very different soil than does the conventional warfare that has marked much of the twentieth century and for which the United States prepared decades ago, and for which the Pentagon and the Congress still appear to be preparing.

The great armies, fleets, and air armadas that defined warfare in the twentieth century all were products of industrial or industrializing nations. Only advanced countries like imperial Japan or Nazi Germany could send aircraft carriers across the Pacific or panzer divisions across the North European plain. Only nations like Great Britain, with brilliant scientists and mathematicians, could devise radar and sonar, and crack the various German codes with an Enigma decryption device. Only a country like the Soviet Union, with its heavy industrial base, could churn out T-34 tanks by the thousands. And ultimately, only the United States could produce so many aircraft, tanks, and ships, as well as food and other supplies, that we could satisfy our own requirements and still have surplus materiel for our allies. That is industrial war. That is the war *of the past.*

None of the countries presently suffering from insurgency (with the special exceptions of China and India, which are faced with limited, separatist insurgencies) have anywhere near the industrial brawn or technological expertise to fight on the scale of the Axis or Allies.

Rather, as I think we have begun to appreciate, war in the twenty-first century will be "down in the weeds." It will be fought by peoples and groups who are largely pre-industrial. It will be fought by people living at the poverty line, some of whom can barely read or write, and many of whom go to bed hungry. It will be fought by people who are angry at their own governments, often justifiably so, and who are prepared to die in order that their children might have a better chance in life.[31]

I also go so far as to say that because the conflicts on the horizon will have little to do with industrial power or technology, these presumed advantages of the First World countries will play little, if any, role in the wars we are likely to face. Rather, the wars to come will be those of desperate people, goaded by high birth rates, ignorance born of illiteracy, and poverty resulting from social conditions and the complicity of inept and criminal govern-

[31] Author readily acknowledges that conventional conflict is certainly possible on the Korean peninsula and in selected areas of the Middle East. However, author doubts that a German-Soviet "rematch" or a renewed Japanese attempt to conquer China or attack Pearl Harbor is likely.

ments. When charismatic and committed revolutionaries fan popular discontent, even our technology will not be enough to save us from the armed upheavals that will take place among the other half of the planet.

Robert D. Kaplan, an extraordinarily perceptive observer of world trends, put his thoughts down more than a dozen years ago in his article "The Coming Anarchy." Kaplan notes many of the social, economic, and environmental conditions that will conspire to bring about conflict in this century. Among these are depletion of natural resources, disease (especially AIDS), the ever-increasing number of refugees and internally displaced persons, the spread of narco-trafficking, and Malthusian population growth. Kaplan's gloomy, but highly plausible prediction of the future is worth quoting at length:

> Over the next fifty years the earth's population will soar from five and a half billion to more than nine billion. Though optimists have hopes for new resource technologies and free-market development in the global village, they fail to note that, as the National Academy of Sciences has pointed out, *95 percent of the population increase will be in the poorest regions of the world, where governments now—just look at Africa—show little ability to function, let alone to implement even marginal improvements. . . .*
>
> While a minority of the human population will be . . . sufficiently sheltered . . . [and] living in cities and suburbs in which the environment has been mastered and ethnic animosities have been quelled by bourgeois prosperity, *an increasingly large number of people will be stuck in history, living in shantytowns where attempts to rise above poverty, cultural dysfunction, and ethnic strife will be doomed by a lack of water to drink, soil to till, and space to survive in.* In the developing world environmental stress will present people with a choice that is increasingly among totalitarianism (as in Iraq), fascist-tending mini-states (as in Serb-held Bosnia), and road-warrior cultures (as in Somalia). [Thomas Fraser] Homer-Dixon concludes that: "as environmental degradation proceeds, the size of the potential social disruption will increase."[32]

---

[32] Kaplan, p. 59. Italics are mine for emphasis. The "minority of the human population" that Kaplan refers to is *us*—the privileged members of the so-called First World.

It must be said that humanity has shown itself capable of adapting to many adverse and even horrific conditions. People are capable of grappling tenaciously with difficulty and do survive, witness the survivors of concentration camps in World War II. That said, if conditions worsen in certain parts of the world, sooner or later there will be a breaking point at which even the most stout-hearted of people will crack under the unbearable weight of desperation. This breakdown will send shock waves even into those of us who today are sufficiently sheltered and oblivious of the coming storm.

Let us conclude this section by quoting an observation made, not by the Soviet Politburo, but by the Vatican Curia over a quarter century ago:

> The seizure of the vast majority of the wealth by an oligarchy of owners bereft of social consciousness, the practical absence or the shortcomings of a rule of law, military dictators making a mockery of elementary human rights, the corruption of certain powerful officials, the savage practices of some foreign capital interests constitute factors which nourish a passion for revolt among those who thus consider themselves the powerless victims of a new colonialism in the technological, financial, monetary or economic order.[33]

Exploitation comes in many colors, shapes, and sizes. Leftist regimes, such as that in Castro's Cuba, equally with rightist regimes, such as that of the Somozas in Nicaragua, have made a mockery of basic rights while fleecing their peoples. We should be mindful of President John F. Kennedy's observation: "Those who make peaceful change impossible make violent change inevitable."[34]

The choice is before us.

---

[33] *New York Times*, 4 September 1984, reporting Vatican statement on "Liberation Theology."

[34] John F. Kennedy, address to Latin American diplomats at the White House, 12 March 1962.

CHAPTER 2

MANY ROADS TO INSURGENCY

I have passed the Rubicon; swim or sink, live or die, survive or perish with my country—that is my unalterable determination.—John Adams[1]

It may be that Americans today, including many military professionals, think of war as being a clash of regular military forces with the winner dictating the terms of peace. Even though World War II is now almost seven decades in the past, its afterglow seems to color what we think about how a proper war should be fought. The American public desires unadulterated *victory* in its wars. It was not impressed by the negotiated ceasefires in Korea or the first Gulf War against Iraq that left armed enemies in place.[2]

After all, in World War II, there was clear Decision. There were heroes and villains; titanic battles on land, at sea, and in the air; the mobilization of entire nations; brilliant landings as at Normandy or heroic escapes as at Dunkirk. Above all, there was a dramatic, and happy for us, decisive conclusion to global war in 1945. Small wonder that novels and films about

---

[1] John Adams, conversation with Jonathan Sewall, Falmouth, Maine, July 1774.

[2] Armistice at Panmunjom in 1953 and the ceasefire in the First Gulf War in 1991 following the liberation of Kuwait. Although it is true that the former left North Korea intact north of the 38th parallel and the latter left Saddam Hussein in power, negotiations end most wars. Indeed, negotiated settlements to limited wars that take due consideration of political realities may be in the interests of all parties. An uncompromising stand—unwillingness to negotiate—risks political isolation and military defeat.

World War II still capture our imaginations. And it is right that this is so. To that Greatest Generation of Americans we owe our survival as a free people. May they be eternally blessed.

A DIFFERENT KIND OF WAR

But the debacle in Vietnam, the later tragedy in Somalia, and the ongoing stalemate in Afghanistan offer other, and very different, ideas about what war is supposed to be. Unfortunately, it may be that some lessons offered about certain kinds of war were never quite digested either by the public or the military. Certainly those of us who became new second lieutenants in the 1960s were steeped during our cadetship in the great campaigns of Grant, Pershing, and Patton against their uniformed foes. We were given virtually no training worthy of the name in either the theory or practice of the strange kind of war we faced in Vietnam. We were told that this kind of war was *just like* all the others, only smaller. To top this off, some wonk in the Pentagon invented the term "low intensity conflict," in contrast, one supposes, to "high intensity conflict."

The defeat in Vietnam, following nearly fifteen years of frustrating struggle, left the American public confused by "people's war," sharply divided politically, and doubtful of its armed forces' ability to deal effectively with insurgency or, as Soviet Premier Nikita Khrushchev liked to say, "wars of national liberation."

Today we find ourselves heavily engaged in Afghanistan pursuing COIN, the unappealing acronym *de jour* for counterinsurgency. Yet, while many talk about this phenomenon, and offer their prescriptions, few show a deep understanding of insurgency. If we are to conduct effective *counter*insurgency we must first understand *insurgency*. As a people we apparently do not.[3]

This is especially ironic as the United States of America won its independence from Great Britain by means of a ten-year-long insurgency aided and abetted by outsiders.[4]

---

[3] Insurgency derives from the Latin *insurgere*, meaning "to rise up." It is related to "insurrection" which is an open revolt against an established authority.

[4] Author is reckoning from the Boston Tea Party of 1773 to the Peace of Paris in 1783. Others trace the onset of the insurgency to the Stamp Act of 1765 or even to the year 1761 when (at that time loyal Subject) James Otis (later turned Revolutionary) perceived the Writs of Assistance to be pernicious to colonial rights. The slogan "Taxation without

It is not that books have not been written about Vietnam or almost every other insurgency, past or present. But there have been relatively few studies on why insurgencies are conceived, how they are born, and how they grow and develop. Therefore, it is often the case that, like overeager new physicians with their first patient, we rush to prescribe cures without having taken time to diagnose either the disease or the patient.

As a backdrop to looking at insurgency, let us first briefly examine five wars involving American forces in the twentieth century. These are: World Wars I and II, the Korean Conflict, the Vietnam War, and the first Gulf War (1990–91.) Vietnam aside, these conflicts were fought as conventional wars between regular, uniformed opponents in an essentially Clausewitzian manner. The strategic idea in each war was a page straight out of *On War*: *destruction of the enemy's regular armed forces thereby compelling him to agree to an armistice or peace settlement.* Had General Ludendorff succeeded in his final 1918 offensive, and broken the British Expeditionary Force, the Allied powers probably would have asked for an armistice. As it happened, the Allies broke the German lines that Fall with the consequence that Germany asked for an armistice.

Had it been within its power, the Imperial Japanese Navy would happily have sunk our aircraft carriers at Midway, occupied Hawaii, and forced us to the peace table. Fortunately, Midway turned out to be a catastrophic Japanese defeat. Chinese intervention in Korea prevented an outright U.N. victory in 1950 and ultimately led to a truce at Panmunjom. As many of us remember, General Schwartzkopf's "Hail Mary" flanking maneuver trapped and destroyed the bulk of the Iraqi forces occupying Kuwait, thus making further Iraqi resistance unwise, if not impossible. Once again, hostilities were ended by an armistice. In four of the five wars the political outcome was decided on the battlefield or at sea between opposing regular forces.

Only in World War II, and then only that part of the war pertaining to Hitler's Germany, was total destruction of the state—unconditional

---

representation is tyranny" is widely attributed to Otis, today virtually unknown. John Adams later wrote: "the child independence was then and there born, [for] every man of an immense crowded audience [in the courtroom] appeared to me as I did, ready to take arms against writs of assistance. . . ."Perhaps the intellectual roots of the insurgency preceded armed force by 14 years and ultimate victory over the British colonial regime by 22 years.

surrender—the political objective. The surrender of Japan was conditioned upon the retention of the emperor as head of state.

Vietnam was a different kind of war. While it is quite true that the North Vietnamese regular army, using mobile warfare, administered the *coup de grace* to the tottering Saigon regime in May 1975, this triumph was made possible only because two decades of persistent, low-level insurgency, heavily focused upon political warfare and subversion, left the southern regime a hollow shell easily toppled. As the end of the war neared, the South Vietnamese piastre was inflating rapidly, the economy was shrinking, civil administration in the provinces was spotty or corrupt, and political leadership in Saigon was a joke. True, the Vietnamese Communists had helped all this along by infiltrating the government, carrying out assassinations of effective civil servants and teachers, promoting the black market, demoralizing U.S. and South Vietnamese troops, and effectively recruiting and mobilizing large numbers of peasants.

Although American units did face NVA regulars, just as we had faced regular armies in all other wars fought in the twentieth century, what made Vietnam different was the involvement of "the people in arms" operating in support of the regulars or, more often, independently. Moreover, the truly significant aspect of the Vietnam War had nothing to do with destruction of our armed forces in battle, but everything to do with the erosion of the political foundations of the losing side, the Saigon regime.

There are those who hold the opinion that the Viet Cong, and therefore by extension the insurgency, had been destroyed in early 1968 during the Tet Offensive. These people contend that from that point on the war was a contest between conventional forces with the issue being decided solely on the field of battle. This view is incorrect for two reasons. First, the armed element constituted only *part* of the insurgency, and then *only the visible part* of a much broader politico-military contest. Political cadres continued their recruitment and indoctrination of peasants and many other Vietnamese long after our forces had retaken the Citadel in Hue. Viet Cong political action was the invisible, albeit ultimately lethal part of the insurgency. Second, the Saigon government's ability to effectively *govern* outside the capital city was steadily declining. Although Saigon, Hue, and other major cities were cleared of armed insurgents in 1968, the provincial countryside was increasingly falling under the administrative control of insurgent cadres. The generals in power in Saigon had no effective means for dealing with the political and administrative challenges they faced from their enemies.

There can be nothing more telling about the relative unimportance of force in deciding the outcome of an insurgency than Col. Harry Summers' exchange with a North Vietnamese officer in 1973. As is well known, the exchange went like this:

> Colonel Summers: You know, you never defeated us on the battlefield.
>
> North Vietnamese officer: That may be so, but it is also irrelevant.

What Colonel Summers evidently missed was that the North Vietnamese strategy was never even remotely intended to destroy American forces. Yes, the NVA did attack our forces, and those of us who served in Vietnam would, I believe, admit that the North Vietnamese were excellent soldiers. But the Vietnamese strategy centered upon gaining effective control over elements of the populace in the South. Its goal was to win to its side as many of the uncommitted peasants, laborers, petty tradesmen and others as possible and isolate the rest. Those who stoutly opposed the local VC political organizer would be given a choice: submit to Viet Cong rule or flee. Those who refused to submit and did not flee often were murdered.

During the war many American soldiers tended to dismiss the Vietnamese people in general, and perhaps "Victor Charlie" as well, with epithets and racial slurs. Some GI's tended to dismiss the VC fighter as a "[insert epithet here] wearing a conical hat and Ho Chi Minh sandals." In other words, we often underestimated our enemies because of the great cultural differences that existed. Moreover, we invariably whipped the Vietnamese when they dared to stand and fight, didn't we?

Or, did they in fact really whip us?

To answer this question we must take a longer view of insurgency *in light of Vietnamese Communist strategy and their war aims.*

Perhaps if we could go back in time and recast the exchange between Colonel Summers and his North Vietnamese counterpart—asking the same question but in a slightly different way—it might have gone something like this:

Colonel Summers: How is it that you won the war when we consistently defeated you on the battlefield?

North Vietnamese: You fought only the enemy you could see, but not the enemy that you could not see. You fought the wrong war.

SO WHAT IS IT?

Insurgency fundamentally differs from conventional warfare for at least three key reasons.

First, it is an internal war. It is not fought as one nation against another, the way that Clausewitz and most other Western thinkers conceived of war. Rather, it is fought by part of the people against the established regime in their own country. Insurgencies can only occur when certain dysfunctional political and social conditions exist. They have distinct life cycles and can be understood in terms of the insurgents' Cause and the people who support that Cause.

Second, an insurgency is "armed politics." It is the involvement of civilians directly in some way, not necessarily militarily, to gain the desired political end. True, insurgent groups may use uniformed elements alongside peasant guerrillas in civilian clothes. For the *real* war, however, the distinguishing feature has more to do with proselytizing, recruiting, organizing, and mobilizing than it has to do with using weapons. In conventional wars, civilians are considered noncombatants. They may get in the way and complicate operations, but basically the people sit and watch as hapless bystanders and await the outcome. In an insurgency *the people* are the political object and are involved in every military or political activity that takes place.

Third, because insurgencies can take place only under certain conditions and involve an insurrection against an established regime, and because the heart of any insurgency is its political basis, the chief weapons are intelligence and counterintelligence, subversion, propaganda and political warfare, passive resistance, sabotage, and *time*.

Insurgency stands Clausewitz on his head in that its centerpiece is the capture of the nation's people politically and psychologically, and the replacement of its government. The destruction of the country's armed forces is achieved through the disintegration of a government rather than by defeating its army in battle. Indeed, the steady erosion of the existing regime from within merely paves the way for the dramatic photo op of tanks crashing through presidential gates. The *war* was already over long before this.

THE GERM OF REBELLION

Let us examine each of the three points in turn.

Insurgencies occur only in lands where a significant portion of the people have become disaffected with their government and its leaders. The ruling group has compromised its legitimacy in the eyes of this body of dissident people through its unpopular, unwise, or criminal policies. The disaffected group, which at the outset of the insurgency may be a minority, may lack competent leadership or a clear vision of what is to be done. If that is so, the ruling group might be able to maintain itself in power indefinitely simply by buying off or co-opting members of the disaffected group or modifying its policies in such a way as to reduce the level of discontent. But the existing regime will do this only if it is politically astute. As it happens, most such repressive or exploitative governments are neither astute nor imaginative.

Colonel Grant Newsham relates an interview conducted by one of his professors, the late Richard Ouderkirk, who was a foreign service officer at the time of Castro's seizure of power in early 1959. Mr. Ouderkirk interviewed a well-to-do Cuban businessman, now a refugee, who had lost everything in the overthrow of the Batista regime. Ouderkirk asked the man, "Why didn't you all just make the small changes that would have addressed so many peoples' grievances?" The businessman-refugee answered wistfully, "You know, we really should have. We just didn't think to do so."[5]

Where educated men and visionaries are in position to exert leadership, especially if the disaffected group views these men as charismatic and dynamic, an insurgent movement may be born. There are only three fundamental ingredients to every insurgency that has taken place or that is likely to take place in the future: a group that is sharply disaffected from its own government, a Cause (the reason or reasons for discontent), and a

---

[5] Colonel Grant Newsham, USMC, personal letter to author.

dynamic opposition leadership group that astutely manipulates the Cause to organize and motivate the people in ever larger numbers behind its banner.

Insurgencies come in a bewildering variety of political shapes and sizes. No two are exactly the same. Some insurgent movements are nationalist (anticolonial) in nature, others are Marxist, and others separatist. The insurgency in Afghanistan is reactionary in its ideology and heavily ethnic in its coloration. The point being made is that the political coloration of an insurgency will vary in each specific case, but its gestation is based on three factors: angry people, shrewd opposition leaders, and a Cause.

The second consideration is the principle of *total war*: active involvement in the struggle by *the people*. In partial contrast to Clausewitz's ideas, and in total contrast to those of Jomini, *the people are the centerpiece of the war* in an insurgency.[6] They are at one and the same time the primary source of resistance and the political prize sought. There can be no fence sitters in an insurgency. Eventually even the would-be neutrals will be compelled to choose one side or the other. The people themselves are both the "maneuver element" and the zone of the interior. They do not sit by passively watching and waiting, but in fact largely determine the outcome of the war. Bearing arms is merely one way by which the people participate in a war of national liberation. Many more civilians contribute through labor, provisions, intelligence, shelter in time of need, and so on. *Even the cold hostility of a community's passive resistance to the enemy is part of people's war.*

Clausewitz was well aware of the insurrection in Spain following its conquest by the French in 1807. Although Napoleon installed his brother as King of Spain, the majority of the Spanish people never accepted King Joseph and his *josefinos*. Thus, from 1808 until the end of the Napoleonic wars, Spain became ungovernable. Due to Spain being ungovernable Napoleon was compelled to station considerable bodies of troops in the country to battle the insurgency and maintain his brother in power. The British took full advantage of this situation and, at relatively small cost to themselves in lives and money, conducted a small war with Spanish *guerrillas* as allies against French regular armies.

---

[6] See Clausewitz, Book VI, Chapter 26, p. 479; Jomini is silent on this subject.

While some might dismiss the Peninsular War as a British proxy war against Napoleon, the Spanish people viewed this as their own fight against French occupation and did not consider themselves mere servants of British policy. Almost certainly Spanish resistance to King Joseph would have continued whether or not the British chose to help. We might observe that Moscow's fraternal assistance to Hanoi during the Vietnam War, and American and Saudi aid provided to the Afghan *mujahedin* during the Anti-Soviet War, were similar in nature. Great Powers take sides and aid insurgents in order to weaken their adversaries, but it does not follow that the Great Powers cause the insurgencies themselves, or are central to them. Rather, they opportunistically capitalize on a developing situation for their own ends. Certainly that rationale was true of Louis XVI and his foreign minister, the Comte de Vergennes, when they decided to aid the American revolutionaries in their war for independence from Great Britain. But the people involved on the ground, American patriots, viewed their liberation struggle as their own. Although appreciative of French help, American patriots did not consider themselves mere proxies or cats paws of the Bourbon monarchy in Paris.

This leads us back to the primary cause of an insurgency: *perceived illegitimacy of the rulers*. It is this factor more than any other that lies at the root of an insurgency. It does not matter if a government is autocratic as long as it is also popularly accepted and has effective control. Nor does the fact that a regime is democratic save it if that government also is considered illegitimate and is widely despised. This assertion can be proved by citing the example of the Weimar Republic, which millions of Germans viewed as illegitimate. By contrast, the Kingdom of Saudi Arabia is an absolute monarchy, yet the majority of Saudis support their government.

Examining our other historical examples—Napoleonic Spain under King Joseph, French colonial or republican Vietnam under the Ngo family, the Marxist government in Afghanistan under the People's Democratic Party of Afghanistan (PDPA), and British colonial rule in its American colonies after a long history of British political abuses—all lacked or lost the essential element of political legitimacy. After a certain tipping point, none of these regimes, irrespective of their political colorations, could claim wide popular support. Each regime was therefore vulnerable to a political challenge from within.

The American political scientist, Seymour Martin Lipset, describes the twin requirements of stable government in the following way:

> The stability of any given [government] depends not only on economic development but also upon the effectiveness and the legitimacy of its political system. Effectiveness means actual performance, the extent to which the system satisfies the basic functions of government as most of the population and such powerful groups within it as big business or the armed forces see them. Legitimacy involves the capacity of the system to engender and maintain the belief that the existing political institutions are the most appropriate ones for the society.[7]

The point being made is that if a government has lost its legitimacy in the eyes of the people, no amount of military force can possibly regain that essential factor. Lipset describes four kinds of regimes: those that are legitimate and effective; those that are legitimate, but ineffective; those that are effective, but illegitimate; and those that are neither legitimate nor effective.

A table might be helpful to understand the relative stability of the four types of regimes:

Legitimate	Effective	=	Least vulnerable to insurgency, most stable and highly likely to defeat an insurgent challenge
Legitimate	Ineffective	=	Vulnerable to insurgency, but capable of rallying most of the people most of the time
Illegitimate	Effective	=	Vulnerable to insurgency; if the insurgents can capture the banner of legitimacy they will win
Illegitimate	Ineffective	=	Highly vulnerable to insurgency, least stable; the regime will collapse even with massive third-party aid

[7] Lipset, p. 64. I have substituted the word "government" for Lipset's original word "democracy" as I believe his observation has applicability to governmental forms other than democracies.

Perhaps Lipset's criteria could be applied in reverse to insurgent movements. If so, it would be vital for those movements early on to capture the banner of legitimacy and to prove their effectiveness as an "alternative government" to the regime in power. Thus, insurgent movements showing themselves to be both legitimate and effective would almost certainly go on to victory whereas other movements shown to be ineffective, and especially illegitimate, would perhaps be more vulnerable to defeat, but to *political* defeat, not necessarily military defeat. The regime still has to demonstrate its own legitimacy and relative effectiveness.[8]

When Lipset's factors are applied against specific countries, it is somewhat easier to predict which governments are more likely to be susceptible to internal conditions leading to upheaval and which are less likely. Again, it must be said that nothing is certain. The only assertion being made here is that those countries whose societal roots are diseased are more likely to fall victim to an internal war than are countries with healthier societies.

A country like Oman, for example, is blessed with both legitimacy and effectiveness. We might therefore bet that it is less likely to experience a new challenge than would be, say, the Democratic Republic of Congo, which falls at the other end of the scale.

The policymaker is therefore presented with a dilemma. The countries most vulnerable to an insurgency are those that are hardest to assist. The temptation is great to rush in to help stave off collapse. But as we've seen in the case of South Vietnam, whose military regime was neither legitimate nor effective, massive American military and financial aid ultimately proved useless. As mentioned elsewhere in this work, it is a near miracle that U.S. power kept the feeble regime in Saigon alive as long it did.

The American government and people tried valiantly to "save" South Vietnam from Communism. Anyone who visits the Vietnam Memorial on the Capital Mall will come away sobered by the human losses that the American people accepted toward that goal. And yet, upon close inspection, what was there to save?

In the case of Vietnam, even during the period of the Ngo family's rule from 1955 to 1963,[9] it cannot be said that there was much (if any) "civil

[8] Author is indebted to Colonel Newsham for raising this issue (which author then pondered).

[9] The family consisted of Ngo Dinh Diem, his brother's wife, Madame Nhu, and brothers Ngo Dinh Nhu, Ngo Dinh Canh and Ngo Dinh Thuc, all of whom "governed" parts of

society" supporting the government. Yes, there were civilians: fishermen, pedicab drivers, rice farmers, petty tradesmen, laborers, and so on. But South Vietnamese society lacked any binder, any sense of internal structure or rationale that an ideology might have given. We might speculate that even had there been no serious political challenge from the North, eventually the Ngo family would have been overthrown or exiled. In fact, the Ngos, who were devout Catholics, went out of their way to alienate the Buddhists and other key groups, thus undercutting their own regime. There simply was nothing binding the rulers to the ruled.[10] The national government of South Vietnam was in a very real sense the person of Ngo Dinh Diem . . . and little else.

The Ngo family's government was largely a regime of the capital city, Saigon. It did not extend into the countryside. Yes, there were Saigon-appointed officials in all provinces and many districts. But the question must be asked whether these officials tied in with any important groups such as the peasantry. Except for the conditional yes of the Catholic refugees who fled North Vietnam after 1954, unfortunately the answer is, no. Moreover, the administrative effectiveness of the regime in rural areas left much to be desired.

After the fall of the Ngo family in November 1963, a constantly changing palace guard of Vietnamese generals took their place. "Government" became the will of the leading generals. Civil administration, always weak, virtually collapsed. For all intents and purposes, beyond the Saigon city limits, the government of the Republic of Vietnam (GVN) was the Army of the Republic of Vietnam (ARVN).

Colonel Harry Summers, noted scholar and fine officer that he was, postulated that the collapse of the South Vietnamese regime in May 1975 had nothing to do with insurgency and was instead the result of massive conventional invasion. He was wrong. In point of fact, the government of the South had collapsed many years earlier. What is surprising, therefore,

---

the country as if these parts were private fiefdoms. Another brother, Ngo Dinh Khoi, was buried alive by the Vietminh. In November 1963 the Ngos were overthrown in a military coup; Ngo Dinh Diem and his brother Nhu were later murdered.

[10] A symptom that South Vietnamese society was dysfunctional was the self-immolation of Buddhist monks prior to the downfall of Diem and his government. The monks were not in the pay of Ho Chi Minh.

is the fact that at enormous cost we Americans managed to stave off the inevitable for so long. I believe it is fair to say that had we not intervened militarily South Vietnam would have been brought under Communist rule by the mid-1960s largely due to the ineptitude and unfitness to govern of its own rulers and further undermined by Viet Cong subversion. The North Vietnamese May 1975 capture of Saigon was merely the delayed result of internal political and economic decay that had taken place in the South over a prolonged period. There was nothing left for the South Vietnamese *people* to defend.

Let us be clear that insurgency is much more than simply guerrilla warfare. Many military professionals, who should know better, often equate the two. They think that guerrilla warfare is insurgency and insurgency is merely guerrilla warfare. While it is true that guerrilla warfare can play a considerable role in the process of insurgency, it is merely one tool of many in the insurgents' tool box. Another tool is "regular" warfare, that is mobile warfare with uniformed troops, which also plays a part, especially near the end of a protracted war when the target regime is near collapse. But the historical record makes clear that insurgents also employ acts of terrorism, sabotage, infiltration of the regime and various organizations, economic warfare, and omnipresent, often highly sophisticated, propaganda and political warfare aimed at building support. Given a politically vulnerable regime this almost invisible activity is the true centerpiece or heart of insurgency.

Insurgency is a broad political process aided by military means; it is armed political competition. Its core is the persuasion of the people of a given country or territory to support the aims of the insurgent movement, to withdraw their support from the existing governmental institutions, and to join in forming a new government to replace the regime that is being overthrown.

HOW INSURGENTS THINK

The leadership of an incipient insurgent movement almost invariably is drawn from the middle and upper classes of a country like Wikitania that is subject to many serious dysfunctions. The leaders themselves may be and often are personally above all or most of these dysfunctions, but are nevertheless keenly aware of their society's problems. Not surprisingly, this awareness of society's ills is most often found in university students. In Islamic lands, revolutionaries may be found among bright young men given intensive religious training over a number of years. Whether educated in western-style universities or trained in *madrassas*, these young people become the core of the insurgent leadership.[11]

Casual observers of insurgencies tend to assume that all revolutionaries and insurgent leaders are, *ipso facto,* Marxists. But revolutionaries come in all shapes and sizes and in all political hues. The leaders of our own revolution were men deeply influenced by the European Enlightenment. Islamists leading insurgent movements tend to be theologically extremely conservative. In fact, they are reactionaries, not radicals as some pundits would have us believe.[12] True, the best known insurgent leaders of the twentieth century—Mao Tse-tung and Ho Chi Minh—were indeed influenced by Marxism. But other leaders, notably Michael Collins in Ireland and George Grivas in Cyprus, were true nationalists. While Grivas and Collins were both insurgent leaders, neither man had much Enlightenment ideology, each had only slight religious motivation, and neither had a drop of Marxist blood. Yet both men were committed revolutionaries.

The point is that the *political language* of an insurgent movement may vary from one insurgency to another. Indeed, the political language *must* vary from country to country, precisely because the needs and aspirations of the people in each country have different cultures, different needs, and different expectations. Insurgent leaders are obviously aware of their own societies. Successful insurgent movements are tailored to those societies.

What matters is that an articulate individual or group of individuals, having studied the problems of their own country, undertake to formulate a set of proposed solutions aimed at correcting a society's perceived ills. Some insurgent leaders may see the solution to their country's problems as the establishment of a republic with a laissez-faire economy in place of a monarchy that strictly controls trade. Others may believe that Marxism holds the answers for their land's dysfunctions. In recent years we note that

---

[11] Colonel Newsham poses the intriguing idea of comparing the decision-making processes used by the old-style Marxist or nationalist insurgent leaders with those of contemporary Islamist leaders. Author commends this as a vital research effort for a "think-tank" or military university researcher.

[12] See Annex B on so-called "Islamic radicalism."

Islamic leaders have put forward the idea that only a return to strict practices found in the Holy Qur'an, or an imagined Golden Age of the early caliphs, can solve man's ills. At the end of the day, the would-be leader or leaders put forward a political program in which they diagnose their country's woes and specify the proper remedy. This is the basis on which the insurgent's vital political mobilization campaign is built. In Robert D. Kaplan's words:

> Beyond its stark, clearly articulated message, Islam's very militancy makes it attractive to the downtrodden. It is the one religion that is prepared to *fight*. A political era driven by environmental stress, increased cultural sensitivity, unregulated urbanization, and refugee migrations is an era divinely created for the spread and intensification of Islam, already the world's fastest-growing religion.[13]

GETTING THE REBELLION UNDERWAY

As its very first move an astute insurgent leadership takes stock of its opponent: the leadership of the regime it seeks to replace. It is sometimes the case that insurgent leaders not only have a clear understanding of their adversaries, they are personally acquainted with some key figures in the target regime.

The insurgents therefore are well aware of the attitudes, preferences, personalities, quirks, virtues and vices, and mental abilities of their foes. These attributes are significant because taken together they influence how the target regime leaders will formulate policy and in particular, how the regime will react to the insurgent challenge.

Even when the insurgents are not personally acquainted with their foes, they nonetheless go about studying the key leaders of the government-in-being and the policies promoted by those leaders. This is done to discern where splits, weak points, or other operationally relevant vulnerabilities exist. The insurgent leadership will be certain to focus upon these vulnerabilities in its political warfare strategy, the object being to play upon tensions and, where possible, to exacerbate those tensions.

Along with a focus upon the regime leadership, the insurgents will make a broad study of society and the contradictions that exist between

---

[13] Kaplan, p. 66.

groups in society and the government-in-being, especially where those contradictions have been caused or aggravated by the sitting government. The insurgents invariably spend much time and effort gaining detailed knowledge of each social group's reaction to the contradictions. Indeed, understanding how the shoe fits is vital to the insurgents as it furnishes them with the *means for conducting the all-important campaign of subversion and recruitment upon which victory chiefly depends.* For it is these groups, motivated to support the aims and goals of the insurgent movement through agitation and propaganda, that provide manpower, intelligence, food, shelter, portage and other logistical services, and a host of other goods and services essential to the triumph of the insurgency.

Insurgent leaders must necessarily take into account the political orientations of the many groups making up the body politic of their countries, for this knowledge will help shape the strategy that is formulated to defeat the government-in-being.

A good example of this thinking is seen in Mao's writings of the 1920s and 1930s in which he spends a great deal of time discussing political and economic conditions as opposed to strictly military tactics. As is well known, China suffered from gross inequity in land holdings which was one of the key political problems Mao believed to be at the root of the country's ills. The following excerpt is taken from his November 1928 report "Struggle in the Chingkang Mountains":

> *The land situation in the border areas.*
>
> Roughly speaking, more than 60 per cent of the land belonged to the landlords and less than 40 per cent to the peasants. In the Kiangsi [Province] sector, landownership was most concentrated in Suichuan County, where about 80 per cent of the land belonged to the landlords. Yunghsin came next with about 70 per cent. In Wanan, Ningkang, and Lienhua there were more owner-peasants, but the landlords still owned the bulk of the land, i.e., about 60 per cent of the total, while the peasants owned only 40 per cent. In the Hunan [Province] sector, about 70 per cent of the land in both Chaling and Linghsien Counties belonged to the landlords.[14]

---

[14] Mao, *Selected Military Writings*, p. 35.

By carefully examining each district's situation, Mao and his colleagues became more familiar with the economics and politics affecting the people living in those localities than were the appointed government officials sent out from Nanking. With Mao having greater knowledge of the land question he was in a better position than were government officials to make political use of it. Indeed, focusing on political concerns at the "worm's eye level" of the peasantry made it possible for the Chinese Communists to *build their military power as their political influence grew.*

The excerpt quoted above is not only of significance in terms of what it tells us about the insurgents' concern with local politics, but also gives insight into what was of greatest intelligence concern to the insurgents. I find it highly likely that Mao and his associates had more detailed information, not merely about land questions, but about the people and political conditions at *hsien* level, than did the government. The operational consequence of this knowledge was that the Chinese Red Army, as it was then known, could survive and operate in the Hunan-Kiangsi border area despite the advantages in weaponry and manpower of its national government enemies. Several times from 1928 to 1934 the Nationalists launched encirclement campaigns to trap Mao and his guerrilla forces. Inevitably these failed. To an extent, this was due to stupidity and incompetence on the government side, but it was also due in considerable part to the aid and comfort given the Red Army by peasants who viewed the Chinese Communists as representing their interests in the land question. This is the heart of armed politics.

Not least, many of the more developed insurgent movements will pay close attention to the *international* politics affecting the insurgency. The North Vietnamese and Viet Cong orchestrated a robust effort to isolate the Saigon regime from the international community and, if possible, cut off its foreign sources of support. The Taliban appear to be doing much the same to deprive the Afghan government of foreign assistance.

Lest you come away thinking that political organization of the people for an insurgency is something only Mao or Ho Chi Minh could do, let us examine an insurgency of a very different type. Let's turn to General Georgios Grivas and his struggle during the late 1950s and 1960s with Britain over Cyprus.

General Grivas, Cypriot nationalist and anti-Communist, wrote:

> A revolutionary movement and a guerrilla war, in particular, stand no chance of success, whatever the qualities of their leader, unless they have the complete and unreserved support of the majority of the country's inhabitants, for it is to them the movement will turn for assistance of every kind (cadres and fighters, hiding places, concealment of equipment and men, liaison agents, food supplies, propaganda, etc.) My own military career has taught me that the collapse of the front usually begins from the rear. Consequently, I devoted my attention to organizing the population in order not only to get it actively to participate in the struggle but also to enable it to hold out, seeing that our struggle was above all a matter of time and endurance.[15]

The political question on Cyprus was not inequitable landholding or a corrupt comprador class that exploited the Cypriots. The issue was Greek nationalism, Cyprus having been a British protectorate from 1878. The Cypriots desired incorporation into Greece or, failing that, the establishment of their own independent republic.

Every insurgency has its armed element. After all, insurgency is "armed politics." If arms were not needed to attain the revolutionary movement's goals, there would be no need to resort to violence. In a sense, violence is a political message intended to tell the government-in-being or foreign occupier that *the pain will continue until you grant our political wish.* In this sense, insurgency is indeed "a matter of time and endurance," as General Grivas observed.

THE POLITICAL GUTS OF INSURGENCY

As I've tried to make abundantly clear, the core of any insurgency is its political aim. There would be no insurgency if a certain collage of dysfunctional conditions did not exist. Likewise, there would be no insurgency if certain major groups were unaffected by those conditions. The actual specifics of the dysfunctions vary from country to country. No two are exactly the same.

In the preceding chapter we made a whirlwind trip around the globe

[15] Grivas, p. 11.

and touched upon some of the key issues that could bring about the conditions necessary for an insurgency.

In the examples of China and Cyprus—two vastly different countries with almost totally different kinds of societies, cultures, economies, and political situations—we note that the roots of conflict lay in perceived dysfunctions. In the case of China, one contributory cause was the matter of land distribution, along with usurious interest rates, unreasonable rental fees, and extortionate taxation of the peasantry. It is probable that the peasants in Hunan or Kiangsi were illiterate or nearly so, their income was a pittance, and the pressing issue was access to a bare minimum of food. In the case of Cyprus, the people were literate (in 2009, literacy stood at 97.7 percent) and GDP is about equal to that of Panama or Jordan, not wealthy, but by no means destitute. Yet both China and Cyprus had insurgencies that ultimately triumphed against their respective rulers.

If we examine some of the factors that spark insurgencies, we could group them into three broad categories: political and administrative; social advancement; and economic discontent. It should be understood that factors tend to spill over from one category to another. Often a shortcoming or dysfunction in political life will have economic consequences, economic problems have social impact, and so on. Countries vulnerable to insurgencies will have a variety of ills, often touching upon all three categories.

POLITICAL-ADMINISTRATIVE

The political-administrative category includes such issues as the structure and effectiveness of government. Foreign control, as in the heyday of European colonialism, may give rise to anticolonial movements. The insurgencies leading to the expulsion of the French from Indochina and Algeria, and the Portuguese from their African colonies are good examples. The revolutionary's appeal is obviously nationalist in nature and sets out a credible vision of home rule.

One-party and oligarchic systems also may be cause for disaffection. We have mentioned the impact of the Ngo family on the former South Vietnam. The Somoza dynasty in Nicaragua is another poster child for misrule. Personalist politics, especially when nepotism and corruption are rife, is a magnet for disaffection. Politically aware elites who are shut out from government tend to agitate for a share of political power.

Inept as well as corrupt administrative services are a classic source of popular grievances in many developing lands. The irony is that peoples at the very bottom of the socio-economic heap, like Niger or Mali, or societies in which tribal, ethnic, or religious groups look to their tribal or religious group to provide basic services, the ineptitude of the government ceases to be a factor. The logic is much like the old saw: *Blessed are they who naught expect, for they shall not be disappointed.* The government is not expected to provide anything, so therefore no public expectations are bruised.

There is, of course, the vital consideration of the police and armed forces. Where those security services are brutal, corrupt, and inept, they are a source of enormous discontent. The Quan Canh police in the former South Vietnam, known to many G.I.'s of that era as the "White Mice," regularly extorted bribes from peasants and tradesmen. They were loathed. While it is vital for a government to have a presence throughout the territory it controls, *the quality of that presence is vital.* Corrupt police are a worse presence than would be no police at all. Depending upon their conduct, the military can also be a trusted source of security . . . or a cause of volcanic discontent among the people. Thievery, brutality and rape do not inspire affection.

Often overlooked is the effectiveness of a country's legal system. Frequently, major sources of discontent are malfunctioning courts and lack of access to justice. In the Islamic world the legitimacy of a ruler is based upon his ability to administer justice. In developing countries it is often the case that judges are bought by the rich elites; "justice" becomes whatever the highest bidder is willing to pay.[16]

A mark of an advanced political system is the presence of an organized political party (or parties) that function in an institutionalized way, even if dominated by a strong figure. The absence of such parties, combined with abstruse systems of voting, if voting is even permitted, can be another

[16] A key Afghan grievance against the Karzai regime is perceived widespread corruption of the courts and system of justice. The Taliban seized upon this failing and turned it to advantage by instituting their own courts based on *shari'a* or Islamic law. Although Islamic justice is harsh, many observers state that the Taliban's brand of justice administration is both impartial and swift.

irritant to the body politic. Again, in lands where parties and voting are not culturally familiar this might not be an issue. But in other countries that are shambling toward mass participation in decision-making, weaknesses or corruption in the way parties campaign, and widespread balloting fraud serve only to breed public cynicism.

Afghanistan may be something of a political mule.[17] On the one hand, under Western tutelage, voting and democracy are strongly encouraged. On the other hand, traditional power structures based on cultural factors remain the political bedrock. It is hardly surprising, therefore, that many Afghans are puzzled or dismayed by democracy while Western capitals profess to be disappointed and embarrassed by vote fraud.[18]

Another factor on the political side is the presence or absence of open media and public access to newspapers, radio and television, the internet, and other sources of information. Ironically, lands like the former Iron Curtain countries, having official newspapers[19] and radio stations, may be less prone to violence and upheaval than countries in which such unconstrained media flourish. It was possible in former days to keep a lid on public disaffection by carefully controlling what the public was allowed to know. Whether such tight controls are possible today, except in lands like Myanmar and North Korea, is quite doubtful. Literacy and the internet are inherently revolutionary.

SOCIAL ADVANCEMENT

Turning toward social advancement, the single most vital signal of dysfunction is the existence of a sharp gap between the common people, the

---

[17] That is, neither a horse nor a donkey, but something in between. Politically, Afghanistan is neither a democracy nor a monarchy though it exhibits some elements of both forms.

[18] Colonel Newsham reports seeing a BBC clip from the 2010 elections showing "a bearded, beturbaned Afghan stuffing ballots in a box. [Newsham's] instinctive reaction [was] what the hell is he supposed to do?" Before pointing fingers, we should note ballot irregularities in some of our own great cities.

[19] A Soviet joke of the Cold War era had to do with the official paper, Pravda, which in Russian means truth and the news service, Izvestiya, which in Russian means news. The joke went: "In Pravda there is no truth, and in Izvestiya there is no news." (*V Pravdu nyet Pravdi; v Izvestiyu nyet Izvestii.*) Given widespread cynicism about their own media, the Russian public sought news from foreign broadcasts and, when they could get them, from foreign newspapers.

masses, and the elites. This disparity between the few at the top and the many below becomes even more significant if social inequality is augmented by established political or legal barriers. The white minority regime in South Africa under *apartheid* was a classic example of this condition. The effect of *apartheid* legislation was to polarize society, largely along racial and class lines. El Salvador's "Fourteen Families" (or *"Catorce"*) is another well-known example of a mass-elite gap.

In the previous chapter we discussed the importance of literacy and public education. Where a country's literacy is spotty, but is not totally lacking, there is the possibility of social divisions along educational lines. (For obvious reasons these divisions may closely conform to the mass-elite gap). People with higher education either receive higher paid jobs in their native countries or, if this advancement is denied, may gravitate toward revolutionary activity. One great danger is that for want of jobs some of the country's smartest and best-trained people may leave their homeland for countries that offer better employment opportunities creating a "brain drain" that further weakens their native country.

Standards of public health are critical to a country's overall human resources and thus to the economy. If infectious disease is widespread it indicates that a land's administrative structure is ineffective and does not meet basic human needs. This condition often is found in countries of the Lower Half of the scale. With governments short on money, public health and preventive medicine are some of the basic services that are often shorted. Should cuts in health services be due to obvious malfeasance by government officials, public anger at the regime is sure to result. Unfortunately, this situation is familiar to many Africans.

Closely related to public health is the issue of nutrition and also associated issues of adequate clothing and shelter. A limited supply of food is often a cause for public disturbances and has been known to trigger revolutions. People who are desperately hungry are often desperate indeed. Food supplies may be catastrophically reduced due to drought or pests. If so, many people, especially the less educated, will interpret this as an Act of God. But if food supplies are substantially reduced due to diversions by corrupt officials, or sharp price increases resulting from manipulation of supplies, it is likely public anger will know no bounds If perpetually hungry due to Acts of God, a nation's population may stolidly accept their lot without complaint. But if people are used to a certain level of nutrition and it is lowered by Acts of Man they will not sit idly by.

Yet another consideration in the social advancement category concerns peasant or what can be called "traditionalist" values and attitudes. Societies undergoing transformation from traditional social patterns frequently spark discontent when modern values and ideas are promoted by the regime that conflict with time-honored values and ideas. This cause of dysfunction is widespread in post-colonial societies, such as those in Africa and Asia, and in some Islamic countries attempting to promote secular education.

ECONOMIC DISCONTENT

Sources of economic discontent are many and varied. Many Third World countries depend upon a very limited portfolio of commodities and crops for the bulk of their national income, sometimes a single crop or commodity. Should prices collapse or even decline the country will be in serious trouble. First, local export businesses will fail. Second, unemployment spreads virtually overnight as almost everyone with a job is, by definition, connected to the export crop or commodity. Third, secondary losses will quickly follow since many other tradesmen derive their income from persons who receive their wages from the export crop or commodity. High unemployment quickly becomes a political problem.[20]

In many Third World countries the economy is not diversified enough to be able to withstand the shock of a drop in price of a major export crop like sugar, coffee, or cacao. Because of this the possibility of self-sustained growth is sharply constrained. Lacking internal sources of growth a country is in danger of becoming dependent upon outside sources of income: aid donors. To the extent that a regime becomes dependent on outsiders it tends to lose credibility in the eyes of the people. Its "nationalist credentials" are called into question. Moreover, the political interests of the donor country may overshadow the national interests of the recipient. This was certainly true of aid given to many countries by the former Soviet Union.

---

[20] Even leftist governments such as that presently in Venezuela are subject not only to world economic vicissitudes, but to their own policies that create price distortions, inflation, and economic dislocation. The question facing the policy community is whether the eventual transfer of power from Hugo Chavez to his successor will be peaceful and orderly or will be brought about by other means.

The lack of a well-developed capital infrastructure—highways, railroads, seaports and airports, and all that is necessary to keep them in good repair—is a major handicap to a country's economy. Even if crops are abundant in one area of a country, if there are no roads, or the roads are in horrible condition as in Afghanistan and many other such countries, transport is difficult if not impossible. The irony is the possibility of super-abundance in one region (and consequent waste) with starvation and misery in another region of the same country.

A stable currency and a modern, reliable (honest!) banking system is a requirement for any serious economic growth. Most countries outside the developed world lack such a banking system and many lack viable currencies. A *hawala* system,[21] though remarkably efficient for *transferring* funds, fails utterly in the primary function of a bank: providing capital for investment in commerce, agriculture, and industry. Often, banks in Third World countries are run by relatives of those in power and merely serve to export money to safe havens such as Singapore, Dubai, Zurich, and New York. In effect, rather than making funds available to farmers and traders for development, these crony banks siphon away much-needed value from a country's economy. We must also admit with shame that certain well-known First World banks have, in fact, encouraged and colluded in this draining away of much-needed investment capital from poorer countries.

Not least, underdeveloped lands generally lack a skilled, trained, disciplined labor force, and with few exceptions, also lack managerial expertise. Workers come and go as they please, and a task may or may not be completed on time. Quality of work is spotty, and often a unit of labor is actually more costly than it would be in a more advanced economy. This is because, in addition to the quality and time factors—low productivity—there are also the issues of waste of materials, theft, damage of equipment, the higher frequency of accidents, and ever-present demand for "squeeze."

In lands where a robust work ethic is absent, productivity is low and costs are high; there is little incentive for a businessman or entrepreneur to invest. With no incentive to risk capital where it almost certainly will be lost or wasted a vicious cycle ensues: no economic growth will take place for lack of venture capital.

---

[21] The term comes from the Arabic *awala* "a bill of exchange" and *ala* "to change."

Agriculture is the foundation of civilization. Every country on Earth requires a reliable food supply. Sadly, most lands in the Lower Half lack reliable food supplies. This is partly because in many Third World countries farming techniques are primitive and require time-consuming hand labor. (After all, machinery and chemical fertilizers are expensive whereas labor is cheap). In part, lack of reliable food is due to pests and crop disease, exhaustion of the soil, spoilage, and weather. But there is also a special problem in underdeveloped countries: successful farmers, especially large landowners, are more interested in using their best soil to produce valuable cash crops for export, not inexpensive food products for local consumption. As a consequence, Wikitania might well be a leading agricultural export country according to published statistics . . . while people in the lower socio-economic strata in rural areas of the country slowly starve.

TAKING STOCK

We have now made a whirlwind survey of a number of political, economic, and social factors that may affect a great number of countries in the middle and Lower Half of the GDP (gross domestic product) and PPP (purchasing power parity) spectrum. It is possible to construct an analytical framework in which these factors are arrayed on a chart and compared with known conditions observed in Wikitania or any other country we may choose to study. To the extent that such conditions exist, and to the extent that they are severe and growing worse, a fair judgment can be made that the conditions for the outbreak of an insurgency also exist.

Taking Lipset's criteria as our yardstick we can draw up a list of those lands having regimes viewed by the people as legitimate. We can also make judgments about governments that are effective. Where both criteria are present we likely will find that political stability is the norm. However, where one or the other quality is absent, it is possible that the conditions required for insurgency exist. And where a regime is neither effective nor legitimate, clouded by some or all of the political, social, and economic factors noted above, trouble is almost certain to occur.

We have made this grand tour of various socioeconomic dysfunctions because it is vital that a practitioner fully understand that insurgency has roots in those dysfunctions. The presence of deep problems creates political conditions favorable for the growth of an internal resistance movement.

Were it not for the existence of many of the conditions noted in a country there would be no insurgency. So long as those conditions persist and affect significant numbers of people there will be no end to the insurgency.

CHAPTER 3

A PEEK AT WESTERN STRATEGIC THINKING

In 1787, Tom Paine wrote, "War involves in its progress such a train of unforeseen and unsupposed circumstances that no human wisdom can calculate the end. It has but one thing certain, and that is to increase taxes."

Since the days of the ancient Greeks until very recent times, Western strategy has been thought of almost exclusively in the military context. Indeed, the Attic Greek term *strategos* had the literal meaning of "leader of the army" or, as we would translate the sense of the term, "general." Certain Greek civil leaders such as Pericles doubled as the leader of the army, the *strategos*. Despite the collapse of the Western Roman Empire in 476 A.D., the ancient concept of the *strategos* lived on in the eastern continuation of the Roman Empire, Byzantium.

STRATEGY

Although the term *strategos* is archaic in the West,[1] the Greek word *strategia*, that which the *strategos* or general formulates, came into the French language in the eighteenth century as *strategie* and ultimately into English as strategy. Its original meaning was limited to the general's deployment of his forces prior to battle, tactics being the means by which he used those forces on the battlefield. Clausewitz initially held this very limited view,

[1] To this day the Greek army uses the term *strategos* to denote its commander.

although he soon came to understand that strategy was something broader than merely the placement of troops.

Even with this explanation as background, it should be understood that the concept of strategy is still hard to define. Several European military thinkers—we will briefly examine concepts by four great strategists: Jomini, Clausewitz, Liddell Hart, and Delbrueck—differ in their meaning and interpretation of strategy. It should not surprise us that each of these thinkers should differ with one another.[2] But one thing should be kept in mind: all four of these great thinkers have Western philosophical roots and share common ownership of the Western cultural heritage. With the partial and special exception of Liddell Hart, their thinking necessarily was colored by their culture.

Strategy is conceived from the viewpoint of the strategist and the physical capabilities and limitations, the objective conditions, as well as the political structures existing in his time. The elements of strategy that were applicable in the Age of Napoleon are not necessarily appropriate to the conditions that existed during the conflicts of the twentieth century. Nor will these elements necessarily be appropriate to the wars we are likely to face during the twenty-first century. As we will see in a later chapter, insurgency has its own distinct strategy that differs in significant ways from classic strategy as understood by great European thinkers of the past. This should not be surprising, because insurgency is fundamentally different from the kind of war the West is used to seeing, and it is practiced, by and large, in non-European settings.

As the twentieth century opened, it became apparent that there were several varieties of strategy to be considered: traditional military strategy, certainly, but also the idea of a higher-level grand strategy appeared in the late nineteenth century having to do with the strategy employed by nations to achieve their own goals. This higher level or grand strategy took account of national resources and capabilities as well as the nation's aims.

Political strategies have been recognized since Nicolo Macchiavelli's publication of *The Prince* in the sixteenth century.[3] Grand strategy and

---

[2] The reader should be aware that many thinkers have contributed to the theory and practice of strategy. Because of space limitations only these four better known authorities will be cited.

[3] Macchiavelli, much maligned by those who have never read *The Prince* and who misunderstand his reason for writing this tutorial for princes, might be considered the first true "pol-mil" strategist.

military strategy had not diverged into distinct entities until well into the nineteenth century because for the most part the head of state also was the chief of the armed forces. For example, Gustavus Adolphus, Frederick the Great, Tsar Alexander, and Napoleon combined both military and political authority in their persons.[4]

As modern nations grew ever more complex in the nineteenth and twentieth centuries they were compelled to divide responsibility between military specialists and political leadership.

Interestingly, during the last forty years or so strategy and strategic thinking has entered the commercial marketing world through the writings of contemporary scholars such as Dr. George Steiner. Political and military specialists would do well to read some of the theoretical works and primers produced by American marketing experts.

In a paper titled "Strategy: Definitions and Meanings" intended primarily for marketing students, author Fred Nickols made the following observation:

> Strategy, then, has no existence apart from the ends sought. It is a general framework that provides guidance for actions to be taken and, at the same time, is shaped by the actions taken. This means that the necessary precondition for formulating strategy is a clear understanding of the ends to be obtained. Without these ends in view, action is purely tactical and can quickly degenerate into nothing more than a flailing about.[5]

Nickols goes on to state that "The risks of not having a set of company-wide ends clearly in view include missed opportunities, fragmented and wasted effort, working at cross purposes and endless internecine warfare."[6] In Nickols's view, a lack of strategy can lead to poor morale, confusion, divided counsels, and the possible collapse of the affected organization.

Clearly, the necessity of strategy applies to a variety of disciplines: military, political, commercial, and governmental. The views expressed by Nickols to his marketing students might also apply to a military officer, a political candidate seeking office, or to cabinet members considering how

---

[4] Upon his deathbed, Napoleon's last words reportedly were: "Chief of the Army . . ."

[5] Nickols, p. 6

[6] *Ibid.*

best to steer the ship of state. In simplified form, strategy is a methodical way of thinking about capabilities that leads to a desired end.

Let us briefly examine the strategic views of four of the most influential European thinkers of the last two hundred years as background to our later examination of insurgency. We will visit insurgent thinking on strategy in the next chapter and examine how in some ways it mirrors conventional ideas, but diverges significantly in others.

JOMINI

Antoine Henri Jomini (1779–1869) was a Swiss officer who served with distinction in both the French and Russian armies and in 1805 was the author of his first great writing on military strategy, *Traité des grandes opérations militaires* (*Treatise on Grand Military Operations*). This and his other writings on military subjects influenced not only the armies of Napoleon and Tsar Alexander, but exerted considerable influence on the military thinking of both Union and Confederate generals during the American Civil War. In many ways, Jominian thinking still influences modern armed forces, particularly those forces that depend more heavily on advanced technology and operate in environments where the impact of human factors on military operations is minimal.

In a Jominian Universe, policy and war dance a kind of minuet. The two barely touch, and policy is almost a thing apart from the military forces sent forth on its behalf. As Professor John Shy put it, "The lesson was clear: [Jomini believed that] a government should choose its ablest military commander, then leave him free to wage war according to scientific principles."[7] In conducting its battlefield maneuvers, Jomini's army would follow a quasi-mathematical program leading inevitably to victory. The deployment of troops on a battlefield, the placement of artillery and supporting arms, and their methodical movement and coordination are all-important to victory, and are done based upon *immutable* Jominian principles. Victory won, the military then hands off the battlefield decision to the sovereign's diplomats to sort out the spoils. A man of the late eighteenth century, Jomini believed that discoverable scientific laws lay behind all aspects of warfare, just as they lay behind all aspects of the physical world.

Jomini's theories of strategy have textbook precision and a formulaic

[7] Paret, *Makers of Modern Strategy*, p. 161

nature. Jomini set down certain observations as "principles of war" that commanders were to observe at all times. Until very late in life Jomini said little about politics, psychology, motivation, or morale. For Jomini war was analogous to a game of chess between two skilled masters with opposing units of comparable size theoretically equal, much as one rook to the other. Perhaps Jomini instinctively believed that each opponent would use the same Marquis-of-Queensberry rules in battle. One is tempted to believe that Jomini viewed war as a kind of noble jousting, filled with chivalry and colorful banners.

The U.S. Army's Principles of War, enshrined in FM 100-5, and a staple of American infantry doctrine, are the intellectual children of Antoine Jomini. In his article "Scientific Optimism: Jomini and the U.S. Army," Major Gregory R. Ebner connects Jomini solidly not only with these principles of war, but with the military decision-making process(MDMP). According to Major Ebner:

> American reliance on decisive points and the scientific application of military theory to provide the commander with solutions to problems in war are further suggest [sic] the Jominian character of the U.S. Army. In schools of tactics, U.S. Army officers repeatedly study the use of the military decision-making process (MDMP) as the predominant tool for deriving solutions for operations in war. If the Principles of War are Jomini writ short, then the MDMP is Jomini in full glory. *Through a scientific, step-by-step calculus, the MDMP promises to assist planners in finding a suitable solution to any military problem that they may face. Its systemic approach to problem solving relies on simple rules governing the movement of forces, the synchronization of their effects, and the discerned application of maximum power at decisive points on the battlefield. The clarity and optimism of the MDMP relies on Jominian hopes that war can be controlled and that the studious theoretician can master the application of violence. The lucidity and precision of the MDMP trumps Clausewitz's friction and fog and offers the Army officer the ability to maintain command of the chaos of war.* [emphasis added][8]

[8] Ebner, *The U.S. Army Professional Writing Collection*, p.2.

Major Ebner goes on to say much more about the Jominian approach to war, largely based on calculation of everything from the combat power of friendly and enemy battalions of equal size down to the measurements of the "space between trees, and the very diameter of the trees. . . . "[9] Jomini's quest was for simplicity, symmetry, and scientific order in warfare with the highest goal being attainment of mathematical precision.

It is worth noting, however, that later in his article Major Ebner observes: "The extreme opposite of the linear battle, guerrilla wars of a national character, shake Jominian ideals to their very core. He [Jomini] recommends avoiding them altogether."[10] Jomini had served in Spain, and was therefore only too familiar with the *guerra de guerrillas* fought there. However, he adopted a kind of ostrich view regarding "wars of opinion" as he called them. They did not fit his paradigm, and he knew it.

Professor Shy notes that Jomini was profoundly shocked when one night an entire artillery company of Ney's corps was wiped out by angry peasants led by a priest. Only one man of the company survived. Jomini wrote, "all the gold in Mexico could not buy the combat intelligence needed by the French forces in Spain."[11] Yet, unlike Clausewitz, Jomini chose not to investigate this strange phenomena of "the people in arms" that was so completely opposite his own conception of war.

Interestingly, Jomini's rules approach strikes one as being almost a model for the more technological naval and air services. In a military environment where *the people* hardly matter, that is, on the high seas or in the stratosphere, Jominian-like calculations such as circular error probable [CEP] or probability of kill [PK] may well be appropriate.[12] Jomini on steroids, perhaps? It must be conceded that mathematics and physics apply in a technological world where only machines fight machines. The point

---

[9] Ibid.

[10] Ibid. Major Ebner cites John Shy, "Jomini," *Makers of Modern Strategy: From Machiavelli to the Nuclear Age*, ed. Peter Paret, p. 171.

[11] Shy, *Makers of Modern Strategy*, op. cit., p. 170.

[12] Both naval ships and military aircraft are concerned with range, speed and payload, as well as fixed bases, and complex logistical systems capable of meeting demand for parts, repairs, and supplies. All this is catnip to Jomini. Even so, as Colonel Newsham, USMC, reminds us, admirals may be subject to the very same "fog of war" based on deception, error, and bad luck, as are generals on land. Newsham cites the Battle of Leyte Gulf in

being made is that warfare at sea, pitting naval ships against enemy ships, or pilots against enemy aircraft, more nearly approaches Jomini's ideal. In the case of land forces, however, intimate knowledge of the myriad cultural, political, and psychological factors of the people living in the area of operations—and not computer algorithms—will shape the outcome of land operations, especially insurgencies.

That having been said, we may speculate how scientific rules apply to battles fought by foot soldiers or guerrillas, especially where political and psychological factors are paramount. Jominian thinking may well lead to disasters when applied to insurgency.

CLAUSEWITZ

Karl von Clausewitz (1780–1831) was a Prussian officer of Polish ancestry who served under the great Prussian general Gerhard von Scharnhorst during the Napoleonic wars. Captured following the disastrous battle at Jena, Clausewitz was a prisoner of war in France for two years. After his release from captivity Clausewitz helped Scharnhorst reform the Prussian army. He entered Russian service in 1812 and was instrumental in bringing about an alliance between Prussia and Russia that ultimately doomed French control of Germany. After the War of Liberation (1813–1814) Clausewitz taught at the *Kriegsakademie* in Berlin and set down his observations and thoughts in what was to become, after his death, *Vom Kriege*.

In a Clausewitzian world, warfare is politics by other means, or the extension of a nation's political aims through arms. Clausewitz saw little precision or mathematical beauty in armed conflict. Instead, he saw war as foggy and uncertain, mitigated only by courage, perseverance, and luck. Clausewitz even made the limited comparison of war to a game of cards in which the chance drawing of the cards themselves, supplemented by bluffing and deception, shaped the outcome. The centerpiece of his con-

---

which Admiral Halsey was fooled into chasing a decoy fleet commanded by Admiral Ozawa, thereby leaving the critical San Bernardino Strait unprotected. Disaster was averted only when Admiral Kurita—himself subject to error, misjudgment and confusion—withdrew without destroying vulnerable American transports. Perhaps Clausewitz also applies to naval operations. Even so, the movement of fleets or air squadrons seldom is shaped by cultural or political factors peculiar to local areas or tribes, or other factors quite alien to Jomini's thinking.

ception of war was the employment of powerful forces to locate, engage, and overwhelm the main force of a foreign enemy with the object of seeking a decisive victorious battle:[13]

> Conquering Moscow and half of Russia in 1812 was of no avail to Bonaparte unless it brought him the peace he had in view. But these successes were only part of his plan of campaign: what was still missing was the destruction of the Russian army.[14]

To Clausewitz, victory and defeat were absolutes that were decided on the field of battle. Generally ignored, even by the German General Staff, was Clausewitz's conception of *wars of limited aims* as well as wars aimed at total destruction of an enemy. In his concept of "total war," once an enemy's army had been defeated in accordance with the nation's political aim, the foreign ministers would take over from the generals and establish a temporary peace. But Clausewitz also considered that a limited war would be fought for carefully limited objectives that could be traded for desired political goals at the peace table. Clausewitz never believed that peace was, or could be, permanent. It was merely a pause between wars. But war would forever be a servant of policy.

Unlike Jomini, Clausewitz left behind no formulae or rules of war or a body of principles. With a smile, he might well have believed as Napoleon did, that the best troops are those that prove victorious.[15]

Unlike his Swiss contemporary, Clausewitz took notice of the Spanish resistance—he called it "the people in arms"—but saw in this new form of war only a useful adjunct to conventional state-versus-state military operations. The concept of true insurgency, *internal war against one's own leaders*, lay in the future.

---

[13] A naval officer might be shocked at the suggestion that Alfred Thayer Mahan was the equivalent on the sea of Jomini on land. But the fact remains that Mahan advocated certain rules leading to command of the sea which, in turn, would lead to victory. Giulio Douhet, father of the theory of airpower, might also be considered a Jominian in that his principle was to gain air supremacy, thus rendering the enemy heartland naked to aerial bombardment.

[14] Clausewitz, Book VIII, Chapter 3, p. 582.

[15] It is said that Madame de Montholon asked Napoleon which troops were the best. Napoleon replied, "Why, Madame, those that are victorious!"

Clausewitz also saw a necessary difference between the commander of troops and his political master. Perhaps he admired the ability of a genius like Napoleon to combine political with military power, using the latter as *means* to advance the former *ends*. But if so, Clausewitz wrote for monarchs who would not command their soldiers in the field, perhaps a Prussian king like Frederick William III, not known for his military prowess. Even so, Clausewitz never deviated from his view that political factors determined by the king and his advisors must guide military operations in the field.

To add to what has been said, we must also note that Clausewitz recognized the need of policy for limited campaigns, that is, as has been said, a strategy dictated by political factors to gain limited advantages. In a war of limited aims, the objective might be seizure of a particular city or province that could be used as a bargaining chip by negotiators at the peace table. Hans Delbrueck, the third of our strategists, was to amplify this view in his historical studies, especially in his analysis of the campaigns of Frederick the Great.

The relationship between political ends on the one hand and force (as a means) on the other is made clear in Book Eight of *On War*, where Clausewitz ponders the idea of escalation beyond a point where means (military force) become meaningless or even counterproductive relative to the policy ends sought:

> The degree of force that must be used against the enemy depends on the scale of political demands on either side. These demands, so far as they are known, would show what efforts each must make; but they seldom are fully known—which may be one reason why both sides do not exert themselves to the same degree.
>
> Nor are the situation and conditions of the belligerents alike. This can be a second factor.
>
> Just as disparate are the governments' strength of will, their character and abilities.
>
> These three considerations introduce uncertainties that make it difficult to gauge the amount of resistance to be faced and, in consequence, the means required and the objectives to be set.
>
> Since in war too small an effort can result not just in failure

> but in positive harm, each side is driven to outdo the other, which sets up an interaction.
>
> Such an interaction could lead to a maximum effort if a maximum could be defined. But in that case all proportion between action and political demands would be lost: means would cease to be commensurate with ends, and in most cases a policy of maximum exertion would fail because of the domestic problems it would raise.[16]

Had Erich Ludendorff considered this relationship of means to ends before the United States declared war on Germany in 1917 we may speculate that the Great War might have had a very different ending with more positive downstream consequences for Germany, Europe, and the world. A negotiated peace in 1916 may well have spared Germany and Europe from the horror of the Nazi Reich and a second world war.

With reference to insurgency, we might note that almost by definition the two sides will find themselves facing vastly different situations and conditions. Factors such as the government's strength of will, character, and abilities will differ from those of an insurgent challenger. We will examine these differences in a later chapter.

DELBRUECK

The third of our selected strategists, Hans Delbrueck (1848–1929), who unfortunately is today less well known than Clausewitz or Jomini, was a professor of history specializing in the campaigns of the Greek and Roman armies, as well as those of Frederick the Great. He had served as a soldier in the Franco-Prussian War (1870–1871) and later as a member of the Reichstag. Delbrueck was an outspoken critic of imperial Germany's strategy in World War I. A true scholar, Delbrueck developed a philosophy of war through his numerous publications. He may have been the first civilian scholar to study war from the historical viewpoint.

Delbrueck's first task was to analyze a number of the great battles of history with the intention of understanding more clearly how the battles were fought and what were the key elements of victory. In so doing, Del-

---

[16] Clausewitz, Book VIII, Chapter 3, p. 585.

brueck examined ancient battles such as Marathon and Cannae, often patiently sifting out fact from fiction and embellishment. He used reasoning to debunk fanciful accounts of Persian troop strength and battle plans as at Marathon, or logistical factors as with Caesar's campaigns against the Helvetii (ancestors of the Swiss). Only after establishing a reasonably accurate picture of these battles did Delbrueck then attempt to understand what factors led to victory or defeat.

Delbrueck went beyond his predecessors in at least two important ways. Clausewitz had put forward two concepts of war: total and limited. The first concept envisioned the encirclement and total destruction of the enemy's armed force, thus leading to a dictated peace. The second concept focused on carefully limited aims leading to a negotiated peace. In contrast, Delbrueck thought in terms of annihilation versus attrition.[17] Both men agreed, however, that politics must guide military action, and that political aims must form the core of strategy.

Delbrueck saw Napoleon, Caesar, and Alexander the Great as generals who pursued a strategy of annihilation, whereas Frederick the Great and Gustavus Adolphus necessarily used attrition due to the strength of their foes and the political situations in which they found themselves. Delbrueck firmly believed that to assure victory the political and military aspects of a campaign had to be fully and completely integrated so that one did not disrupt the other. He recognized that annihilation would be appropriate in some circumstances and attrition in others. The trick, of course, is to know which is most appropriate to the situation. Gordon A. Craig, a scholar of German diplomatic history, noted that Delbrueck understood that strategy is shaped by the situation at hand:

> Yet the military critics completely missed the deeper significance of Delbrueck's strategic theory. History showed that there could be no single theory of strategy, correct for every age. Like all phases

[17] The German terms are "Niederwerfungsstrategie" and "Ermattungsstrategie." "Niederwerfen" is a verb meaning to "throw down, put down, or crush." The noun form, "Niederwerfung" means "suppression." "Ermattung" in German means "exhaustion" and comes from the verb "ermatten," to weary, weaken or fade. Many English translations use the terms annihilation and attrition, respectively. The author holds the opinion that more accurate translations into English might lessen potential misunderstanding.

> of warfare, strategy was intimately connected with politics, with the life and the strength of the state.[18]

Delbrueck's own words reflect the importance of political considerations in the ancient wars: "Here as always it was politics that determined the administration of the war and that prescribed to strategy its course."[19] He believed that Frederick the Great's true brilliance as a general lay not in his military victories, such as the Battles of Rossbach and Hohenfriedberg, but rather in his political acumen and ability to make good use of those successes toward attainment of Prussia's limited political objectives.

Unlike Jomini, Delbrueck paid considerable attention to the impact of logistics on past campaigns along with economic and political limitations. He reasoned that, as in the case of the Romans or Frederick the Great, success in battle or statecraft depended directly upon *not* exceeding one's available resources.

Unfortunately for Delbrueck, and probably for Germany as well, the total victory in 1870 over Napoleon III and the French army at Sedan convinced many German military professionals, notably Erich Ludendorff and Paul von Hindenburg, that mass armies and the strategy of annihilation were the wave of the future. The idea of war fought for limited political objectives, as practiced by August Neidhardt von Gneisenau and others, was drowned by a tsunami of nationalistic hubris.

When World War I broke out in 1914, Delbrueck was almost alone in advocating that Germany pursue a strategy of limited objectives and negotiate peace as soon as possible. This view was far from popular in Wilhelmine Germany which greatly desired a repeat of the thumping victory of 1870. However, after the failure of the first drive on Paris during summer and fall of 1914, Delbrueck concluded that a cataclysmic battle of annihilation to destroy the French army simply was not possible and that thereafter Germany would find itself fighting a defensive war of attrition. The change in approach did not imply that victory was beyond reach, but that it would have to be gained by means other than simple force-on-force combat. The Powers would have to negotiate a peace.

---

[18] Gordon A. Craig "Delbrueck: The Military Historian" in Paret, *Makers of Modern Strategy*, p. 343.

[19] *ibid.*

Throughout the war Delbrueck pleaded for Germany's leaders to adopt a reasonable and flexible political approach that would lessen growing European suspicion of German war aims. As early as 1915 he suggested that the imperial government open negotiations and issue clear disclaimers about territorial ambitions. Delbrueck stoutly opposed Germany's use of unrestricted submarine warfare and predicted that it would draw the United States into the war. His pleas for a political strategy fell on deaf ears. In writing about Delbrueck's views toward the Great War, Craig observed:

> In his desire for a political strategy that would be effective in weakening the resistance of the enemy, Delbrueck was bitterly disappointed. It became apparent as early as 1915 that strong sections of German public opinion regarded the war as a means of acquiring new territory not only in the East but in the West. When Delbrueck called for a declaration of willingness to evacuate Belgium, he was greeted with abuse and was accused by the *Deutsche Tageszeitung* of being "subservient to our enemies in foreign countries." The changing fortunes of war did not diminish the desire for booty and the powerful *Vaterlandspartei*, the most important of the annexationist groups, exercised a strong influence on national policy. Not only did the German government not make any declaration concerning Belgium but it never made its position clear on the question of a negotiated peace. When the Peace Resolution was being debated in 1917, Hindenburg and Ludendorff threatened to resign if the Reichstag adopted the measure.[20]

We leave off with Delbrueck with one final observation. As the war ground on, with the German general staff looking desperately for a knockout annihilation blow that would end the war with a glorious victory, Ludendorff and Hindenburg displaced what remained of the civilian government. The German army itself came to be the maker of national policy. In turn, that policy had only the narrow goal of achieving a military victory by means of pursuing annihilation of the opposing armies, a strategy that was increasingly beyond Germany's steadily dwindling military means. The

---

[20] *ibid.* pp. 348–349.

high command largely ignored the political, psychological, and moral aspects of war. Policy was now subordinate to military operations. The result ultimately was collapse.

LIDDELL HART

The last of our thinkers is Basil Henry Liddell Hart (1895–1970), a military historian and journalist who had served in World War I as an infantry officer and between the wars as a correspondent for *The Times of London* and several other newspapers. Like many other strategists, especially Clausewitz, whose phraseology he echoes, Liddell Hart espouses the general idea that "Strategy depends for success, first and most, on a sound calculation and co-ordination of the end and the means. The end must be proportioned to the total means. . . . "[21]

Liddell Hart is perhaps best known as one of the earliest advocates of armored warfare and mobility. Throughout the 1920s Liddell Hart, along with prominent British military theorist J.F.C. Fuller, extolled the virtues of the firepower and shock action of tanks. While Fuller believed that highly mobile armored forces could bring victory by themselves, Liddell Hart considered that a mix of infantry and armor was necessary. Liddell Hart believed that the tank would return maneuver to the battlefield and "restore generalship in place of mechanics."

Despite his association with armored warfare, Liddell Hart produced other theoretical works on strategy and several biographies of famous commanders, among them T. E. Lawrence. Liddell Hart is credited with writing *The Strategy of Indirect Approach* and formulating two important principles of interest to our discussion of insurgency: first, to upset the enemy's equilibrium or plan of action, and second, to avoid making direct attacks on one's opponent using instead an indirect approach intended to exhaust and wear down the enemy. This latter idea seems to mirror some of Delbrueck's ideas about *Ermattungsstrategie,* a strategy of wearing down or exhausting one's adversary.

Although speculative, it is possible that Liddell Hart's conception of an indirect approach may have been inspired by the example of T. E. Lawrence in Arabia. Lawrence clearly was an expert practitioner of indirect

---

[21] Liddell Hart, p. 336.

forms of warfare. Lawrence never took on the main Ottoman forces, as did General Allenby in Palestine, but preferred instead to disrupt Turkish lines of communication in Arabia and thus isolate and tie down the enemy's regular forces. He used relatively small, but highly mobile forces to immobilize far larger forces. Indeed, the Turkish army stationed in Medina was never able to make its inherent power decisive in Arabia, nor could it provide reinforcements to Turkish units opposing Allenby's British army in Palestine. Immobilized, the Turkish garrison in Medina had become more of a liability than an asset to the Ottomans.

Liddell Hart's theory of strategy is crystallized in "Aim of Strategy," chapter XIX of his book *Strategy* and is reminiscent of the strategic thinking of Sun Tzu more than two millennia earlier:

> The perfection of strategy would be, therefore, to produce a decision without any serious fighting. . . .
>
> Let us assume that a strategist is empowered to seek a military decision. His responsibility is to seek it under the most advantageous circumstances in order to produce the most profitable result. Hence *his true aim is not so much to seek battle as to seek a strategic situation so advantageous that if it does not of itself produce the decision, its continuation by a battle is sure to achieve this.* In other words, dislocation is the aim of strategy; its sequel may be either the enemy's dissolution or his easier disruption in battle. Dissolution may involve some partial measure of fighting, but this has not the character of a battle.[22]

Liddell Hart goes on to say that dislocating an adversary can be accomplished by a variety of means, some of which are tactical and others psychological. The greatest degree of success, however, is to entrap an enemy through a well-mixed combination of physical and psychological effects:

> In the psychological sphere, dislocation is the result of the impression on the commander's mind of the physical effects which we have listed. The impression is strongly accentuated if his realization

[22] *Ibid.* pp. 338–339. Italics are Liddell Hart's.

> of his being at a disadvantage is *sudden*, and if he feels that he is unable to counter the enemy's move. *Psychological dislocation fundamentally springs from this sense of being trapped.*[23]

Perhaps more fully than any previous theorist, Liddell Hart recognized that psychological and physical elements were intertwined, and that both were required for success:

> The profoundest truth of war is that the issue of battle is usually decided in the minds of the opposing commanders, not in the bodies of their men.[24]

It should be recalled that earlier strategists, Sun Tzu and Clausewitz among them, specifically commented on this aspect. Napoleon had quipped, "The moral is to the physical as three is to one." Not least, the master of insurgent warfare, Mao Tse-tung, is quoted as saying: "The mind of the enemy and the will of his leaders is a target of far more importance than the bodies of his troops."[25] The point to be made is that all of these strategists and men of action recognized the importance of psychology in battle. Indeed this intangible aspect is just as vital an element of strategy as is availability of oil, ammunition, and food.

From the foregoing, it can be seen that in some of his theoretical writing Liddell Hart mirrors the strategic ideas held by Mao Tse-tung. Although it is doubtful that either man had any influence on the other's thinking, we can see elements in Liddell Hart that can be applied to insurgency and irregular warfare. Not least, along with Clausewitz, Liddell Hart recognized the importance of intangible elements such as strength of belief in a Cause, high morale, and even humane conduct on the battlefield:

> Moreover, fighting power is but one of the instruments of grand

---

[23] *Ibid.* p. 340. Italics are Liddell Hart's.

[24] B.H. Liddell Hart quoted by Prof. Lawrence Friedman in *The Times.* The author is Professor of War Studies at King's College, London.

[25] Mao Tse-tung, *On Guerrilla Warfare*, p. 23.

> strategy—which should take account of and apply the power of financial pressure, of diplomatic pressure, of commercial pressure, and, not least of ethical pressure, to weaken the opponent's will. A good cause is a sword as well as armour. Likewise, chivalry in war can be a most effective weapon in weakening the opponent's will to resist, as well as augmenting moral strength.[26]

Having taken a quick peek at four of Europe's leading strategic thinkers, and noting their differences, we must also take notice of one important similarity. All were speaking in terms of strategy as it might be applied by one nation against another. Clausewitz alone explicitly considered strategy as it might apply in an internal war, an *insurgency*, although, as stated earlier, his principal concern was state-on-state conflict.

Three of the four, Clausewitz, Delbrueck, and Liddell Hart, recognized that political considerations must guide and direct military strategy, and indeed political factors must be thoroughly integrated into any use of military power if success is to be achieved. Liddell Hart and Clausewitz also recognized the importance of psychological factors in battle, either directed against an opposing commander and his troops, or against an enemy civilian population. None of these European thinkers, however, understood the methodical use of political and psychological factors in rousing popular discontent against a sitting regime. This was left to the strategists of insurgency.

CARVED IN MARBLE?

To continue with our discussion of strategy we should examine whether specific strategies are fixed or may be flexible enough to meet changing times and conditions.

Strategy is malleable and can change. Indeed, it *must* change as gains or losses are noted in material resources or other advantages. The means at hand can change for better or for worse, thus greatly shaping a strategy. In other words, a strategy is not carved in marble for all time, but is flexible

[26] Liddell Hart, op. cit., p. 336. Author generally agrees with Liddell Hart's views on chivalry in war, but with the caveat that non-European enemies may have very different ideas of chivalry than does Liddell.

and dynamic; it is a "living roadmap" leading us from where we are to where we want to be.[27]

Of course, deciding where we want to be is not always easy to do. Recall that Nickols advises us to have an "end clearly in view." Elbert Hubbard, a well-known American journalist who died with the sinking of the Lusitania in May 1915, was quoted as saying: "It does not take much strength to do things, but it requires great strength to decide on what to do."[28] The truth of Hubbard's observation as it relates to the formulation of strategy, that is to say the "end clearly in view," is apparent to anyone who examines in depth the bitter debates between the Americans and British in World War II (or for that matter, between the U.S. Navy and U.S. Army) over strategic aims and the allocation of resources to support those aims. Even the issue of Overlord, the great Allied landings in Normandy, was the subject of heated dispute and doubt until very late in 1943.[29]

We normally think of resources in the physical sense: money, oil, steel, shipping, aircraft, and so on. An obvious strategic advantage—or disadvantage—is a country's geography and location.[30] Time, when available, is a major strategic advantage. And, if available in sufficient quantity and quality, manpower is another valuable strategic resource.[31]

In formulating strategy it is imperative not merely to tally one's resources and advantages, *but to coldly assess deficiencies of material resources and the lack of certain advantages.* If sober appraisal of the minuses, as well as plusses, is not made and these debits are glossed over or ignored, serious

---

[27] My own definition is: *Strategy is the intelligent use of all available resources and advantages to achieve clearly defined goals or conditions that create promising options for future action.* If a strategy is successful, ideally the advantages one enjoys and the material resources available should increase. However, the author adds to this Goethe's cautionary observation: "Genius is knowing where to stop."

[28] Hubbard, p. 65.

[29] See Cray, especially Part III.

[30] Both Poland and Switzerland share borders with Germany. Poland, however, is basically flat, good tank country. Switzerland is sharply mountainous, not good even for mountain infantry operations. The nature of the topography of each country is therefore a factor in formulating a viable strategy.

[31] The Chinese have a brilliant observation about the value of Time : *An inch of Time is an inch of gold. But an inch of gold cannot buy an inch of Time.* In Mandarin Chinese, this aphorism rhymes: *Yi tswun guang-yin, yi tswun jin; twsun jin nan mai yi tswun yin.*

negative consequences are absolutely certain to follow. This is because the strategic goals have been disconnected from the means available to achieve them, and have thereby become unrealistic or impossible to achieve.

For example, if neither time nor sufficient manpower (or shipping, or oil, etc.) are available, these deficiencies will force a change in strategy. Perhaps it is possible to find compensating resources and advantages. To buy time, one may trade distance, as the Russians did during the Nazi onslaught of 1941. Where manpower is in short supply technology in the form of laborsaving equipment may be available. When a vital material such as natural rubber was no longer available due to Japanese conquest of Southeast Asia during World War II, American chemists invented a comparable synthetic product. However, if it proves impossible to find compensating advantages and resources for those you lack, it follows that no strategy will be successful. The master strategist is therefore the one who is best able to *assess what he has and what he lacks* in light of what he wants to do, and successfully finds means either to compensate for what he lacks or adjusts his goals appropriately.

Devising a viable strategy should never be mistaken as a completely rational, scientific Principle of Nature, or as a thing apart from human nature. Formulation of strategy is not a science, as Jomini would have us believe, but is rather something of an art. It must be kept in mind at all times that developing a strategy is terribly vulnerable to the foibles and flaws in our human nature. History is replete with examples where potentates and their ministers, generals, and admirals let wishful thinking, pet peeves, personal ambitions, or sheer fantasy influence the formation of strategy. Personality conflicts, ideological concerns, political favors, ambition, even demagoguery have colored the strategies pursued by nations and their armed forces. Most often these irrational and erratic influences on strategy have led directly to ruin.

Consider the strategy pursued by Adolf Hitler. After his conquests of Poland, Norway, Denmark, the Low Countries, and France, his intuition replaced all rational thinking in relating attainable ends with available means. Very soon Nazi Germany found itself well beyond its available means to attain Hitler's apparently limitless political ends. These goals proved overly ambitious and ultimately unattainable. Making matters worse, as setbacks mounted, Hitler's pathological personality further gutted

German strategy through irrational outbursts, paranoia, threats, and unreasonable demands.

There is a line in Fyodor Dostoyevsky's *The Brothers Karamazov* that describes the Hitlerian situation perfectly:

> A man who lies to himself, and believes his own lies, becomes unable to recognize truth, either in himself or in anyone else. . . . Having no love in him, he yields to his impulses. . . .[32]

Let me present you with a truly chilling thought. Let us suppose that, instead of being nasty, pigheaded, and capricious, Hitler had been calm, rational and willing to listen to wise counsel (though, to be sure, remaining *Evil Incarnate*). Imagine a Fuehrer reasonable, thoughtful, and genuinely interested in the knowledge, views, and ideas of others. Let us further suppose the Fuehrer had asked the following questions in a calm and rational way and *acted* upon the advice of Albert Speer and Erich von Manstein: *What are we trying to do, and how do we get there? Are our goals beyond our available means? Can we compensate for what we do not have, or must we adjust our goals accordingly?*

Had Hitler been rational, Nazi conquest of Britain, defeat of the Soviet Union, and isolation of the United States may have been possible *if these ends had been tackled sequentially, allowing sufficient time for the recuperation of German industry, society and armed forces.* Fortunately for us, and probably for Western Civilization, Hitler defeated himself by attempting something then impossible for Germany: making war on all three Powers simultaneously. By waging war on Great Britain, the Soviet Union, and United States simultaneously, Hitler compelled the three Powers to put aside for the moment their fundamentally differing national interests, and combine their efforts to overwhelm Nazi Germany through "British brains, American brawn, and Russian blood."[33]

In a similar fashion, the myopia of the Japanese militarists in 1940 was

---

[32] Dostoyevsky, Book II, Chapter 2, "The Old Buffoon," p.49.

[33] This quip, British of course, referred to British intelligence successes and inventions like radar, the incomparable industrial power of the United States, and the horrific losses of Russian soldiers and civilians that resulted in the defeat of Nazi Germany.

laid bare by a Japanese writer, Hasegawa Nyozekan, in his 1952 book *The Lost Japan*:

> The war was started as the result of a mistaken intuitive "calculation" which transcended mathematics. We believed with a blind fervor that we could triumph over scientific weapons and tactics by means of our mystic will. . . . The characteristic reliance on intuition by [the] Japanese had blocked the objective cognition of the modern world.[34]

Summarized succinctly, the Japanese allowed mythology and wishful thinking to displace sober assessment and hardheaded planning.

To conclude this chapter, we can say that modern European strategy evolved gradually from the seventeenth century idea of placement of troops on a battlefield, through the great minds of Jomini and Clausewitz of the eighteenth and nineteenth centuries, to eminent thinkers of the late nineteenth and early twentieth centuries such as Hans Delbrueck and B.F. Liddell Hart.

What must always be kept in mind as one critiques the thinking of this or that strategist is that all were men of their times,their Western European cultural heritage, and the historical cases they studied. Each man analyzed the conflicts of his day (or as with Delbrueck historical cases), and they also examined the political structures and conditions that brought about those conflicts.

These factors must be borne in mind by the practitioner as he goes about applying one or another of the precepts advanced by earlier strategists. We will see that some ideas of the great European strategists do apply in insurgencies and upheavals, but other concepts that may be appropriate for conventional forces or in a European context either do not apply or must be modified.

---

[34] Nyozekan, page unknown, quoted in Bartlett. Hasegawa's true name was Hasegawa Manjiro, Nyozekan being a pen name. A social critic and journalist, he was jailed by the Japanese militarists for his views. He lived between 1875 and 1969.

CHAPTER 4

NEITHER KARL NOR ANTOINE

Divide our forces to arouse the masses, concentrate our forces to deal with the enemy.—Mao Tse-tung[1]

We will now turn our attention to the development of a viable insurgent strategy. As noted in the preceding chapters, insurgencies must have distinctive environments in which they can germinate, incubate, and grow. Were it not for a special set of political and economic circumstances existing in a particular country or region, there would be no insurrection. Indeed, there could be no insurrection simply because the necessary conditions did not exist.

THE POLITICAL IMPERATIVE

Insurgency is not primarily a military operation; insurgency is a political competition. The centerpiece is neither the regime's armed forces nor even a country's level of socio-economic development *per se*, although both are important factors.

Rather, given the necessary conditions, it is the nature of the political

[1] Mao Tse-tung, *Selected Military Writings* "A Single Spark Can Start a Prairie Fire," p. 72. Mao goes on to say: "These tactics are just like casting a net; at any moment we should be able to cast it or draw it in. We cast it wide to win over the masses and draw it in to deal with the enemy. Such are the tactics we have used for the past three years." [1930]

leadership of the opposing sides and the attractiveness of their competing political visions that sets an insurrection in motion. It is the nature and credibility of the competing political programs advanced by the government-in-being and by the insurgent or revolutionary movement that will determine the course of the struggle. It is the ability of one side or the other to mobilize the people and get them to act in ways that aid the goals of the insurgent command (a shadow government) or the established government.

In the majority of historical cases where a government-in-being has taken steps to correct its own shortcomings it has, in fact, won the struggle with the insurgents. Indeed, if a regime takes the necessary steps early on to put its house in order it can defeat the insurgent movement even before the movement has fully formed. This is because the people will rally to the side that it believes gives them the best deal. If landholding is the central political issue, why should peasants fight as guerrillas for a bit of land when the government willingly distributes it to the tiller? If home rule is the issue, but the occupying regime has taken concrete steps toward granting independence, there is no point for nationalists to take up arms. People will avoid risk unless no other option for the resolution of perceived ills can be found.

Reform and political advantage shape the nature of the ongoing contest between potential rebels and established authority. It is only in cases where the government totally abdicates its responsibilities as a government—when it busies itself alienating the people, when it has no inspiring leadership or vision, and *especially when the regime has no intention of correcting its flaws*—that an insurgency is likely to rise and eventually triumph. Even when confronting an oppressive, intransigent regime, however, insurgents are not guaranteed success. They still must have a clear policy and viable strategy, essential elements for victory.

The distinction must always be made between policy and strategy. While they are tied at the hip, strategy is about the means of attaining the goals specified by policy, but not about the formulation of policy itself. And yet, it is an inescapable fact that *ends*, the essence of policy, cannot exceed the *means* available for their attainment. Put another way, goals (ends) and means must be in balance even though remaining distinct entities. Means lacking an attainable policy framework are aimless, even pointless, while policy goals without sufficient means readily at hand are feckless, even absurd. Again, means and ends must always be in comfortable balance.

Well-known consultant and former executive director of Educational Testing Service (ETS) Fred Nickols, speaking from the corporate world, gives interesting insight into strategic thinking and the means by which a viable strategy is devised from corporate policy. Replace the phrase "company-wide" with "insurgent" or "regime," and his article is entirely appropriate for our consideration:

> How does one determine, articulate and communicate company-wide ends? How does one ensure understanding and obtain commitment to these ends? Some quick answers are as follows:
>
> The ends to be obtained are determined through discussions and debates regarding the company's future in light of its current situation. Even a future-oriented SWOT analysis (an assessment of Strengths, Weaknesses, Opportunities and Threats) is based on current perceptions.
>
> The ends settled on are articulated in plain language, free from flowery words and political "spin." The risk of misdirection is too great to tolerate unfettered wordsmithing. Moreover, the ends are communicated regularly, repeatedly, through a variety of channels and avenues. There is no end to their communication.[2]

The path advocated by Nickols places the CEO as the "keeper of the vision" and although responsible for keeping the organization focused, the Chief also seeks out information and advice from members of his company.

In dictatorships and absolute monarchies, policymaking is streamlined in the sense that it is not subject to anything more than suggestions from the dictator's politburo or the king's ministers. Moreover, once policy has been determined, execution normally follows swiftly: the command goes out to the minions for action. Heads will roll for failure to execute the command . . . or simply for failure. I have no idea whether this model of decision-making and action applies in Corporate America, but suspect that it does.

---

[2] Nickols, op. cit., p.7.

In republics and constitutional monarchies, policymaking tends to be a convoluted process that involves not only the input of cabinets and special advisors, but also the wishes of legislators, special interest groups, and ultimately the people through their support as expressed by votes cast and taxes paid. This makes policy formulation slow and contentious, with competing groups heatedly debating the merits of suggested policies, compelling political figures to stay abreast of public opinion. James A. Garfield, twentieth president of the United States, once quipped: "All free governments are managed by the combined wisdom and folly of the people."

Even after a policy has been decided upon—which in a democracy is often merely a compromise between the interests and desires of opposing groups—its execution may be slow. Those called upon to execute policy may have agendas and ideas of their own. They know that, at worst, failure to carry out directives can result only in dismissal, not in a firing squad. Moreover, some failures and dismissals might even result in promotion, or at least some nice royalties from their published memoirs.

Policy has its roots in an idea, a vision of how the world should be. At its broadest and most general conception, parliamentary democracies have certain views of how the world should be, whereas autocrats typically have diametrically opposing views. Different groups hold differing views of themselves and the regional or global reality of which they are a part. It is at this point where the formation of competing strategies occurs. The political foundations of a governing group necessarily color its outlook and attitude toward competing groups, third parties, and even potential allies and enemies. And, as we've taken pains to point out, the political goals also direct and shape strategy.

In a previous chapter we briefly mentioned two historical insurgencies: the well-known Chinese revolution and the less well-known Cypriot uprising. These examples were selected because Cyprus and China are about as different as can be imagined in terms of their size, location, social patterns, geography, culture, history, economies, and much else. This necessarily makes the political issues of the two countries completely different. Yet the insurgent leadership in both China and Cyprus shared one thing in common: each leadership group set forth a clear political idea as the central goal or policy end around which all else revolved. It is time to take a closer look at those two insurgencies.

Our objective is to gain deeper understanding about how insurgents think, how they go about forming insurgent movements, and how insurgents develop strategy.

GEORGE (GIORGIOS) GRIVAS

George Grivas (1898–1974) was a Greek Cypriot from a middle class family living in the Famagusta District of eastern Cyprus. When he was eighteen, Grivas decided upon a military career and left British-ruled Cyprus to enter the military academy in Athens. Later, he graduated from the Ecole Militaire in Paris, the same institution where Napoleon had been a student 130 years earlier. As a young army lieutenant Grivas was assigned to the Greek forces then attempting to conquer parts of western Anatolia populated by ethnic Greeks under Ottoman Turkish rule. This campaign ended disastrously with the Greek army being smashed and thrown into the sea by Turkish forces under command of Kemal Pasha, who later became better known as Ataturk.

Grivas went to Paris for further study in the mid-1920s, after which he returned to Greece for a series of assignments including service as an instructor at the military college. He was promoted to major in 1935 and then was made a divisional chief of staff in 1940 when the Italians attempted to invade Greece.

Sadly for Greece, early in 1941 the Germans took over the task of conquering the unfortunate land from their bumbling Italian allies. In these new circumstances, the issue was no longer in doubt and within a matter of weeks the Wehrmacht had defeated Greece and occupied the country, later conducting a spectacular, albeit costly, airborne invasion of Crete.

Grivas, now a colonel, remained in occupied Greece, but organized a small resistance cell that operated principally in Athens. Although this organization did not play a major role in the liberation of Greece, it nevertheless provided useful assistance to British and Greek royalist forces as they battled Communist insurgents in 1945 and 1946. Grivas retired from active service in 1946 and his thoughts turned once again to Cyprus.

Grivas may have returned to Cyprus by the early 1950s. In any event, he and Archbishop Makarios III, another Cypriot nationalist leader, began laying the groundwork for an insurgency to free the island from British rule. It is highly probable that Grivas's World War II experience with clandestine underground operations helped shape his thinking about the liberation struggle before him. Concealment, deception and covert communications would play major roles. However, the decisive factor would be mobilization of the Greek Cypriot people toward self-determination.

During the Cypriot liberation war, Grivas remained on the island, moving frequently from one hiding spot to another using the *nom de guerre* "Digenis" for communications and using disguises when necessary. Grivas escaped capture on at least three occasions despite strenuous attempts by the British authorities to get him in their clutches and despite a large reward offered for information leading to his arrest. He never left Cyprus and was never captured. Archbishop Makarios was exiled in 1956 thus compelling General Grivas to assume supreme political as well as military leadership.

GENERAL GRIVAS AND INSURGENCY

Let's begin by looking at Cyprus in the mid-1950s, a British Crown Colony, but one that was increasingly restive under the pressure of cultural awareness. In the chapter on strategy in his book *General Grivas on Guerrilla Warfare*, Grivas makes the following observation:

> *The moral factor*. Our struggle, like any other struggle, was mainly a tussle of wills, in which the upper hand would be gained by the one whose moral stamina was higher and his will stronger. I always reckoned on this factor. Throughout the struggle I succeeded in keeping up the morale both of combatants and non-combatants at a very high level. There was never any sign of yielding. *An important contributory factor was of course faith in the justice of our cause, whereas the British soldier on the contrary was well aware that he was fighting in order to keep a people in subjection.* Thus it was that the ranks of our fighters, even when depleted by casualties or when hard hit, remained unbroken and were quickly reconstituted, and with increased cohesion.[3]

Interestingly, the British commissioner in Larnaca in a dispatch sent to the colonial secretary in London on 28 July 1955 forecast widespread disorder in his area of Cyprus, but went on to say that severe measures,

---

[3] Grivas, p. 43. Italics are mine.

even if widely applied, would not be successful unless the roots of the population's discontent were addressed.[4]

The commissioner further reported that the rural populations had lost their confidence in the British colonial administration, making it necessary to carry out programs to quickly improve conditions in the villages in order to restore the people's confidence.[5] It soon appeared, however, that instead of offering a political carrot, the British government intended only to apply the military stick.

Grivas and his EOKA[6] guerrillas believed that the October 1955 arrival of Field Marshal Lord John Harding with British troops ruled out an immediate political solution to the crisis. As governor of Cyprus, Lord Harding intended to apply a policy of a strong hand. This led the Cypriot resistance to focus its attention on the use of armed operations and sabotage aimed at "disrupting the police; wearing down the [British] army; putting out of gear the Intelligence Service's information network." The general's military goal was to "hold the greatest possible number of the enemy forces in the maintenance of order in towns and inhabited places, and deliver sudden attacks on these forces in suitable spots . . . thereby causing casualties and lowering enemy morale."[7]

Here we see a classic use of *Ermattungsstrategie* (wearing down) as urged by Delbrueck. In fairness, the Cypriots had very little choice in formulating their strategy; the British army and the British-backed police had overwhelming firepower and mobility with helicopters and armored vehicles at their disposal. But Grivas knew that in a war of attrition it was possible to offset these British advantages through maintaining the initiative and by mobilizing his people. EOKA organized anti-British unarmed demonstrations in many cities, which served to tie down the British security forces. The British were not willing to fire on unarmed demonstrators, but had to use significant numbers of police and possibly army personnel to control the crowd.

The political objective—Cypriot independence from Britain —was a powerful Cause and had the desired effect of mobilizing a high percentage

---

[4] *ibid.*, pp.36–37.

[5] *ibid.*, p. 37.

[6] EOKA = Ethniki Organosis Kyprion Agoniston or, in English, "National Organization of Cypriot Fighters." The British branded EOKA a "terrorist" organization but, in fact, it was a broad based insurgent movement which used terrorist acts as a political tool.

[7] *ibid.*, p. 39.

of the islanders. Grivas correctly noted that a British Tommy was in Cyprus as an unwanted occupier, without a real Cause to fight for, far from home in a peacekeeping role that restricted his scope for action. Here an intangible factor tipped the scales heavily in favor of the Cypriots and against the better armed, equipped, and trained British. That was the moral factor, and it became a vital element of the insurgent strategy.

The Cypriot insurgency combined political and military aspects smoothly. Archbishop Makarios served as head of the political wing while George Grivas was the military chief. The two worked closely until the British removed the archbishop and sent him into exile. Thereafter, Grivas combined both political and military responsibilities in his person. To be sure, Greece clandestinely made available some supplies and permitted the operation of a radio station intended to conduct influence operations directed at the islanders and at potentially sympathetic nations. But Greek help was not decisive.

The cost to the British of conducting military security operations on Cyprus, in addition to the normal costs of colonial administration, rapidly made the undertaking unpalatable back in London. Wars must be paid for. And in democracies wars are ultimately paid for by taxpayers. Parliament was increasingly sensitive to the fact that Cyprus was costing more than it was worth. It is believed that at his strongest General Grivas had only 1,250 EOKA guerrillas opposing some 40,000 British soldiers and police, a ratio of nearly 32 counterinsurgents to each insurgent fighter. One source claims that the total cost to EOKA of its operations over four years was a meager £50,000.[8] We may take it as a safe bet that British military and civil costs were far higher.

In the political sense, the Cypriot insurgency was a *total* war from the perspective of the Cypriot people, their objective was freedom from British rule, and the war involved nearly every Greek-speaking islander. A compromise or negotiated solution might theoretically be possible, and was, in fact, eventually agreed to, but a compromise always is fragile. The question of contested sovereignty leaves little room for splitting the difference. To summarize the competing political goals, the Cypriots' policy was to gain independence from Britain for which they were willing to negotiate, but the political *end* of self-determination was not negotiable.

---

[8] Joseph S. Kraemer, "Revolutionary Guerrilla Warfare and the Decolonization Movement," in *Polity* 4 (2): 146, Winter 1971, found in Wikipedia.

The British policy was to retain Cyprus as a Crown colony.

In support of the insurgents' strategy was the factor of *time*: the Cypriot people lived right there on the island and at any time could boycott the British, obstruct their attempts to govern the island, frustrate British military and security plans, and waste British time and resources at little cost to themselves. A disadvantage was, of course, the tiny size of the island and the fact that the British had total control of the surrounding sea and command of the air. The smallness of Cyprus was offset by the element of *manpower*. Although General Grivas had but 1,250 armed men he could draw upon the resources of the civil population for demonstrations and passive resistance at no cost to the insurgency. In contrast, the British could bring in additional army regiments and police reinforcements only when they could be spared from other commitments, and then only with sufficient logistical support, which was costly. Neither sea power nor air supremacy could contribute much to British strategy.

Negotiations in Zurich concluded in August 1960 by granting the Cypriots independence, though at Turkish insistence the agreement forbade a political union with Greece.[9] The Republic of Cyprus was born.

Before we leave the Cyprus example, a final key observation is in order. As we have taken pains to point out, insurgency is a war of *the people in arms*. An insurgent movement that is cut off from daily contact with the people is in danger of shriveling up and eventually blowing away. Hear what General Grivas has to say about the British counterinsurgency plan and EOKA's vulnerability:

> In May and June 1956 Lord Harding launched a large-scale offensive with strong forces against our mountain units. It should be noted that Harding, from his first arrival in Cyprus, devoted his main effort to the mountain units to which he obviously attached a major importance. This was the first time that we saw the enemy apply a definite plan. It consisted in covering a wide area with small detachments of men acting independently who carried out searches with the support of helicopters. But if the plan in question at first sight appeared logical, it nevertheless fell flat. . . .

---

[9] A second key Cypriot political goal was *enossis* or union with Greece. This goal could not be achieved because of opposition by the Turkish Cypriot minority and the Turkish Republic. Ultimately this cultural divide resulted in Cyprus being partitioned into Greek and Turkish areas.

> It is a moot point whether the enemy should have started with operations against the guerrilla units in the mountain areas, or whether he would have done better to start from the towns and villages. *For it was obvious that the guerrilla units were entirely dependent, for supplies and liaison, on the inhabited centres, and if the enemy had succeeded in paralysing all activity and dislocating our organization in those centres, it would have been a serious blow to the very existence of our guerrilla units.* [emphasis added][10]

We might ask why the British did not apply a sophisticated, true counterinsurgency strategy aimed at the people in the towns and cities as hinted at by Grivas. In Malaya and in Oman the British combined political and military elements in their strategy. In Cyprus they did not. It is sometimes instructive to study failures along with successes.

Let us now move to a different part of the world and examine another successful insurgency, and how it succeeded over its enemies. Here we will examine the well-known Chinese example from its inception in 1927, but from a perspective that is rarely studied by experts on the subject of insurgency.

MAO TSE-TUNG

Mao Tse-tung (1893–1976) was born into a peasant family in Shaoshan village, Hunan Province, in south central China. As a boy he worked part of the day in the fields while he also attended the village school, where he was an exceptional student. He had memorized the Confucian *Analects* by age ten and he loved reading, especially tales of ancient China's legendary heroes. Two of his favorite books were *Water Margin* and *Romance of the Three Kingdoms*, historical novels filled with intrigue and clever military operations. As an adolescent, Mao also read pamphlets and books by Chinese authors who were alarmed by Chinese backwardness and the encroachments of foreign powers on the country.

Struggling against poverty, and against his peasant father who saw little value in book learning, Mao made his own way to a district school for a year and then to a provincial-level school in Changsha, capital of Hunan Province. Here he learned of the failed attempts by modernizers like Liang Ch'i-ch'ao and K'ang Yu-wei to introduce reforms and modernity into

---

[10] *ibid.*, p. 40–41.

China and of repression under the Manchu Dynasty. He also learned of a Manchu governor who, during a famine, taunted the starving people by saying: "How come you have nothing to eat? There's a lot of rice in the city. Look at me. I can always find plenty to eat." A mob of angry, starving people stormed the governor's palace.[11]

Mao's education was distinctly colored by the major events sweeping China after 1908. Revolutionary discontent seethed in China after its humiliating defeat in 1895 by the Japanese. Some Chinese patriots, like Liang and K'ang, favored converting the absolute monarchy into a constitutional monarchy. This attempt at political reform was blocked by Dowager Empress Tzu-hsi. Another patriot favored overthrowing Manchu rule and establishing a republic. This man was American-educated Sun Yat-sen. Mao was deeply impressed by Sun and had, in fact, read Sun's tract *The People's Strength* in which Sun wrote:

> China has fallen to the lowest place among the nations: we are 400 millions on an immense territory, but our Government does not govern. The Court sells positions and dignities, the nobles and mandarins are also all for sale, and brigands are everywhere unchecked.[12]

China was in the throes of the Revolution of 1911 and a train of events followed that led to warlordism, foreign intervention, economic collapse, civil war and chaos. Mao joined the revolutionary army that year and then returned to his studies. It might be said that Mao was formed by revolution and upheaval and later became master of it.

At the Hunan Provincial Library and the First Normal School Mao read voraciously: Adam Smith's *The Wealth of Nations*, Charles Darwin's *The Origin of Species*, John Stuart Mill's *System of Logic*, Herbert Spencer's *Study of Sociology*, Montesquieu's *Esprit des Lois*, and everything he could lay hands on by Rousseau. It is entirely possible that during this period he read something about military theory. Mao's later theoretical writings show a touch of Jomini and a deep understanding of Clausewitz. Mao was obviously quite familiar with the *Sun Tzu Ping Fa* and its commentaries;

---

[11] Biographic materials summarized from Anne Fremantle who, in turn, drew upon Edgar Snow.

[12] Anne Fremantle, p. xv, quoting a passage from Sun Yat-sen's works read to the students at Changsha.

these had a profound impact on his thinking.[13]

In 1918, just as World War I was ending and Japanese imperial encroachments on China were beginning, the well-read and partially self-educated Mao entered Peking University. Later, in Shanghai in 1921, he attended the founding session of the Chinese Communist Party.

A Westerner unacquainted with China's history and culture cannot understand the formation of Mao's thinking. Anyone not familiar with allusions to figures from ancient China's history, or even the tumultuous events of the Century of Humiliation (from1839 to 1949 and commemorated by a marble obelisk in T'ien-an-men Square) would find Mao's writings abstruse or even bizarre. However, if the historical and cultural context of Mao's formative years are understood, much of his thinking becomes clear.

Mao was first and foremost a Chinese patriot in the mold of Sun Yat-sen. A product of the late nineteenth and early twentieth centuries, Mao saw China in danger of being divided by Japan and the European powers into spheres of interest and ultimately foreign colonies, with the Chinese people subjected to alien, colonial rule. Much like Sun he also viewed the Manchu government as being both corrupt and inept, and essentially a handmaiden to the imperialist powers.

Mao was a brilliant, well-read scholar and student. While deeply impressed by what he read, Mao was equally impressed by the practical world around him. Son of a peasant, he understood the peasant mind and social condition. Mao had a special gift that enabled him to speak on equal terms with peasants and scholars. Although his active military service was brief (and somewhat mundane), Mao quickly grasped the practical elements of soldiering and gained familiarity with strategic principles.[14] Not least, Mao let practice shape theory; he was above all else both practical and capable of changing his views once experience proved his theory to be flawed.

---

[13] Literally "The Soldier's Way of Master Sun," begun about the fifth century B.C., but commented on by successive generations of Chinese generals for well over fifteen hundred years.

[14] This is not unlike Abraham Lincoln, whose only active service was as a militia captain in the Blackhawk War of 1832. Yet Lincoln had a superb understanding of strategy and a clear grasp of the relationship of policy to strategy. Mao shared this talent.

The place to begin comprehending Mao's unique view of revolutionary war, his theory of internal warfare, is in his 1930 essay "A Single Spark Can Start a Prairie Fire." Until 1927, the fledgling Communist Party had been allied with the Nationalists against the warlords. This alliance lasted until the "White" Kuomintang (KMT) turned on the Reds and viciously mauled them late in that year. Moreover, by early 1928 the Red forces had been expelled from all the coastal cities and defeated even in Changsha, Hunan's provincial capital, which the pro-Russian faction in the Party had insisted unwisely on capturing and holding. As Mao had foreseen, the weak Red forces were incapable of defending the city and were quickly driven out by government forces. Loss of Chinese Red Army fighters and cadres had been heavy and morale was low leading to the downfall of pro-Russian Chinese Communist leaders, which created opportunities for new leaders like Mao.

Rather than pen a martial tract laying out a program of attacks and violence, armament and maneuver, Mao instead laid bare the sociopolitical conditions affecting China and told his comrades to take heart despite the setbacks; their political tinder was dry:

> In the wake of imperialist commercial aggression, Chinese merchant-capitalist extortions, heavier government taxation, etc., comes the deepening of the contradiction between the landlord class and the peasantry, that is, exploitation through rent and usury is aggravated and the hatred of the peasants for the landlords grows. Because of the pressure of foreign goods, the exhaustion of the purchasing power of the worker and peasant masses, and the increase in government taxation, more and more dealers in Chinese-made goods and independent producers are being driven into bankruptcy. Because the reactionary [ed. Nationalist] government, though short of provisions and funds, endlessly expands its armies and thus constantly extends the warfare, the masses of soldiers are in a constant state of privation. Because of the growth of government taxation, the rise in rent and interest demanded by the landlords and the daily spread of the disasters of war, there are famine and banditry everywhere and the peasant masses and the urban poor can hardly keep alive. Because the schools have no money, many students fear that their education may be interrupted;

> because production is backward, many graduates have no hope of employment. Once we understand all these contradictions, we shall see in what a desperate situation, in what a chaotic state, China finds herself. We shall also see that the high tide of revolution against the imperialists, the warlords and the landlords is inevitable, and will come very soon. All China is littered with dry faggots which will soon be aflame. The saying, "A single spark can start a prairie fire," is an apt description of how the current situation will develop. We need only look at the strikes by the workers, the uprisings by the peasants, the mutinies of soldiers and the strikes of students which are developing in many places to see that it cannot be long before a "spark" kindles "a prairie fire."[15]

We would do well to put ourselves mentally in the shoes of those Chinese who felt that taxes were too high, fees arbitrary, interest rates usurious, crime and disorder rampant. These were, in fact, the conditions that prevailed in much of Nationalist China throughout this government's twenty-year existence. It's more than idle speculation to imagine that the Nationalists might yet be in power on the mainland had they taken effective steps to lower taxes, curb usury, and establish honest, effective administration. Perhaps, like the Cuban refugee in Chapter 1, the ousted Nationalists might say about these reforms: "You know, we really should have. We just didn't think to do so."

In the excerpt above Mao examines the conditions then existing in China—all factual, by the way—and notes the weaknesses that would permit the growth of revolutionary political power. The key element of strategy for Mao was the patient and methodical building of support from each of these major groups: landless peasants, exploited urban workers, national industrialists wiped out by foreign competition, university and other students, disaffected government soldiers, citizens negatively affected by high taxation as well as usurious rental or interest rates, and persons living in dangerous or desperate circumstances.

Mao considered all these dysfunctions from the perspective of Chinese history. When dynasties fell from power, their decline and weakness was invariably marked by peasant uprisings, soldiers who became bandits,

---

[15] Mao Tse-tung, *Selected Works,* p. 69.

collapse of production and famine, and general disaffection. He knew that in the past rebels like Ming Hung-wu, founder of the Ming dynasty, had been able to rally the disaffected people of that time to his standard and defeat the ruling, but now discredited, dynasty. Mao believed that with socioeconomic conditions deteriorating so badly, the political foundations of the Nationalist government in Nanking, now headed by Chiang Kai-shek, were failing and would eventually cause its collapse.

The second key to understanding Mao's strategy is to be found in his May 1938 essay "On Protracted War." In this essay Mao describes the means by which discontent would be transformed into political power:

> What does political mobilization mean? First, it means telling the army and the people about the political aim of the war. It is necessary for every soldier and civilian to see why the war must be fought and how it concerns him. . . . Secondly, it is not enough merely to explain the aim to them; the steps and policies for its attainment must also be given, that is, there must be a political programme. . . . Without a clear-cut, concrete political programme it is impossible to mobilize all the armed forces and the whole people to carry the war against Japan through to the end. *Thirdly, how should we mobilize them? By word of mouth, by leaflets and bulletins, by newspapers, books and pamphlets, through plays and films, through schools, through the mass organizations and through our cadres. . . .* [emphasis added] Fourthly, to mobilize once is not enough; political mobilization for the War of Resistance must be continuous. *Our job is not to recite our political programme to the people, for nobody will listen to such recitations; we must link the political mobilization for the war with developments in the war and with the life of the soldiers and the people, and make it a continuous movement. This is a matter of immense importance on which our victory in the war primarily depends.* [emphasis added][16]

This is Mao's prescription for mobilizing the people. In carrying out his revolution, Mao Tse-tung understood that every military action had to

[16] Mao Tse-tung, *Selected Military Writings*, p. 229. One can substitute "the Nationalists" for "Japan" without changing the meaning of this passage, which is vital to understanding Mao's strategy.

be designed to support some political aim, however local, however humble. At no time was force to be used unless it served some political purpose.

This brings us to the key point. Whereas the European strategists thought in terms of a contest between regular forces put into the field by opposing governments, with either a limited goal in mind or conversely, the total destruction of the enemy force, Mao almost disregarded the armed forces and focused instead on political warfare against the "internal enemy," the regime in power that had forfeited its right to rule. To destroy that internal enemy, what was required was slow and steady recruitment of individuals and groups, and the erosion of the regime's remaining base of support.

None of the Europeans, Liddell Hart included, had concerned themselves with the internal dynamics of a society. Like the military establishments from which they came —France, Germany, Great Britain, Russia— the European strategists viewed ordinary civilians as mere bystanders, not as key participants. While three of the four Europeans acknowledged the connection of war with politics, they interpreted politics as being what the monarch and his advisers deemed it to be. *The idea of mass politics—the will of the people—playing the key role in military affairs never occurred to the Europeans.* The relationship of political guidance to strategy was clear, but only Mao thought in terms of fusing warfare and mass politics into one metal.

Despite his focus on mass politics, we should not conclude that Mao eschewed the use of force, as did Mohandas Gandhi in his non-violent struggle with the British Raj. Rather he prescribed force to be used selectively either to expand political penetration of government-held or occupied areas, or to exhaust the government forces, the enemy. Delbrueck comes closest to Mao's thesis of stretching the regime until it exceeds its own resources and collapses.

We are also mindful that Liddell Hart, probably based on the accomplishments of T. E. Lawrence with his relatively small force of Arabs and a handful of British advisers, advocated the indirect approach: avoiding enemy strongpoints and hitting vulnerable weak spots. Although it is doubtful Mao's thinking was influenced by Delbrueck or Liddell Hart, his military strategy appears to mirror both approaches. And yet, it is distinct.

There are several other elements of Mao's unique strategy we must examine. During the anti-Japanese war (1937–1945) Mao considered the relative strengths of China and Japan and how he might best offset Japanese advantages. He noted that China was a large continental country and had an enormous population, albeit at a lower socioeconomic level than was the norm in Japan. In contrast, Japan was an island nation with a smaller, but more homogeneous population, with higher levels of education, literacy, public health, and so on. Japan had an industrial base, ships, and skilled labor. China lacked all of these assets, especially after 1937 when the Japanese seized the coastal cities from the Nationalists. Therefore, Mao settled upon a war of attrition, using mainly the indirect approach of tying down and immobilizing as many Japanese units as possible. He thought in terms of China's huge manpower advantage and especially the advantage of *time*. The Japanese had a modern, highly proficient army. However, that army required constant reinforcement and resupply from Japan. In China it would operate from cities and need unobstructed access to China's railroads to maintain its logistical support.

Time as an element of strategy is a subjective quality having positive impact in certain circumstances and negative impact in others. For Mao, time was an advantage. For the Japanese War Cabinet in Tokyo, it was a disadvantage, although in 1938 it's possible that the Cabinet had not yet recognized this fact. The problem for the Japanese was that the longer the war lasted, the greater the drain on the treasury and on the nation's relatively limited manpower. Men taken from rice fields and factories for military service reduced agricultural and industrial output, thereby putting additional pressure on an already strained economy. The Imperial treasury found it hard to keep pace with the military's demand for armaments, particularly for naval forces, and increasingly difficult to find funds for nonmilitary governmental functions.

SUN TZU AND MAO

No discussion of military operations in support of an insurgent movement would be complete without reference to Master Sun ("tzu" is Chinese for master) and to his spiritual heir, Mao Tse-tung.

It is worth quoting from Book III, "Offensive Strategy," of the *Sun Tzu Ping Fa* as translated by Samuel B. Griffith:

Sun Tzu said:

1. Generally in war the best policy is to take a state intact; to ruin it is inferior to this.
2. To capture the enemy's army is better than to destroy it; to take intact a battalion, a company or a five-man squad is better than to destroy them.
3. For to win one hundred victories in one hundred battles is not the acme of skill. To subdue the enemy without fighting is the acme of skill.
4. Thus, what is of supreme importance in war is to attack the enemy's strategy. . . . [17]

Clearly understood was Sun Tzu's emphasis on avoiding, if possible, a titanic clash with enemy forces and a fight to the death. Rather, Master Sun saw value in using means other than arms not only to defeat his enemy, *but to absorb him*. This is a unique idea that is found nowhere in European strategic thinking: the idea of absorbing an army or a state into one's own organizational structure is distinctly non-Western.

We might infer that to Sun Tzu war was far more of a mental than a physical process. His conception was to win by maneuver, deception, and ultimately, persuasion.

In this respect, Master Sun's thinking more nearly resembles B. H. Liddell Hart's idea of indirect approach. Sun Tzu also understood the value of psychology in warfare and the value in manipulating the mind—and foibles—of the enemy commander. He also advocated measures intended not merely to deceive enemy forces, but to frustrate and demoralize them.

Sun Tzu's writings have been studied and commented upon by Chinese commanders over many centuries. Indeed, the *Sun Tzu Ping Fa* and its commentaries remained the standard textbook for military officials well into Ch'ing Dynasty times (1644–1911). Mao's works quote from Sun Tzu more than any other source. His *Selected Military Writings* are replete with quotations and examples drawn from Sun Tzu and Chinese antiquity.

Many Americans overlook the fact that Mao Tse-tung was a scholar and historian of no mean achievement. Thoroughly familiar with China's

[17] Sun Tzu, p. 77. Samuel Griffith (1906–1983), a highly decorated Marine Corps officer, served in the Pacific during World War II and retired as a brigadier general. He was a scholar of Chinese language.

history, as we have already said, he was widely read having served in his early years as a librarian at Peking University. Mao certainly had read and absorbed the precepts of the *Sun Tzu Ping Fa* as well as classics such as the *Romance of the Three Kingdoms*, a record of the great generals Tsao Tsao and Chu Ko-liang who were active around the third century A.D. It also seems possible that Mao was familiar with the contemporary example of T.E. Lawrence's operations against the Turks during World War I.

In May 1938 Mao succinctly outlined how it was possible for his weak, predominantly irregular forces, to withstand the *conventionally* superior Japanese army:

> If we take the War of Resistance as a whole, the fact that Japan is a strong country and is attacking while China is a weak country and is defending herself makes our war strategically a defensive and protracted war. As far as the operational lines are concerned, the Japanese are operating on exterior and we on interior lines. This is one aspect of the situation. But there is another aspect which is just the reverse. *The enemy forces, though strong (in arms, in certain qualities of their men, and certain other factors), are numerically small, whereas our forces, though weak (likewise, in arms, in certain qualities of our men, and certain other factors), are numerically very large. Added to the fact that the enemy is an alien nation invading our country while we are resisting his invasion on our own soil,* [emphasis added] this determines the following strategy. It is possible and necessary to use tactical offensives within the strategic defensive, to fight campaigns and battles of quick decision within a strategically protracted war and to fight campaigns and battles on exterior lines within strategically interior lines. Such is the strategy to be adopted in the War of Resistance as a whole.[18]

Later in the same theoretical piece Mao emphasizes that in guerrilla operations there can be no true *defensive* warfare. Guerrillas must appear suddenly, conduct a swift attack, and then fade into the woodwork. They cannot stand and fight a defensive campaign, certainly not against a superior force. (This was the key lesson of Changsha.) Rather, their protection

---

[18] Mao Tse-tung, *Selected Military Writings*, p. 157.

is partly in surprise, but more significantly in their clandestine nature. All conventional military men understand the need for secrecy in warfare, but only insurgents understand the need for "clandestinity."

In ancient times, Chinese military leaders considered that there were two forms of military power—the *ch'i* (or light) forces and the *cheng* (or heavy) units. *Ch'i* units were capable of rapid movement and quick striking power; *cheng* units were not so flexible but found their strength in numbers of men and in armament. Mao thought of *ch'i* forces as his guerrillas and *cheng* units as the mobile warfare columns he developed over time.

> But the basic principle of guerrilla warfare must be the offensive, and guerrilla warfare is more offensive in its character than regular warfare. From the fact that the enemy is strong and we are weak it necessarily follows that, in guerrilla operations in general even more than in regular warfare, battles must be decided quickly, though on some occasions guerrilla fighting may be kept up for several days, as in an assault on a small and isolated enemy force cut off from help. Because of its dispersed character, guerrilla warfare can spread everywhere, and in many of its tasks, as in harassing, containing and disrupting the enemy and in mass work, its principle is dispersal of forces; but a guerrilla unit, or a guerrilla formation, must concentrate its main forces when it is engaged in destroying the enemy, and especially when it is striving to smash an enemy attack. "Concentrate a big force to strike at a small section of the enemy force" remains a principle of field operations in guerrilla warfare.[19]

Elsewhere in his writings Mao reduced this thinking into the aphorism: *My strategy is one against ten; my tactics are ten against one.* On the strategic defensive, the Chinese Communist Eighth Route Army, far smaller than its adversaries, would merely preserve itself and threaten the Japanese (or the Nationalists) while avoiding combat as much as possible. But on the tactical offensive, when conditions were ideal, guerrilla or semi-regular units would rapidly encircle, overwhelm, and destroy smaller isolated enemy forces.

The Chinese example was well known to Vo Nguyen Giap and Ho

[19] *ibid.* p. 158.

Chi Minh, and translated well within the distinct political and cultural framework of French Indochina. A reading of *People's War, People's Army* is recommended for all students of insurgency and revolutionary war, but the reader will find that Giap's writing is merely a distillation of Mao's original thinking.

SO WHAT?

Cyprus and China: two examples, chosen from vastly different societies facing totally different local circumstances, give some insight into the mechanisms of insurgency. Both examples are now fading into history, and neither may be applicable in all aspects to would-be insurgent leaders of the twenty-first century contemplating uprisings in their own countries. However, the analytical process of Mao in defining the ills affecting huge elements of the Chinese populace and General Grivas's demonstrated ability to conduct his war clandestinely against the technologically superior British stand as examples of what might yet be done by others.

What is clear is that for an insurgency to appear, there must be certain political, social and economic conditions that affect a wide number of people in the country or territory that will become the field of operations. The exact nature of these conditions will vary from country to country. Even so, the insurgent leadership must have a clear, concise political goal to set before the people, a goal that crystallizes the causes of the ills felt by the people while at the same time prescribing the cure. With the political goal defined, insurgents then need to propound that idea and the steps for its accomplishment. In small, relatively homogeneous countries like Cyprus that have a high literacy rate political mobilization is relatively easy. In large, heterogeneous countries like China, which at the time was relatively illiterate and had virtually no mass media, political mobilization is a far more difficult but still achievable task. Popular mobilization in Cyprus, given the widespread desire for independence and union with Greece, could be achieved in months. It took years for Mao and his educated cadres to set up literacy programs for peasants, to conduct lectures and debates for the intellectuals, and to reach tens of millions of Chinese with Mao's central message of a *new* China free of exploitation and foreign interference.

So far as operations were concerned, manpower was no problem for

Mao, but was more of a challenge for Grivas. Clandestinity was an absolute hourly requirement for the survival of EOKA and its leader Digenis. Mao could afford to live more or less in the open as his base in Yenan was too far distant from his Japanese and Nationalist enemies for them to seize him. Hit and run tactics suited both Mao and Grivas, for neither could conceive of the possibility of destroying in open battle the Japanese or British armies respectively, though following the World War II surrender of Japan Mao was eventually able to completely annihilate in battle, or win over by adroit propaganda, huge Nationalist armies as the Chinese civil war drew to a close in late 1948 and early 1949. The point was therefore to conduct a sustained, systematic limited war to exhaust the enemy.

There is also the consideration of the enemy regime and its forces. Both Japan and Great Britain had been industrialized, modern countries for many years. Their armies were organized pretty much like all other modern armies to handle heavy weaponry and equipment manufactured in the home country (or, in post-World War II Britain's case, in the United States). Troops and equipment are costly. Sending troops and equipment abroad to wage expeditionary warfare is costly. Soldiers require huge supplies of food, good medical care, occasional home leave, housing, and much else. This necessarily entails a sophisticated and efficient logistical system. Such logistical systems require considerable manpower and transportation resources. Logistics are therefore costly, as well.

These costs must be borne by the national treasuries and ultimately by the taxpayers of the home country. Neither imperial Japan nor post-imperial Britain could afford their wars. Both governments found themselves unable to fund other pressing nonmilitary requirements, and the taxpayers in Britain saw no compelling need for ever-increasing tax levies to support what many people considered foreign adventures. In the case of the Nationalist Chinese, logistics was less a concern than for the British or Japanese.[20] But the already weak Nationalist economy could not sustain the cost of war. As the war dragged on, the Chinese yuan inflated in value until, like the German mark of the 1920s, it was in the millions per one U.S. dollar. Indeed, as its 1949 collapse drew ever nearer, the National Government

[20] The deployment of Nationalist armies into Manchuria, hundreds of miles from their nearest secure base, was patently foolish, but nonetheless dictated by Chiang Kai-shek. They were cut off and destroyed.

could not pay its troops, civil servants, suppliers, or, for that matter, anyone else. For all intents and purposes, the black market was the economy in Nationalist China, and the U.S. dollar was preferred to Chinese currency.[21]

Both Chairman Mao and General Grivas understood that relatively small armed forces, if shielded by a sympathetic populace from harm by a superior adversary, could survive and inflict painful, though not life-threatening injury on their opponents. The point was not to destroy the enemy, but merely to frustrate and exhaust him, and to convince him that reaching a political accord is a wiser course of action than sustaining casualties and costs indefinitely.

From a purely numerical standpoint, Grivas won his war despite a thirty-two to one advantage held by his British foes. In a later chapter we will see why force ratios, so beloved by many counterinsurgents, are basically meaningless. Mao's ratios are harder to compute because of questionable numbers on both sides, but all observers agree that until the last year of the Chinese civil war he was numerically weaker than his enemies.

The final "So What?" is that insurgencies can be contained by military force at great cost in blood and treasure, but they can only be defeated by a thoughtful and systematic political strategy incorporating genuine reform that addresses the grievances of the people and is supported by skillful employment of a competent civil-military approach. This concept is something new, something completely beyond the European view of strategy.

Neither Jomini nor Clausewitz can help us here.

[21] Jim Rogers, a contemporary venture capitalist quipped: "You know a country is falling apart when even the government will not accept its own currency."

CHAPTER **5**

THREE CAUTIONARY TALES

Always ask the question, "If not?" Few people have good strategies for when their assumptions are wrong.—Moses Shapiro[1]

There is a tendency to believe that insurgency is a modern invention. This view is completely incorrect. While it is true that technology and social change have greatly influenced the process of insurgency, the idea of people's wars is actually quite a venerable one. In a previous chapter we briefly mentioned the Spanish uprising against Napoleon's brother, King Joseph, and the resulting *guerra de guerrillas* intended to expel the French and their puppet king from Spain. Clausewitz also was undoubtedly aware of the failed insurgency in Tyrol under the Austrian patriot, Andreas Hofer.

The point is that if we look to history we will find numerous examples of rebellions that flared into insurgencies of varying lengths and types. As has been stated, there are three basic factors needed to spark an insurgency: widespread anger, a leader or leadership group, and a *Cause*.[2]

American military officers would do well to study in some detail the 1780–1781 campaign of Lord Charles Cornwallis during the American

[1] CEO John Malone quoting Moses Shapiro (1920–1990) former senior executive, labor attorney, and member of the War Labor Board during World War II.

[2] Dr. Michael Shurkin, an expert on Jewish history, notes that the campaign of the Maccabeans to expel the Seleucids in the 2nd century B.C. has all the features of an insur-

Revolution, General Francois Achille Bazaine, French commander of Napoleon III's forces in Mexico from 1864 to early 1867, and General Henri Navarre in French Indochina in 1953 and 1954. Each of these examples—deliberately chosen because they are in different lands and in different historical times—tells a cautionary tale about the wisdom of attempting to employ conventional forces conventionally against insurgents enjoying at least a measure of popular support.

LORD CORNWALLIS VS. NATHANIEL GREENE

Friday 12 May 1780 was a black day for the cause of American independence. On that day General Benjamin Lincoln was forced to haul down the national colors and march out of Charleston in surrender. The American regular force defending Charleston consisted of fifty-four hundred soldiers, plus artillery and a variety of other armaments. This defeat marked the worst drubbing received by the Americans during the Revolutionary War.

At the head of his triumphant army of fourteen thousand men Sir Henry Clinton and his deputy Lord Charles Cornwallis watched the surrender of their American enemies with contempt.[3] Surely the rebellion, as they saw it, would soon be suppressed and British colonial rule fully restored. Indeed, His Majesty's Government had concluded that a strike into the southern colonies would cause thousands of Tory Loyalists to rise up, join His Majesty's forces, and destroy the rebels. The plan looked good on paper.

With eight thousand men Lord Cornwallis moved inland into South Carolina. During the summer of 1780 he met with almost continual successes. The unwise General Horatio Gates, victor of Saratoga, was humbled at Camden in August when he attempted to oppose Cornwallis in conventional battle. Nine hundred American soldiers lay dead and another one thousand were made prisoners as Gates himself ignominiously fled 160 miles to safety.

Cornwallis and his notorious cavalry commander Banastre Tarleton

---

gency, as does the later Bar Kochba uprising. Author also offers the suggestion that the early struggles of the Prophet Mohammed and his followers might be defined as a transformational insurgency aimed at breaking Meccan power, unifying the peoples of the Arabian Peninsula, and overcoming external interference.

[3] Sir Henry Clinton was supreme commander and had brought down additional troops and ships from his headquarters in New York, but Lord Cornwallis would be field commander in the South. The British had concentrated some fourteen thousand men augmented by Admiral Arbuthnot's fleet in Charleston harbor.

destroyed smaller rebel forces at Waxhaws and Fishing Creek with great savagery. A neutral observer reporting to his superiors in September 1780 would probably have concluded that the American Revolution, at least in the South, had been decisively defeated.

But was it? It was certainly true that a good number of Tories did rally to His Majesty as Cornwallis's victories convinced them of the inevitability of a royal triumph. However, at the same time, the viciousness and cruelty of the British army, especially Tarleton and his troopers, enraged large numbers of settlers in the Carolinas. In effect, the British invasion only polarized the political struggle in the southern colonies—neighbors now set out to kill other neighbors—but the invasion itself did little to cement royal control in the South. Ignored by many historians was the savagery of the British military toward civilians in areas occupied by Cornwallis, and the mounting violence between American Tories and Patriots.[4] Enraged colonists uttered the phrase "Tarleton's Quarter," meaning take no prisoners, and vowed to fight to the death against the hated British.

The lack of a political strategy for the restoration of British colonial rule in the South was perhaps more fatal to Lord Cornwallis than was his decision to ignore Sir Henry Clinton's advice about staying close to the Atlantic to receive support from the Royal Navy. Instead of following a policy of reconciling those colonists having grievances against the Crown, winning the sympathy of neutrals and giving active support to Loyalists, Lord Cornwallis punished the rebels, antagonized the neutrals and kept the Loyalists in decidedly subordinate roles. He flatly refused to restore civil rule in South Carolina, preferring to serve as that colony's military governor. In effect, General Cornwallis declared South Carolina to be a conquered enemy state rather than liberated friendly royal territory under its own civil, albeit pro-British authorities.

Given South Carolina's condition of lawlessness, Cornwallis' military strategy and lack of a viable British political strategy resulted in widespread violence throughout the Carolina Piedmont. Tory Loyalists now fell upon their neighbors who were suspected of Patriot sympathies. For their part, colonists who held anti-British sympathies and desired independence clashed with their Tory neighbors. Much of this bloodletting is only

---

[4] The film, *"The Patriot,"* starring Mel Gibson, captures the flavor of this neighbor-on-neighbor savagery and the enormous price that was paid by ordinary citizens to gain our independence. Without stretching the point, the American Revolution was "a people's war" against their British colonial masters.

poorly documented, but it was nevertheless quite real.

Moreover, the absence of responsible civil authority in the Carolinas capable of maintaining some semblance of order left the region ungovernable by either side and vulnerable to the spread of insurgent units that menaced the roads on which Cornwallis depended. This meant that in reality Cornwallis did not have a secure rear area. He was therefore unwittingly advancing steadily forward into a quagmire of his own making.

British fortunes changed decidedly for the worse with sharp defeats at King's Mountain in October 1780 and at Cowpens in January 1781. Although Cowpens, a clever double envelopment of the British, is justly regarded as the American Cannae, I believe the Battle of King's Mountain is more instructive. This is because it was fought between eleven hundred Tories under Major Patrick Ferguson and some fourteen hundred Virginia and Carolina militia and Tennessee "Over-mountain men"; many were sharpshooters. *All participants in this battle except Major Ferguson himself were Americans.* The Patriots surrounded and totally annihilated the Tory forces.[5]

> This disaster [King's Mountain] combined with widespread disorders in South Carolina, led Cornwallis to abandon a planned invasion of North Carolina. He retreated to winter quarters at Winnsborough, N.C., and took stern measures against rebellious colonists.[6]

We may rest assured that Cornwallis's "stern measures" did not make these rebels loyal subjects of the Crown. Moreover, Lord Cornwallis probably perceived that his army was now far from its coastal bases and the protection of the Royal Navy. Indeed, it was deep in a countryside swarming with guerrillas, such as those led by Andrew Pickens and Francis Marion, and surrounded by a populace that was at best coldly sullen and often actively hostile.

The year 1781 offered new prospects to Cornwallis, but once again

[5] The Patriots, goaded by hatred, annihilated the Tory unit, shooting many even as they tried to surrender. Some three hundred Tories were killed and seven hundred captured. After the battle, ten captured Tories were tried and hanged for plundering the homes of colonists suspected of Patriot sympathies.

[6] Dupuy and Dupuy, p. 719.

obstinate resistance by the colonists—both uniformed and civilian—ultimately frustrated his plans. General Nathanael Greene had replaced the impetuous Gates, and though untutored as a military man, he conducted a skillful retreat and delaying action that exhausted the British forces.

After his humiliation at Cowpens, Cornwallis attempted a conventional pursuit of Greene to the Virginia state line. Undoubtedly his thinking was that if he could catch Greene he could destroy him. And, if he destroyed Greene the campaign would be won. Or so he thought.

Greene was well aware that his militia forces were no match for British regulars in an open, conventional battle. Instead, he employed distance and time to defeat Cornwallis. This resulted in the famous "race to the Dan River" in which Greene steadily withdrew ahead of Cornwallis, refusing to stand and fight, but instead causing the British commander to pursue him across many rivers and deeper into the wilderness. Greene won the race to the Dan; Cornwallis's army was now exhausted and probably dispirited. We may also infer that, having destroyed his baggage train in his vain attempt to catch Greene, Cornwallis's remaining soldiers were hungry and in need of supplies. As the British were now far from sources of help along the coast and deep in hostile country, Cornwallis had no choice but to withdraw.

Greene followed cautiously, his only battle being that at Guilford Courthouse in March 1781. Perceiving an opportunity, Cornwallis immediately attacked Greene's forces even though his army was depleted to about nineteen hundred men. History records Guilford as a British victory. But although Cornwallis held the field, and Greene withdrew, British losses greatly exceeded American losses: clearly it was a Pyrrhic victory.

After his "victory" at Guilford Courthouse, Cornwallis realized that he could not hold the Carolinas or Georgia. He had neither the military strength nor the support of the people, not even a sham civilian government to maintain his position in the South. This left his only path a retreat to the coast to Wilmington, North Carolina, to obtain supplies and reinforcements, followed by the move of the remnants of his army of about fourteen hundred men to Virginia. The southern campaign was over. Despite their many victories on the battlefield it was a strategic defeat for British arms.

Morale in Cornwallis's army plummeted as it became ever clearer to the officers and men that they had achieved nothing and that their presence in the South was not only unwanted by the bulk of the population, but in fact had been counterproductive. Not only was popular support lacking for the British invasion but passive resistance by the colonists steadily mounted as the British occupation continued.

One British officer stationed in Charleston wrote a letter to a friend in London in late May 1781 that was published months later in the Philadelphia-based *Pennsylvania Packet* newspaper. It gives a stark picture of the low state of British morale and the colonists' policy of noncooperation:

> The retrograde progress of our arms in this country, you have seen in your newspapers, if they dare tell you the truth. This precious commodity is not to be had in the government paper which is printed here, for a fell licenser [censor] hangs over the press, and will suffer nothing to pass but what is palatable; that is, in plain terms, what is false. Our victories have been dearly bought, for the rebels seem to grow stronger by every defeat, like Antaeus, of whom it was fabled, that being the son of the goddess Tellus, or the earth, every fall which he received from Hercules gave him more strength, so that the hero was forced to strangle him in his arms at last. I wish our ministry would send us a Hercules to conquer these obstinate Americans, whose aversion to the cause of Britain grows stronger every day.
>
> If you go into company with any of them occasionally, they are barely civil, and that is, as Jack Falstaff says, by compulsion. They are in general sullen, silent, and thoughtful. The King's health they dare not refuse, but they drink it in a manner as if they expected it would choke them.
>
> The assemblies which the officers have opened, in hopes to give an air of gayety and cheerfulness to themselves and the inhabitants, are but dull and gloomy meetings; the men play at cards, indeed, to avoid talking, but the women are seldom or never to be persuaded to dance. Even in their dresses the females seem to bid us defiance; the gay toys which are imported here they despise; they wear their own homespun manufactures, and take care to have in their breasts knots, and even on their shoes something that

> resembles their flag of the thirteen stripes. An officer told Lord Cornwallis not long ago, that he believed if he had destroyed all the men in North America, we should have enough to do to conquer the women. I am heartily tired of this country, and wish myself at home.[7]

What we can take away from this example are several facts that offer a cautionary tale to conventional forces operating in an insurgent environment. Cornwallis won most of his battles, with the notable exceptions of King's Mountain and Cowpens, whereas his main opponent, Greene, won none of his. Despite consistent losses in the conventional sense, Greene nonetheless proved the victor *strategically*. The British did rally a large number of Tory supporters,[8] as they had hoped, but this was more than offset by the number of enemies they created thanks to their savage behavior toward the people. Although they were able to surprise and defeat Thomas Sumter, they failed to catch or neutralize Andrew Pickens and "Swamp Fox" Francis Marion who remained painful thorns in their "rear areas." Indeed, it may be said that the British did not really have a secure rear area as the combination of an enraged populace and Patriot irregular forces prevented the British from establishing any form of stable political control.

Conventional force-on-force operations, such as those favored by American General Gates, were doomed to failure against an opposing force superior in numbers, armaments, discipline, and technical training. But the application by Nathanael Greene of a different approach—if you will, a pre-Maoist approach of avoiding pitched battles, withdrawing before the enemy's advance, cautiously following his retreat, and using time and distance to wear down his British enemy—ultimately proved successful. Greene also benefited from the fact that a great number of colonists in the Carolinas now considered themselves to be "Americans." They would aid his movements, not impede them.

Later in life, reflecting upon his unfortunate American experience, Lord Cornwallis wrote that Nathanael Greene was the one American general whom he feared.

---

[7] Moore, pp. 506–507.

[8] Today we call most descendants of these Tories "Canadians."

GENERAL BAZAINE VS. BENITO JUAREZ

Mexico under Emperor Maximilian offers us a similar cautionary tale. In late 1861 the French emperor Napoleon III had decided that Mexico, which had been independent for the previous forty years, would be the ideal base for a new French colonial empire in the Americas. After hoodwinking his British and Spanish partners in a debt-collecting effort, Napoleon III landed six thousand soldiers under General Comte Charles Ferdinand Latrille de Lorencez to conquer Mexico.

This general, completely contemptuous of the ragtag Mexican force of four thousand sent to block his way at Puebla, wrote in April 1862 to the French Minister of War:

> We are so superior to the Mexicans in race, organization, morality, and elevated sentiments that I beg Your Excellency to inform the Emperor that at the head of six thousand soldiers I am already master of Mexico.[9]

General de Lorencez spoke prematurely. Disdaining his Mexican foes as being perhaps two steps above animals, the Frenchman sent his cavalry directly up the steep slopes of the Cerro Guadalupe, over a wall, and across soggy ditches. The result was over a thousand French dead and dying. The date was 5 May 1862.

History records this as the Battle of Puebla. Mexicans (and some of the rest of us) celebrate the battle as "Cinco de Mayo" to this day.

But Cinco de Mayo was merely the opening shot in what was to be an increasingly costly and deadly French war in Mexico, a war pitting an element of a modern European army against poorly-armed insurgent forces under the political leadership of Benito Juarez.

Cinco de Mayo was a stinging defeat for France and its emperor. Indeed, it was the first time since Waterloo that a French army had been defeated. Making matters worse in Emperor Napoleon's eyes was the fact that this humiliation was at the hands of the Mexicans, a subject people. The French defeat shocked Europe and galvanized an enraged emperor into taking stronger measures to bring his colony to heel. He now despatched an army of 28,000 under three of his most experienced generals to conquer Mexico.

---

[9] Fehrenback, p. 423.

The French conquest of Mexico began in earnest in March 1863 with Puebla being captured in May. The road to Mexico City now lay open, so Juarez evacuated his government to the north. The French, now under General Elie Frederic Forey, entered the capital on 10 June 1863 and were "welcomed by jubilant church dignitaries and rich Catholic Creoles. In the great cathedral, Te Deums were sung at solemn high mass celebrating Mexico's deliverance from the hated government of Juarez."[10]

In the very hour of their triumph, however, the French committed a series of political blunders that were to undermine their colonial scheme. General Forey set himself up as virtual dictator of Mexico, sent a memo to Napoleon III asking that Austrian Archduke Maximilian be sent out immediately, and refused Church requests for restoration of lands seized by the Juarez government under the *Ley Lerdo* of 1856.[11] Although Napoleon III was well aware that Maximilian was to be his puppet emperor in Mexico, he wished it to appear that the people of Mexico had requested Maximilian's presence, certainly not the French commander. Forey was recalled to Paris. A sham plebiscite was held early in 1864 that ostensibly called Maximilian to the throne. It should be understood, however, that Maximilian had no popular base of support; he was an Austrian and the French were viewed as outsiders.

The new French commander, General Francois Achille Bazaine proceeded to push the republican forces under Juarez ever northward. Napoleon III now felt that it was time to send forth Mexico's new emperor to take charge of the country. In April 1864, after a rash of parties in Paris thrown by Louis-Napoleon in his honor, Maximilian and his consort, Carlotta, embarked for the New World.[12] Even before the imperial couple set sail, the U.S. Congress passed a resolution in keeping with the Monroe Doctrine unanimously opposing the establishment of monarchy in Mexico.[13]

---

[10] McHenry, p. 136.

[11] *Ley Lerdo*, written by Mexican liberals at the time of the constitution, appropriated all Church lands other than the buildings themselves. This amounted to tens of thousands of hectares of productive land. This law (*ley*) was named for Miguel Lerdo de Tejada, the treasury secretary at the time.

[12] Maximilian was the younger brother of the Austrian (Hapsburg) emperor, Franz Josef. Maximilian's wife was Charlotte, daughter of King Leopold I of Belgium. As he set out for Mexico, Maximilian was forced to renounce all claims of inheritance to the imperial crown in Austria, a painful act for him.

[13] Act of Congress, 4 April 1864, cited in Wikipedia.

History views Maximilian as honest and idealistic, but nevertheless as a dupe of Napoleon III's imperial schemes. Brother of Emperor Franz Josef of Austria, Maximilian may have yearned for an imperial diadem of his own. Certainly that was true of Carlotta, who consistently believed that she was being treated well below her true station in life. While Maximilian apparently believed that he was to be a servant of the people of Mexico, his wife was much more focused on the pomp and ceremony of being an empress. Clearly, events would prove that Maximilian was far out of his depth in confronting the myriad economic and political problems that faced Mexico. He imagined that after being crowned emperor many of these difficulties would simply resolve themselves. It is said that on the six week voyage to Mexico, Maximilian busied himself, not with studying Mexico's many problems, but with writing a six-hundred-page tome on court etiquette.

Militarily, the situation in Mexico became steadily less secure for the French. Although General Bazaine invariably occupied city after city, town after town, the moment that French troops departed, these occupied cities and towns reverted to the republicans. A true insurgency, the national resistance was everywhere and nowhere, exhausting the French occupation forces. Although a Mexican imperial army was created, it was relatively small and only occasionally effective. This army consisted largely of Indians led by officers from France, Austria, and Belgium. The Belgian Foreign Legion and elements of the Austrian army joined the French and imperial forces in Mexico.

Politically, the situation was equally discouraging. Although considered by many to be honest, charming, and a gracious host, Emperor Maximilian very quickly undermined the political base upon which his imperial regime rested. A fair-minded man, Maximilian was philosophically something of a liberal himself. He did not restore church lands as had been expected, he did not abrogate the civil and political rights won by Mexicans under the Constitution of 1857, and he did not govern as an autocrat.

> Maximilian was too quixotic to make a good emperor. He built his government on democratic principles much to the chagrin of the clergy and the rich Creoles who since 1823 had been longing for a centralized monarchy modeled after the governments of the viceroys. As he showed no inclination to repeal the hateful laws of

> Juarez, nor to restore church land, the conservatives, only six months after he arrived, denounced him as a liberal in royal trappings, no better, basically, than their archenemy Juarez.[14]

By early 1865, and perhaps even by late 1864, the foundations of the Empire of Mexico were crumbling. Juarez had removed himself to the far north, indeed to Paso del Norte, today renamed Ciudad Juarez. Though in exile, his government continued to resist the French occupiers and the Mexican conservatives. Insurgent forces operated in many parts of the country, and the northern areas of Mexico fronting on the United States were firmly in his hands. In an effort to overwhelm the insurgents, Napoleon III had increased the number of French troops in Mexico by 1865 to forty thousand.[15]

Emperor Maximilian's base of support decreased almost daily as he alienated or disappointed those who had hoped to regain lost lands, fortunes, and social status. Insurgent groups had spread throughout the country and the French army found that it held only what it could physically occupy. Worse, the rebel groups were increasingly better armed, trained, and supplied than had been the case only a year earlier.

At the close of the American Civil War, with Texas now firmly in Union hands, a covert war against the French in Mexico was stepped up. The Baton Rouge arsenal, with thousands of muskets and other weapons now surplus to the Union's needs, was made the base for equipping Juarez's army.

General Sheridan was appointed to lead the American force along the Rio Grande. Many of the fifty-two thousand troops sent to Texas were seasoned combat veterans. All were superbly armed and trained, and well led by former Union army officers.

> Wrote Grant to Sheridan: " . . . concentrate at all available points in the States an army strong enough to move against the invaders of Mexico, if occasion demanded."[16]

---

[14] McHenry, pp. 138-139. Even the Mexican reactionaries now spoke of the regime as being foreign. It had lost credibility and it never had political legitimacy. The empire was a French occupation regime.

[15] Wikipedia, Philip Sheridan.

[16] McHenry, p. 140. The official U.S. Army history (*American Military History*) gives a total figure of fifty-two thousand troops deployed in three corps along the Mexican border. Vigorous patrolling along that border was intended to be observed by any French or imperial forces or scouts in the area.

At the same time as the U.S. Government sent forces to the border, it widened its covert assistance to Benito Juarez and his followers:

> During the American civil war a trickle of supplies in arms and munitions was crossing the Texas border and reaching Juarez forces, but when Lee surrendered to Grant, that trickle became a gushing stream, although it ran surreptitiously beneath legal channels. Wrote Phil Sheridan in his papers: " . . . we continued covertly supplying arms and munitions to the liberals, sending as many as 30,000 muskets from Baton Rouge arsenal alone."[17]

Elsewhere in his memoirs, Sheridan described how the covert resupply process worked so as to provide the U.S. Government a fig leaf of plausible deniability.

> Sheridan later admitted in his memoirs that he had supplied arms to Juárez's forces: ". . . supplied with arms and ammunition, which we left at convenient places on our side of the river to fall into their hands."[18]

General Bazaine now found himself in a quagmire. Although he could, and did, defeat bands of guerrillas, new bands would spring up in areas Bazaine thought he controlled. Captured guerrillas often were sprung from jail by Mexicans sympathetic to the national cause. French troops were assailed from every quarter. With his situation growing more desperate by the day, Bazaine requested that Maximilian sign a decree empowering the French to summarily execute any captured guerrillas. Maximilian was reluctant to sign such an authorization, but gave way and did so on 5 October 1865.[19] The signing of the Black Decree, as it came to be known, resulted in the summary execution of Juarist prisoners on 21 October. The war then became pitiless as each side, French and Mexican, gave no quarter to the other.

---

[17] *ibid.* p. 140.

[18] Wikipedia, Philip Sheridan. Section quotes Sheridan's memoirs about his involvement along the border.

[19] This decree was to become Maximilian's own death warrant. It was the key piece of evidence put before the court-martial that convinced the officers that he was deserving of the death penalty.

American covert aid to Juarez continued throughout 1866 and almost certainly contributed to placing the republican forces on a more equal footing with the French occupiers. The muskets given to Juarez covertly by the U.S. Army were modern and replaced many of the antiquated pieces used in May 1862 by the defenders of Puebla.

Emperor Napoleon's situation grew markedly difficult in 1866. In a sense, he was a victim of his own imperial success. French armies now were scattered around the globe and thus the French Empire suffered from what has been called imperial over-stretch. The war in Mexico was not only a costly drain on the French treasury, but tied down forty thousand men who might be needed elsewhere. Indeed, the elsewhere increasingly appeared to be France itself as Napoleon III became acutely aware of a rising threat in the form of Prussia and its wily Iron Chancellor, Otto von Bismarck.

Adding to the French emperor's worries about Berlin came an ultimatum from far off Washington, D.C. In January 1866, through a sharply worded diplomatic note the United States government demanded the immediate withdrawal of French forces from Mexico.[20] A similar demarche was also sent to the imperial court in Vienna complaining of the many Austrian volunteers in the Mexican imperial army.

Facing the pressures of land threats in Europe and in America, Napoleon III secretly instructed General Bazaine to begin withdrawing French forces from Mexico. This was to be done in three stages: Bazaine was to pull out the first tranche in November 1866 followed by withdrawals in March and December 1867.[21] As a courtesy, Bazaine advised Maximilian of his orders to begin phased withdrawals. He also counseled the emperor to abdicate his throne and depart with the French army.

Historians agree that Maximilian, a thoughtful and moderate man, was inclined to heed Bazaine's advice. However, the moment Empress

---

[20] Chapter 13 of *American Military History* notes that "Major General John M. Schofield was then on a special mission in France to make this point clear." (p. 282) Napoleon III must certainly have been aware that in May 1865 the Union army had over a million soldiers on its rolls, although it is true that most were volunteers on limited enlistments. Even though by the end of 1865 that number had been reduced to fifty-four thousand regulars and a further two hundred thousand plus volunteers, it was clear that this smaller force nevertheless presented a serious threat to the French in Mexico.

[21] The withdrawals were accelerated. The last French troops departed Mexico on 5 February 1867.

Carlotta heard of this she flew into a rage and insisted upon confronting Napoleon III. Her position was clear: "She was an empress and would remain an empress."[22] Carlotta set sail for France on 9 July 1866.

Despite Carlotta's pleadings and ravings before Napoleon III, the die was cast. The Council of State told Napoleon what he already knew: France could no longer afford its war in Mexico. He personally conveyed this message to Carlotta. "Though he spoke gently and judiciously, his message threw Carlotta into raving hysterics."[23] Soon thereafter, Carlotta lapsed into insanity and eventually was taken home to Belgium where she died in 1927 at the age of 87. She was never to see her Emperor Maximilian again.

As 1867 opened, the end was in sight for the French imperial adventure in Mexico. Insurgent forces had already gained control of Guadalajara, Monterrey, Tampico, and Oaxaca. It was clear that they soon would be at the gates of Mexico City. General Bazaine implored Maximilian to leave Mexico at once. Indeed, Maximilian seriously considered departing with the French in January, but at the eleventh hour reversed himself. Maximilian's army of twenty thousand did have contingents of Belgian, Austrian, and French volunteers, but despite its technical proficiency, it was no match for the tens of thousands of republican insurgents who enjoyed quiet help from across the Rio Grande.

On 5 February 1867 Emperor Maximilian and some friends watched General Bazaine lead the last French troops out of Mexico City on their way to Veracruz. In a masterpiece of total misperception of the true situation, Maximilian is reported to have said: "Now, gentlemen, at long last I am free!"[24] It apparently never occurred to Maximilian that with French military support gone the handwriting was on the wall for his kingdom.

The last act in this tragedy was played out north of Mexico City on the Hill of the Bells (Cerro de las Campanas) in the city of Queretaro. After a lengthy siege and series of battles, Maximilian and his staff were captured there on 14 May 1867. Tried by a court-martial, Maximilian was sentenced to death for treason. He and two of his senior commanders were executed by a firing squad on 19 June 1867.

---

[22] McHenry, p. 141.
[23] *ibid.* p. 142.
[24] *ibid.* p. 145.

As with the earlier example of Cornwallis in the Carolinas, the impossible dilemma faced by Bazaine in Mexico was to trap and destroy *a political idea*, not merely an opposing army and its leader. While both Bazaine and Cornwallis came to realize that they were fighting in a sea of angry citizens, neither may have fully understood that the more they employed the superbly trained regular forces under their command, their respective situations became steadily worse, not better.

Bazaine could go from tactical victory to tactical victory and still lose the war. Indeed, rising costs and external pressures eventually made his occupation of Mexico untenable.

HENRI NAVARRE VS. HO CHI MINH

When the United States dropped its second atomic bomb on Nagasaki on 9 August 1945, Japanese troops were in firm control of what had been French Indochina: Cambodia, Laos, and the three regions of Vietnam: Tonkin, Annam, and Cochin-China. The French had come to Vietnam in the 1860s under Napoleon III, and by the end of the century had annexed all of Vietnam to its border with China. As it had for centuries, the Vietnamese imperial family continued to live in Hue, but the emperors were reduced to puppets under control of a French governor general.

Following the surrender of France to Nazi Germany this situation changed with the landing of Japanese soldiers in Tonkin in 1940. The profascist Vichy regime lamely approved the Japanese occupation of Hanoi, although the Japanese permitted Vichy officials to remain nominally in positions of authority. Real power, however, lay with the Japanese army.

Although Vietnam itself had been absorbed piecemeal by the French between 1858 and 1893, the Vietnamese people retained their cultural identity and a sense of nationhood that was to give rise to several nationalist movements in the twentieth century. One of the many such groups advocating the reestablishment of Vietnamese independence was the Indochinese Communist Party, which was founded in 1930. A key organizer of the ICP was a man born in 1890 as Nguyen Sinh Cung. Later he became Nguyen That Thanh (Nguyen the accomplished one), then Nguyen Ai Quoc (Nguyen the patriot), and finally Ho Chi Minh (He who enlightens).

The Japanese came to Vietnam, not as liberators, but as occupiers.

Vietnamese nationalists therefore had two enemies to choose from: their old masters, the French, or the new colonialists in Asia, the Japanese. During the course of World War II the ICP operated small units inside occupied Vietnam, which on some occasions were sponsored by the American Office of Strategic Services (OSS). The OSS found the organization known as Viet Nam Doc Lap Dong Minh Hoi (League for the Independence of Vietnam), which was founded on 19 May 1941, to be serious about taking on the Japanese and fairly competent at so doing. This group of guerrillas came to be known by the shorter version of their name: the Viet Minh. The Viet Minh collected intelligence on Vichy French and Japanese activities inside Vietnam and occasionally carried out damaging raids and sabotage.

America's use of the atomic bomb brought an abrupt end to World War II and the Japanese formally surrendered on 2 September 1945. That very day in Hanoi Ho Chi Minh and other Viet Minh leaders proclaimed Vietnamese independence with the creation of the Democratic Republic of Vietnam. Since the Japanese had imprisoned the Vichy French officials in March 1945, and had now been ordered by Emperor Hirohito to cease resistance, the Viet Minh found themselves inheritors of a power vacuum. They quickly seized the opportunity to establish an independent government to replace the French colonial regime that had ruled for some eighty years.

Independence was to be short-lived. Below the 16th parallel a British force had landed to take the surrender of the Japanese forces in the Mekong Delta and Annam. Within a few months about two hundred thousand Chinese Nationalist troops arrived in Hanoi to accept Japanese surrender of armies and weapons in the northern part of Vietnam. The French, who were slow to move back into their old colony, initially agreed to Vietnamese autonomy within the French Union. By early 1946 the Chinese had departed, but had turned over the reins of administration to the now-returning French, not to the Vietnamese. The French waffled on their pledge of independence for Vietnam, though both sides agreed to negotiate.

During World War II, the United States indicated to its European allies, the British, French, and Dutch, that the age of colonialism had passed and that independence of former colonies would be welcomed. Franklin D. Roosevelt's death and aggressive postwar acts by the Soviet Union in Europe muted this American policy and France decided to retain

Indochina. Toward this end its policy was reoccupation, and by military means, if necessary. Ironically, French policy was shaped by the Socialist government then in power in the Fourth Republic with the support of the French Communist Party. Armed hostilities commenced in late 1946 and Ho and his government fled Hanoi on 18 December 1946.

Early in 1947 Leon Blum, temporarily head of the French government, asked World War II hero Gen. Jacques Leclerc, who had been instrumental in arranging a 1946 ceasefire with the Viet Minh, to return to Indochina as commander-in-chief and high commissioner. Leclerc declined the positions and told his political masters in Paris:

> In 1947 France will no longer put down by force a grouping of 24 million inhabitants which is assuming unity and in which there exists a xenophobic and perhaps a national ideal. The major problem from now on is political.[25]

Two of Leclerc's detractors, Admiral Georges Thierry d'Argenlieu and General Jean-Etienne Valluy, saw the matter in very different terms. They believed a quick military decision could be achieved over the Viet Minh followed by the unquestioned restoration of French power. They held that anti-Communist groups in Vietnam would unite with the French to oppose Ho Chi Minh and by so doing convert a colonial war into a *mere* civil war. Seeing through this smokescreen, Leclerc declared: "Anti-Communism will remain a useless tool as long as the problem of nationalism is not solved."[26]

And yet, the political paralysis of the ever-changing coalitions of the Fourth Republic and the temptation of a purely military solution prevented serious negotiations. The record shows that the French could have had peace in Vietnam, and possibly retained a leased base there, had they been willing to agree to genuine Vietnamese independence in 1946.

Despite Leclerc's pleas, that was not to be. On 17 May 1947 the high commissioner in French Indochina, Emile Bollaert, told *Le Monde* that

---

[25] Jacques Leclerc quoted in Buttinger, pp. 284–285. Leclerc's true name was Philippe Francois Marie, Comte de Hauteclocque (1902–1947). Jacques Philippe Leclerc was his French Resistance name, and the name by which he is remembered. Posthumously he was made a Marshal of France.

[26] *ibid.* pp. 286–287.

"France will remain in Indochina, and Indochina will remain within the French Union." [27] This was France's final offer.

Not all Vietnamese supported the Viet Minh. Catholics, anti-Communists, merchants and landowners, and many others either opposed the Viet Minh or were highly skeptical of them. There was one problem, however. The majority of Vietnamese also desired an end to French rule. The French had now proclaimed that they were there to stay. The political situation was therefore polarized between the French colonialists and the leading nationalists, the Viet Minh: opposing one meant supporting the other. This left many Vietnamese caught in the middle, and as we have seen, it is very difficult to remain truly neutral during an insurgency.

After chasing the Viet Minh out of Hanoi, the French army under General Valluy then opened its first serious offensive in northern Vietnam by attacking the Viet Minh's main base in the highlands northwest of Hanoi. The Viet Minh blunted this attack, but rather than meeting force with force, they withdrew further into the mountainous areas while keeping up a steady drumbeat of guerrilla attacks. The French found that they could advance in most areas of the North with relative impunity. However, every attempt to trap and destroy the Viet Minh failed because the insurgents simply faded away as French Union forces advanced. Moreover, it appeared that the Viet Minh could not be destroyed in classical ways by cutting their lines of communication or seizing their bases. Valluy had grossly underestimated the Viet Minh and was blind to political reality.

In 1947 and 1948 the French developed strong defenses in the Red River Delta around Hanoi and the port city of Haiphong. However, it soon proved impossible for the French to do more than send out occasional probes into Viet Minh controlled territory in the countryside. The French almost always ended up empty-handed for their pains. By early 1950 the French had lost most of their outposts along the border with China; in any case, these distant and isolated outposts could not be defended with the available French military assets. Still, the French appeared at least to have achieved a stalemate of sorts in the delta.

In the so-called "liberated zones," the Viet Minh continued building both semi-regular and guerrilla units. More significantly, they patiently built their political power. While Viet Minh military forces could operate

---

[27] *ibid.*, p. 290.

only where the French military had little or no presence, Viet Minh *moral and political* forces could penetrate even into areas thought secure by the French high command. Ho Chi Minh issued a code of conduct that bears repeating here. This code, perhaps modeled after Mao's "Eight Points for Attention," featured twelve points:

> **TWELVE RECOMMENDATIONS**
> The nation has its roots in the people.
>
> In the Resistance War and national reconstruction, the main force lies in the people. Therefore, all the people in the army, administration, and mass organizations who are in contact or live with the people, must remember and carry out the following recommendations:
>
> **SIX FORBIDDANCES:**
> Not to do what is likely to damage the land and crops or spoil the houses and belongings of the people. Not to insist on buying or borrowing what the people are not willing to sell or lend. Not to bring living hens into mountainous people's houses. Never to break our word. Not to give offense to people's faith and customs (such as to lie down before the altar, to raise feet over the hearth, to play music in the house, etc). Not to do or speak what is likely to make people believe that we hold them in contempt.
>
> **SIX PERMISSABLES:**
> To help the people in their daily work (harvesting, fetching firewood, carrying water, sewing, etc). Whenever possible, to buy commodities for those who live far from markets (knife, salt, needle, thread, pen, paper, etc.) In spare time, to tell amusing, simple, and short stories useful to the Resistance, but not to betray secrets. To teach the population the national script and elementary hygiene. To study the customs of each region so as to be acquainted with them in order to create an atmosphere of sympathy first, then gradually to explain to the people to abate their superstitions. To show to the people that you are correct, diligent, and disciplined.[28]

Military enthusiasts who study only the tactics of the French war in

[28] Gettleman, p. 88.

Indochina, but not its political and psychological aspects, might dismiss the Twelve Recommendations as mere propaganda. In point of fact, this code was an important means of building popular support among uncommitted Vietnamese. The French had nothing whatsoever that was remotely comparable.[29]

The accession to power in China of the Chinese Communists in late 1949 made possible the training and equipping of larger, regular Viet Minh units, even divisional-size units. With these new, better equipped units, the Viet Minh believed they could challenge the French openly. In this, however, they were to be bitterly disappointed. Tempted to use their newly built large units, the Viet Minh struck at the French positions in the Red River delta in 1951. Viet Minh military leader Vo Nguyen Giap brushes over this period in his book *People's War, People's Army* because the results were disastrous. The Viet Minh tried to fight precisely the kind of conventional battle the French had hoped for.

Late in 1951 General Jean de Lattre de Tassigny, arguably one of France's most able and experienced generals, established a strongpoint at Hoa Binh, well beyond his Red River defenses southwest of Hanoi. Giap, licking his wounds from his ill-considered offensive earlier in the year, thought it wiser to by-pass Hoa Binh and instead attack its vulnerable line of communication.

> Hoa Binh set the pattern: French mobility and firepower could take them almost anywhere in Vietnam, but they could not stay, and could show only wasted resources and time for their efforts. Time, to the French, was a dwindling resource as patience ran out in Paris. To the Vietnamese, time built confidence, and allowed the transformation of popular support for independence into more tangible kinds of strength: training, supplies, and troop strength.[30]

At great cost the French extricated their exposed garrison at Hoa Binh in February 1952. De Lattre, gravely ill with cancer, had returned to France

[29] The Viet Minh were not squeamish about using strong-arm tactics to silence collaborators of the French and others whom they regarded as enemies. It should be remembered, however, that Ho Chi Minh stated his goal as nothing less than total and complete independence of Vietnam from French rule. This nationalist appeal was strong enough to convince many fence-sitters that "Uncle Ho" was the man to back.

[30] Paret, *Makers of Modern Strategy*, p. 849.

in February 1952. De Lattre, gravely ill with cancer, had returned to France where he died in January. His only son Bernard had been killed in combat eight months earlier. The new commander in Indochina, Raoul Salan, merely maintained the *status quo* and passed the baton in May 1953 to General Henri Navarre, France's last commander in Indochina, who planned an active campaign to destroy the Viet Minh.

Navarre enjoyed complete command of the air and, of course, had no Viet Minh opponent at sea. On land he controlled Hanoi and Haiphong as well as most other major cities, and had a total of 482,000 French Union forces under his command.[31]

His opponent, Giap, had no navy or air force, controlled no major cities, and had approximately 300,000 men under his command including regulars and guerrillas. While the Viet Minh received military aid from China, the French had the benefit of some $10 billion in aid (over the course of the war) from French taxpayers, augmented by a further $900 million in U.S. assistance.

In mid-1953 the Board of National Estimates, chaired by CIA but including inputs from all members of the intelligence community, produced a National Intelligence Estimate that laid out a sobering picture of the situation in French Indochina. Despite French material superiority over the Viet Minh, NIE-91 describes in unvarnished terms all that Navarre lacked. This NIE's first five key judgments say it all:

> **CONCLUSIONS**
>
> 1. Unless there is a marked improvement in the French Union military position in Indochina, *political stability in the Associated States and popular support of the French Union effort against the Viet Minh will decline.* [all emphasis in this excerpt added]We believe that such marked improvement in the military situation is not likely, though a moderate improvement is possible. The over-all French Union position in Indochina therefore will probably deteriorate during the period of this estimate.
> 2. *The lack of French Union military successes, continuing Indochinese distrust of ultimate French political intentions, and popular apathy will probably continue to prevent a significant increase in Indochinese will and ability to resist the Viet Minh.*

---

[31] NIE 91; dated 4 June 1953.

3. We cannot estimate the impact of the new French military leadership. However, we believe that the *Viet Minh will retain the military initiative* and will continue to attack territory in the Tonkin delta and to make incursions into areas outside the delta. The Viet Minh will attempt to consolidate Communist control in "Free Laos" and will build up supplies in northern Laos to support further penetrations and consolidation in that country. *The Viet Minh will almost certainly intensify political warfare, including guerrilla activities, in Cambodia.*
4. Viet Minh prestige has been increased by the military successes of the past year, and *the organizational and administrative effectiveness of the [Viet Minh] regime will probably continue to grow.*
5. *The French Government will remain under strong and increasing domestic pressure to reduce the French military commitment in Indochina, and the possibility cannot be excluded that this pressure will be successful.* However, we believe that the French will continue without enthusiasm to maintain their present levels of troop strength through mid-1954 and will support the planned development of the national armies of the Associated States.[32]

Americans who are familiar with the Vietnam War are aware of the catastrophic May 1954 French defeat at Dien Bien Phu. Arguably one of the most significant battles of history, Dien Bien Phu marked not only the end of French rule in Indochina but the beginning of the end of the French colonial empire. The details of the battle are well described elsewhere, particularly in Bernard Fall's *Hell in a Very Small Place.*

Upon his arrival in Hanoi in 1953, General Navarre, an intellectual officer of the old school, determined to take the war to the Viet Minh. During that summer he considered several options for luring the Viet Minh into a general conventional engagement in which he intended to destroy Giap's forces with artillery and air power. Navarre also hoped to disrupt Viet Minh operations in Laos by cutting the insurgents' supply line from northern Vietnam into that country. Over the objections of several subordinates, he selected what he believed to be a suitable chokepoint on that

[32] *ibid.*

supply line for his Operation Castor and commenced an airborne drop onto the site on 20 November 1953.

Apparently Navarre had learned nothing from the near disaster at Hoa Binh scarcely two years earlier. Believing that a fortified airhead at remote Dien Bien Phu would prove irresistible to the Viet Minh commander, the French general hoped to draw Giap's forces into a trap. Hoa Binh was barely twenty miles from the French fortified lines in the Red River delta. Dien Bien Phu was more than one hundred and fifty miles by air from Hanoi and completely surrounded by hills infested with Viet Minh. By late January 1954 the French there found themselves surrounded, and by mid-March it was clear that it was they who had been trapped by the Viet Minh. Seven weeks later the bloody battle ended with more than 7,500 French soldiers dead or wounded and another 11,700 taken prisoner. The Geneva talks began the day after Dien Bien Phu fell.

Although the war in the southern areas of French Indochina did not reach the same level of intensity as in the North, the Viet Minh gradually extended their operations into the Central Highlands. Two months after the disaster at Dien Bien Phu, the French suffered a second serious defeat, this time in the central region of Vietnam. The Viet Minh, marching on foot, trapped the road-bound French Mobile Group 100 on Route 19 between An Khe and Pleiku and virtually wiped it out. The Geneva talks concluded on 21 July 1954, less than a week after GM-100 ceased to exist. French rule in Indochina was at an end.

What needs to be said, and perhaps said repeatedly, is that a modern, fully mechanized, well-equipped army, even if it has complete control of the air, as well as command of the sea, cannot defeat an insurgency that is based in popularly-supported revolt. What was lacking in French Indochina was a realistic political program. Much like Erich Ludendorff in 1918, the various French commanders in Indochina—Valluy, De Lattre, and Navarre—kept looking for a decisive military victory. Absent some political strategy that cut the ground from beneath the Viet Minh, the French effort was doomed from the start. Jacques Leclerc had been correct, almost prophetic, but no one had heeded his advice.

TOO LITTLE, TOO LATE

One of the more intriguing French innovations during the Indochina War was the Groupement de Commandos Mixtes Aeroportes (Composite Airborne Commando Groups) known as GCMAs.[33] A GCMA consisted of up to four hundred men *recruited from the indigenous population in pockets deep inside Viet Minh territory* and led by a lieutenant or captain assisted by three or four NCOs. These were not raider units that sallied forth from the defensive lines on brief missions, but true guerrilla forces consisting of local people with French officers and NCOs who adapted European weaponry and tactics to indigenous customs and capabilities.

The GCMAs had many of the advantages of Viet Minh guerrilla units: they were mobile, depended upon the people for intelligence and logistical support, could "disappear" if the need arose, and were masters of their local terrain. Another great advantage was their relative self-sufficiency. Fall notes that whereas French regular forces at Dien Bien Phu required two hundred tons of supplies *per day* to sustain roughly eighteen thousand men, all of France's GCMAs, totaling roughly fourteen thousand men at the close of 1953, required but two hundred tons of supplies *per month*.[34]

Although some French regular officers scoffed at the GCMAs, their effectiveness is indicated by the following Viet Minh report quoted by Bernard Fall:

> . . . the French imperialists have succeeded in leaving behind them their agents who continue to be a nuisance to us. At the beginning they were only a handful but now, the rebel movement against the Democratic Republic of Viet-Nam has increased . . . .in speed of movement as well as in numbers. There must be at least two thousand of them now.
>
> This movement begins to worry us seriously. *A large part of our forces is pinned down in mopping-up operations against those*

[33] The GCMA's were formed by the French secret service, SDECE, on the model of the maquis of the Resistance of World War II. From 5,000 members in 1952, the units grew to 14,000 by the close of 1953, and to 20,000 men in July 1954. Altogether, the GCMAs tied down 14 battalions of Viet Minh. In December 1953 the GCMAs were renamed Groupement Mixte d'Intervention (GMI) when, belatedly, such units received control of all operations behind enemy lines. We will use the term GCMA for simplicity. See Chef de Bataillon (Major) Philippe Pottier, Master's thesis, U.S. Marine Corps Command and Staff College, Quantico, Virginia; academic year 2003–2004.

[34] Fall, p. 275, and Pottier, op.cit

> *rebels. . . . The reason for the great extension of the rebel movement and why it succeeds in holding out against us stems from the fact that we are not supported by popular opinion.*[emphasis added][35]

Fall goes on to say, "By the end of 1953 some GCMA operations began to assume strategic importance," and mentions several operations with hill tribes and along the Chinese border. By taking a leaf from T. E. Lawrence and Mao, the French had succeeded in tying down larger Viet Minh units with relatively small GCMA units. The GCMAs operated effectively among the T'ai and Meo peoples, where the Viet Minh were not supported by popular opinion. Rather the French, who during colonial times had befriended these tribes, now were rewarded with their loyalty.

As is so often the case when innovation meets stolid conservative doctrine, the new methods were adopted too little, too late. And then, adopted reluctantly. The GCMA concept was developed only during the final two years of the war in Indochina by which time the Viet Minh had consolidated their control over much of the north.

IN SUM

We have now visited three completely different scenarios set in different times and different lands with different conditions. And yet, there are some valuable lessons that the practitioner can draw from each. To begin with, troop strength and firepower are meaningless if the people of a given country consider a military force to be alien and unwanted. It is even possible, as suggested by David Kilcullen in his book *The Accidental Guerrilla*, that the presence of an alien army can serve as a guerrilla maker. Had Cornwallis not conducted his counterinsurgency campaign in the southern colonies as he did, it is possible that many people in the Carolinas would have remained neutral, or even sympathetic to the Crown. French policy in Indochina drove many Vietnamese who might otherwise have opposed the Viet Minh into Ho Chi Minh's open and waiting arms. None of the men behind these campaigns, civil or military, had considered the possibility that the assumptions on which their campaigns were based were wrong.

Time and distance are the great equalizers of the weak in their contest with the strong. Forces operating in an expeditionary mode abroad must

---

[35] Fall, pp. 274–275.

necessarily be sustained by lengthy and costly logistical systems. The British had to supply their troops in America over three thousand miles of ocean. True, they could sometimes buy provisions in their colonies. But passive resistance is also a weapon; many farmers would not sell to the British. As the French alienated the Mexicans in the 1860s and the Vietnamese in the 1940s, the French army found that it was ever more dependent upon Paris for supplies. Moreover, the cabinet ministers found that the costs of the war had spiralled out of control. Time and distance were strategic factors working against them.

Finally, and perhaps most important, it should be clear that no armed force, however well trained and equipped, can defeat hostile public opinion. If the people are for you, you cannot lose. But if the people are against you, you cannot win.

CHAPTER **6**

ROOT AND STEM

Mus tek cyear a de root fa heal de tree.
"You need to take care of the root in order to heal the tree"
according to the Gullah women from the Sea Islands of Georgia.[1]

Indeed, when we consider the nexus between the policy community and the military in tackling an insurgency, the wisdom of these island women is profound. In his "Twelve Recommendations" Ho Chi Minh said, "The nation has its roots in the people." If the roots are sickly, so too will be the tree. The Gullah women were not just describing sound horticultural practice, they were also describing much in life, including societies and the nations they inhabit. If a nation is a great tree, then surely its roots are the people, the nation's citizens. If the roots of a society are unhealthy, then like the tree of the Gullah women, the nation also will be ill.

OF SYMPTOMS AND DISEASES

Insurgencies are thought to be diseases. They are not. Rather, insurgencies are merely the outward manifestations of deeper societal illnesses. Many political scientists mistake the symptom for the disease. The disease is revealed by the visible symptoms—the outbreak of insurgency—but the illnesses affecting a society may be hidden for years. It is only when the disease has progressed to a certain stage that an insurgency may appear.

---

[1] See Brown.

I need to be very clear that I did not use the word "will," but only "may." There is little apart from death and taxes that is certain. However, certain conditions and habits make the onset of disease more likely. It is possible that one person may smoke five packs of cigarettes a day, drink to excess, eat all manner of fatty foods, yet live to be a hundred: this person is lucky. Most people who indulge in unhealthy habits are likely to develop cancer or other debilitating and life-threatening medical conditions. So it is with insurgency. Nothing is certain; we may only venture into what is probable.

If we were to list all the insurgencies that have taken place since 1945, and many political scientists have done just that, we would find that not one took place in a society that was *healthy*, that is, free from the societal ills of bad governance, ignorance, ethnic or religious division, or great disparities of income, landholding, or political power. I hasten to point out that historically an insurgency has not occurred in all societies afflicted by disparities in income, inequitable landholding, or ethnic differences. However, where many of these conditions exist, there is a distinct probability that an insurgency will appear.

As we will come to see in a later chapter, at times the U.S. government has rushed into foreign entanglements without first clearly assessing the unhealthy roots of client regimes requesting our financial or military assistance.

Corruption, exploitation, hunger, and misgovernment have plagued humanity since the dawn of recorded history. The Old Testament prophet Amos spoke out against the cynical and exploitative practices of his day:

> Listen to this, you who grind the destitute and plunder the humble, you who say: "When will the new moon be over so that we may sell corn? When will the Sabbath be past so that we may open our wheat again, giving short measure in the bushel and taking overweight in the silver, tilting the scales fraudulently, and selling the dust of the wheat; that we may buy the poor for silver and the destitute for a pair of shoes?" The Lord has sworn by the pride of Jacob: I will never forget any of their doings.[2]

Chinese philosopher Mencius made much the same observation of the

[2] Amos 8: verses 4–7. *New English Bible.*

destitution and hopelessness of peasants thanks to corruption existing in his day:

> Is it only the mouth and belly which are injured by hunger and thirst? Men's minds are also injured by them.[3]

Again, quoting from the *Book of History*, Mencius noted that the passing of power from dynasty to dynasty and from ruler to ruler was accomplished by the Mandate of Heaven. Asked by a student how Heaven exerted its will, Mencius replied:

> Heaven sees as the people see. Heaven hears as the people hear.[4]

And lest we think that only Old Testament prophets and Chinese sages castigated the elites of society who misuse their positions to exploit and defraud, let us turn to a modern American president who saw the same age-old problems:

> Now the trumpet summons us again—not as a call to bear arms, though arms we need; not as a call to battle, though embattled we are; but a call to bear the burden of a long twilight struggle, year in and year out, "rejoicing in hope, patient in tribulation," a struggle against the common enemies of man: tyranny, poverty, disease, and war itself.[5]

This brief excursion into philosophy has one point: the beginning and ending of politics is not what potentates and presidents or counselors and governmental ministries may think or do, but what the people of a given country think and do. Any strategy proposed by the civilian government to its generals, or by generals to their government that is not centered on the needs and will of the people is nothing more than hot air. If the people's interests are not taken into account, and if these interests do not help shape strategy, that strategy will fail.

Since 1945 the United States has committed itself around the globe

---

[3] Mencius, Book VII, 1:27.1.

[4] Quoted in *Sources of Chinese Tradition.*

[5] Kennedy, Inaugural, 20 January 1961.

to helping some nations while opposing others, all in the name of the national interest.

Following World War II the cornerstone of American foreign policy was containment of the Soviet Union. In a cable to the State Department, U.S. ambassador to the Kremlin George F. Kennan laid out Moscow's ambitions and stated that the best way to deal with Soviet imperialism was to contain it. This strategy was based on American perceptions of Soviet expansionism and recognized the need to bring together countries threatened by Soviet designs. Where this policy was based on the will of the people who were to be protected from Soviet hegemony, as it was in Western Europe, the containment strategy was an unqualified success. However, where our policy of containment did not match up with public opinion, as in French Indochina, it met with only checkered success . . . or outright failure.

Let's briefly examine a series of cases of U.S. involvement overseas in conflicted areas during the containment era from 1945 to about 1993 in search of useful lessons.

PHILIPPINES

Our farsighted political leadership more than seventy-five years ago may be credited with the wisdom to see the inevitable end of colonialism.[6] Virtually alone of the Great Powers, we took concrete steps toward preparing our one and only colony, the Philippines, for its independence. The Commonwealth of the Philippines, under its own president and legislature, took form in 1935 with full independence slated for July 1945.

Thus, when the Japanese imperial army swept down on the Philippines in December 1941, they came not as liberators, but as conquerors. True enough, the Japanese *proclaimed* Philippine independence and installed a puppet government. But even many members of the puppet government knew this was a sham. The Filipinos, alone of all colonial peoples in Southeast Asia, put their lives on the line to fight as guerrillas alongside their colonial bosses, the Americans. The reason? We had a common fight. The Filipinos wanted their independence and we wanted it for them, also.

Cynics may claim that despite granting independence on 4 July 1946

[6] The Tydings-McDuffie Act, also known as the Philippine Independence Act PL 73-127 (24 March 1934), created the Commonwealth of the Philippines and promised full independence by 1945.

we manipulated the Philippine government from "behind the screen." While it is true that we retained both influence and respect in the new republic, that charge does not wash. The Filipinos had been in control of their internal affairs since 1917 and remain so today. After 1946, we retained only Clark Airfield and Subic Bay Naval Base, and even these have reverted fully to Filipino control. And yet, the heritage of Bataan, Corregidor, and the infamous Death March lives on. Filipinos of the older generation still view Americans with respect and even with affection because we suffered together, struggled together, and ultimately triumphed together.

Several years after independence, thanks to the corruption and nepotism of President Quirino's administration, the Philippines found itself facing a potent insurgency in the form of the Hukbalahap, commonly known as the Huks.[7] Because the United States had considerable prestige due to its fair and honest administration of the islands during the time of colonialism, and also because America had fought the Japanese to guarantee true independence, America was able to provide excellent advice to the Philippine government, which eventually helped bring about the defeat of the Huks. The United States sent no troops and relatively small amounts of material aid. Its most valuable aid, however, was the advice provided by Edward Geary Lansdale and his associates.[8] American advice and aid, in the hands of an incorruptible and energetic leader such as President Ramon Magsaysay, were important contributions to the Huks' defeat.

But there is another factor, often ignored, by counterinsurgency theorists. Magsaysay beat the Huks by changing the nature of the Philippine Republic. Before 1953, when Magsaysay became president of the Philippines, the Philippine government was a rats' nest of nepotism and corruption. Both the Armed Forces of the Philippines (AFP) and the civil government were burdened with sinecure positions filled by cronies of President Quirino and other leaders. Major Lawrence Greenberg has written an excellent study of the Huk insurgency and the measures, political as well as military, taken to counter that insurgency.[9] What remains for us is

---

[7] Hukbo ng Bayan Laban sa mga Hapon = People's Army against the Japanese. This was an element of the Communist Party of the Philippines formed during World War II to resist Japanese occupation. Although demobilized in 1945, it reappeared about 1948 with the goal of seizing power in the Philippines.

[8] Edward G. Lansdale, a U.S. Air Force major general, was perhaps the foremost American counterinsurgency theorist of his day.

[9] Greenberg, op. cit.

to understand that by dint of his personality and strong character, Magsaysay *remade* the Philippine Republic, eliminated corruption and inefficiency, regained the enthusiastic loyalty of the people, and by 1955 forced Hukbalahap insurgents to surrender.

EUROPE

The post-World War II European Recovery Plan, which is more commonly known as the Marshall Plan, is likely the greatest political and economic mobilization plan ever devised; it met with universal public approval in the western European countries. Even two East Bloc countries, Czechoslovakia and Poland, had hoped to sign on, but their hopes were squashed by Moscow. The magic of the Marshall Plan was that by advancing funds, equipment, and raw materials, America gave the first turn of the economic wheel, which enabled Europeans to continue turning it thereafter. Within a very short time Europe began a remarkable recovery and, with American encouragement, gradually moved toward political confederation. The North Atlantic Treaty Organization (NATO) grew alongside the economic and political integration of Europe. Taken together, the political, economic, and military advancement of Europe proved beneficial not only to the Europeans, but to the United States. America had true partners, allies, and friends, not subject peoples as in Eastern Europe.

We do not think of modern Europe as being the target of antiregime violence. And yet it is possible that internal violence might have erupted had the United States stood by idly and let the Soviet Union, aided by massive French and Italian Communist parties, take over their respective governments from within. Looking behind the Iron Curtain we find anti-Soviet uprisings in Poland, Hungary, and East Germany that were perhaps premature, did not use classic insurgent means, and were quickly and violently suppressed. Although it is difficult to prove a negative, it is reasonable to believe that the history of the postwar world might well have been fundamentally different had the Communists come to power in Western Europe. It is not a stretch to say that the Marshall Plan prevented political violence in the West.

Perhaps the measure of success in Europe, and the rallying of the democratic principle in the Western European countries, was best captured by George C. Marshall in his speech upon accepting the 1953 Nobel Peace Prize:

> We must present democracy as a force holding within itself the seeds of unlimited progress by the human race. By our actions we should make it clear that such a democracy is a means to a better way of life, together with a better understanding among nations. Tyranny inevitably must retire before the tremendous moral strength of the gospel of freedom and self-respect for the individual, but we have to recognize that these democratic principles do not flourish on empty stomachs and that people turn to false promises of dictators because they are hopeless and anything promises something better than the miserable existence that they endure.[10]

Marshall thought that his speech was a failure. I disagree: it is a masterpiece in laying out a political vision. But what really matters is the fact that the Marshall Plan gave hope to millions, sparked the European recovery, preserved the peace, and profoundly influenced world history.

CHINA

The tragedy of China is one of American misperception and wishful thinking. The United States has a long history of sympathy to China, built up through missionary work during the late Manchu empire and the early republic, educational ties through figures such as Sun Yat-sen and Soong Mei-ling (Madame Chiang), and commercial ties going back to the 1790s. This long relationship was built partly on fact and partly on myth. It led the U.S. government to think of China as united, strong, and democratic. Unfortunately, these perceptions were seriously distorted. In turn, the distortions led to flawed military and foreign policies that were pursued by the Roosevelt and successor administrations.

In the 1940s America fastened upon Chiang Kai-shek as *our man* and provided extensive military and civilian assistance to his government. What we did not know, or chose to ignore, was that Chiang had become a dictator and his wing of the Kuomintang (KMT), or Nationalist Party, had set itself up as a one-party dictatorship. Worse, the regime that he headed was based on tenuous warlord alliances throughout China and by family-based cronyism: the Soong family, for example, controlled vital strings of

[10] Cray, p. 731.

the Chinese economy and had considerable influence over Chinese politics. While the KMT controlled the capital and all major cities, it had little effective reach into the countryside, which was the home of the majority of the population. The National Government was nothing more than the Nationalist Party, but the KMT had its social roots among the landlords and the commercial and banking elites of the cities. It did not represent the great mass of the Chinese people who lived in poverty in rural areas.

Franklin D. Roosevelt and his senior military advisors believed that China could be a great staging area for allied attacks against Japan. That assumption quickly proved wrong as it was never Chiang's intention to use much of his American-provided military equipment to fight the Japanese. Instead, he husbanded as much of this equipment as possible for a postwar fight-to-the-death with Mao Tse-tung's Communist forces following the United States's defeat of Japan. The Nationalists received billions of dollars in aid of various kinds (although the KMT cried that it was never enough) and yet the American *investment* in war material intended for use against Japan proved of little value to our war effort. Moreover, much of the economic aid intended for the people ended up either wasted or pocketed by corrupt Nationalist officials.[11]

Following VJ day, China found itself sharply divided between north and south, between the Communists led by Mao and the Nationalists led by Chiang. George C. Marshall was sent out to negotiate a ceasefire and coalition government, but this was not to be. Although Marshall was an honest broker and applied his considerable talent and prestige to arranging a peaceful solution to the pending crisis, he ultimately failed. This was due in part to Chinese Communist unwillingness to disband and accept a political position decidedly subordinate to the Nationalists. But in greater part, it was due to Chiang's unwillingness to accept anything less than total victory over Mao and his followers. Somewhat in the mold of General Ludendorff on the Western Front in 1918, Chiang believed in one great battle of annihilation to decide the fate of China.

And yet, Chiang had not paid attention to the will of the people. After Marshall had left China, General Albert C. Wedemeyer was directed to make a survey of conditions. Even though Wedemeyer initially was sym-

---

[11] The reader is directed to Barbara Tuchman's excellent political biography *Stilwell and the American experience in China*, or the *Stilwell Papers* on which her book is based, for detailed insight into Nationalist policies and the deteriorating situation in China during the 1940s.

pathetic to the Nationalists, his survey caused him to greatly modify his opinions.

> Wedemeyer was to spend a month in China, gathering information from military and civilian figures alike, traveling from Mukden in the north to Shanghai in the south. Within days of arriving, he cabled Marshall that "the Nationalist Chinese are spiritually insolvent." The people had "lost confidence in their leaders." Public officials held office only to amass through graft what they could before the collapse came. The army had lost the will to fight, while the Communists displayed "excellent spirit, almost a fanatical fervor."
>
> Just before Wedemeyer was to leave, Chiang invited him to address a joint meeting of the State Council and [Nationalist] government ministers on August 22. Wedemeyer delivered an unvarnished lecture, pointing out the rampant corruption and inefficiency of the KMT government, and the lackluster effort of the Nationalist Army against the Communists. The war could not be won without the support of the Chinese people, long alienated, apathetic, and desirous only of peace, he admonished the shocked Chinese.[12]

General Marshall himself testified in January 1947 saying, "The best way to defend against Communism was for the existing [Nationalist] government of China to accomplish such reforms that it would gain the support of the people."[13]

The defeat of the Nationalists on the battlefield in late 1948 and their ouster in 1949 was merely the *coup de grace* for years of inattention to the people, and their many political and economic sins. While it is true that Communist military power brought about that *coup de grace*, ultimately it was Communist *political power* that proved itself in battle.

Veteran foreign service officer and scholar of China O. Edmund Clubb captured the situation clearly and succinctly in his book *Twentieth Century China*:

> The struggle between the Nationalists and Communists had of

[12] Cray, p. 634.
[13] *ibid.*, p. 583.

course extended far beyond the battlefield. The Nationalists had been defeated militarily, true; but it was when they lost the loyalties of the intelligentsia and the "little people" of the towns, and when the agricultural countryside rose in revolt against long neglect and oppression, that the Nationalists finally lost the nation.[14]

KOREA

Many American military men hold up the wars in Korea and Vietnam side-by-side as if they were of one substance. They are not. The war in Korea was a conventional invasion of a sovereign republic that although weak was nationalist in nature and had the support of a majority of the South Korean people. Syngman Rhee, long a foe of Japanese imperialism, had been elected in 1948 when the United States ended its occupation of South Korea.[15] He had a functioning cabinet and at least a rudimentary administrative structure in place throughout the Republic of Korea (ROK).

In June 1950 the North Koreans with Soviet backing, and probably Soviet advisors, sent tanks and infantry south of the 38th parallel to conquer the South. The ROK Army had roughly a hundred thousand men in uniform, but no heavy weapons or armor to speak of. The United States had a military advisory group (KMAG) but very few combat forces in the Republic of Korea because our forces were withdrawn when the postwar occupation ended. The mechanized North Korean army quickly overran both South Korea's army and the small number of U.S. units that were rushed from Japan, such as Task Force Smith. Finally the North Korean invasion was halted at the Pusan Perimeter.

The campaign is well known and does not need to be detailed here. What is significant is that the ROK Army, backed by public opinion in battered South Korea, put up a fight alongside its United Nations allies. Admittedly, it was weak and experienced many setbacks, but the ROKs showed great improvement as the war went on. Today it is a competent, professional armed force, one of the most respected in Asia.

More importantly, the vital political trump card of *legitimacy* was never lost. Syngman Rhee retained his stature as a nationalist leader. The Repub-

---

[14] Clubb, p. 296.

[15] Born Yi Seungman in 1875, Rhee entered anti-Japanese politics in 1897. Educated in the United States, Rhee was president from 1948 to 1960.

lic of Korea was neither a foreign colony nor a puppet, but the recognized government of the South Korean people. Unquestionably, in June 1950, on the eve of the invasion, South Korea was militarily and economically weak. But it had one vital asset: the willing support of its people. *The South Korean government was not at war with its own people.* It could therefore look to the front and not worry about its rear areas.

FRENCH INDOCHINA

Although we've discussed the French Indochina war in some detail elsewhere, one additional comment is in order. In the late stages of World War II the United States made plain its policy of encouraging independence for the colonies of European countries. Following President Roosevelt's death, the United States relaxed its policy of decolonization , though it was never abandoned. However, the actions of the Soviet Union in Eastern Europe and later Korea, and the fall of China to the Communists caused an abrupt change in Washington, D.C.

From 1950 to the end of the war in Indochina, the United States provided extensive military aid to the French. As has been noted, the French strategy was to destroy the Viet Minh in open battle and restore French power in the Associated States. This strategy failed to take into account the wishes of millions of Vietnamese, and likely the wishes of Cambodians and Laotians as well. Once again, this is not to say that all Vietnamese supported the Viet Minh; they did not. But the prospect of continued French suzerainty was enough to force some nationalists into supporting the Viet Minh and others to lose hope and simply lapse into apathy.

The courage and skill of the French Union forces is beyond question. Nor is there any doubt about the heroism of the French infantry commanders and their soldiers.[16] But skill, courage and even heroism were not enough when confronted by a political idea held by the Viet Minh and millions of Vietnamese. The French had heavy weapons, armor, command of air and sea, and 482 thousand men. But they still lost.[17] They had noth-

---

[16] One of the "most heroic" of a pantheon of heroes was certainly Captain Valerie Andre, a medical doctor who was also a skilled helicopter pilot. She is credited with flying her personal Hiller helicopter into very dangerous combat zones, including Dien Bien Phu, to rescue and treat wounded French soldiers. Dr. Andre later flew in Algeria and in 1976 became France's first female major general, a true heroine.

[17] French Union dead (France, French North Africa, and French Indochinese allies) totaled 95thousand.

ing meaningful to offer the Vietnamese people: only continued French rule.

What the French lacked was the willing cooperation of the majority of Vietnamese. Had the leaders of the Fourth Republic heeded Jacques Leclerc in 1946[18] they might have achieved a political settlement in Vietnam that avoided compromising or undercutting non-Communist nationalist parties and leaders while retaining the respect and friendship of many Vietnamese. But French policy was set upon reconquering Indochina, and the French government completely disregarded the desire of the Vietnamese people for independence. Sadly, the French paid dearly for their political myopia.

I think it instructive that our policymakers went against our own anticolonial heritage, our declared policy of decolonization, and the longstanding American desire to avoid foreign entanglements, especially those that were not *our* fight. Despite our policy of containing Communism, some would argue that we went against our own long-term interests in Asia. In helping the French restore their rule, the United States, from fear of Communist expansion under the containment policy, had backed the wrong horse. Fortunately, this unwise policy choice only cost us money, not lives . . . at the time.

VIETNAM

As it was practiced in Asia, the U.S. policy of containment, brought America into conventional war in Korea (1950–1953) and then an unconventional war in Vietnam (starting about 1955). The Geneva Accords of 1954 provided for the partitioning of Vietnam into North and South. The French evacuated the North by fall of 1954, though they stayed on in the South until 1956. South Vietnam came under the rule of Ngo Dinh Diem and his family, though with French advisors. American military advisors began to appear around 1955 and eventually replaced their departing French counterparts.

The Ngo family regime's support rested upon Vietnamese Catholics, landholding elites, merchants, and the Chinese minority living in Cholon and elsewhere. Diem himself could claim a nationalist credential, though

[18] Leclerc's son, as well as the son of General de Lattre, both of whom were French army lieutenants, died in Indochina.

it was hardly as prestigious as that of his northern rival. Had a "free and fair" election been held in 1956, as prescribed by the accords, it is entirely possible, even likely, that Ho Chi Minh would have won. But the prescribed national election was never held. Indeed, with American approval it was Diem who cancelled it. Peaceful reunification of Vietnam by political means would not, could not happen.

Content for the moment with *his* half of the country, Ho Chi Minh spent the next five years consolidating his political hold over North Vietnam. His political methods were by no means Jeffersonian. Ho severely persecuted opponents and others considered security risks, he collectivized land and nationalized industry, and instituted one-party rule. That said, it must also be admitted that Ho Chi Minh commanded considerable popular support despite his strong-arm tactics. He had won his nationalist laurels in battle against the French and the Japanese.

When war was resumed in the South, for a number of years it was conducted through guerrilla operations against the South Vietnamese army,[19] and political warfare to undermine the Ngo family and its military successors. Although leavened by seasoned fighters from the North, many of the Viet Cong were southerners. Even as early as the 2 January 1963 Battle of Ap Bac, these guerrillas had demonstrated their mettle against greatly superior South Vietnamese forces. This battle was tactically insignificant, but had enormous political and psychological consequences. About three hundred Viet Cong held off fourteen hundred ARVN soldiers, inflicting heavy casualties and damaging or destroying valuable equipment. At a cost of eighteen dead, the VC killed eighty ARVN soldiers and three U.S. Army advisors, and put five helicopters and three armored personnel carriers out of action. This victory convinced the North to step up aid to the VC, and alarmed Washington into considering the deployment of regular troops to Vietnam. The battlefield tactics, which were bungled by the South Vietnamese, are unimportant. What is significant is that Ngo Dinh Diem had appointed politically reliable but militarily incompetent cronies to senior positions and threatened to punish commanders who dared to take risks that would result in casualties.

Combat operations such as those at Ap Bac, however, were merely the

[19] ARVN: Army of the Republic of Vietnam (South); PAVN: People's Army of Vietnam (North); VC: Viet Cong (Communist insurgents in South Vietnam)

visible parts of the Vietnam War. The invisible war was political, conducted by slow and steady recruitment and indoctrination, and by means of effective propaganda and political action campaigns including selective use of terror as a psychological weapon.[20] It is ironic, but no less true, that the South Vietnamese regime aided Communist recruitment through its ineptitude, corruption, and simple neglect. While the government of the Republic of Vietnam did have officials, police, and army units in most parts of the country, typically in district capitals, many officials were ineffective as government administrators. Moreover, ARVN did not see itself as a social and political force as did PAVN. Finally, the South Vietnamese national police, the Quan Canh (QC), were thoroughly and viciously corrupt.

It is not our purpose here either to give a blow-by-blow history of the Vietnam War or to refight such battles as there were (viz. Ia Drang, Hue, Quang Tri, etc.) Nor is it to give our opinion on whether victory in the military sense was possible. Rather, it is to look at the situation as it unfolded from a political and strategic standpoint. The conclusion that unfortunately must be drawn is that the South Vietnamese—and the Americans—fought only the enemy they could see, not the enemy they couldn't see.[21]

Below the surface, the Republic of Vietnam was a veritable sea of rural peasants, the great majority of whom had little education and depended on the vagaries of the rice crop for their meager existence.[22] As a general rule, ARVN officers thought only in military terms: planning operations, seeking reinforcements and supplies, etc. They took relatively little notice of the rural population that surrounded them. Many peasants operated on

---

[20] See Annex D. In late 1969 Viet Cong political cadres "abducted" 400 men in Phu Yen province, indoctrinated them about the war and the RVN regime, then sent them back to their villages and rice paddies as a sleeper political force that could be called upon when circumstances dictated. This method of political mobilization, repeated countless times in all parts of South Vietnam with thousands of peasants, was a key element in gradually eroding any remaining domestic support for the South Vietnamese government.

[21] Colonel Newsham notes that the USMC's civic action program, and efforts by U.S. Army Special Forces in the Central Highlands, were attempts to go after the invisible enemy. The fact remains, however, that in Vietnam the U.S. military largely pursued a conventional strategy that focused on the visible enemy.

[22] Author met a number of villagers in Binh Dinh province who did not know where Saigon was.

a narrow margin as share croppers; even if the rice harvest was poor, the landlords and moneylenders always got their share. The QC police were corrupt, nasty, and even cruel, regularly shaking down the peasants. The neglected and exploited peasantry were the true social and political substrata on which the tottering regime in Saigon rested.

Toward the end of the war, the piastre, the RVN national currency, began losing its value as inflation set in. Perhaps the government was rolling the printing presses to pay its bills. Hard-currency black marketing, often involving U.S. dollars and gold, was rife. The elite lived well in Saigon, Nha Trang, and a few other cities. While the rich lived in posh villas, the majority of Vietnamese lived in huts. It should therefore come as no surprise that, apart from the social elite and the soldiers of ARVN, there were few who had a real stake in the regime.

There were plenty of people in South Vietnam who either felt victimized by the regime and actively opposed it, *or simply didn't care whether it survived or fell.*

NICARAGUA AND EL SALVADOR

The last two cases we will examine are more recent and much closer to home. We often think of these two countries, and others in Latin America, in the context of Cuban subversion. While it is true that Cuban advice and aid were provided to revolutionary groups in both countries, it cannot be said that Cuba caused either insurgency.

Though distinct countries, both the "Nicas" and the "Guanacos" are proud, hardworking peoples. However, both Nicaragua and El Salvador shared similar landholding patterns and stratified societies. In El Salvador it is said that "Fourteen Families" controlled some 80 percent of the arable land. Whether this is actually true, it is undeniable that prior to about 1984 a relatively small number of landholding families owned virtually everything worth owning in El Salvador. The wealthy families, in partnership with a military elite, controlled the government to the exclusion of the *little* people.

Nicaragua's social structure was much the same. In the late 1920s an internal disturbance had taken place as a result of a disputed presidential election. In one of history's many ironies, two of the soon-to-be main antagonists, Augusto Cesar Sandino and Anastasio Somoza Garcia, served under the same Liberal party commander, General Jose Maria Moncada. At this moment Juan Bautista Sacasa, a former Nicaraguan vice president, returned from exile in Mexico "with that country's backing for the presidency, including arms and ammunition, and set up a 'constitutional' government in Puerto Cabezas under the protection of General Moncada."[23]

The United States was suspicious of Sacasa's ties with revolutionary Mexico, but apart from that only had the mission of protecting American citizens, their holdings, and other commercial interests. Secretary of State Henry L. Stimson was sent to Managua to mediate the crisis.

History sometimes has unintended consequences. As it happened, Secretary Stimson needed an interpreter and found one in the person of Anastasio Somoza. Somoza had attended business school in Philadelphia and spoke American English. Stimson brokered an agreement between the Liberals and Conservatives to hold elections in 1928 under U.S. supervision, and also to set up a nonpolitical national guard that would provide internal security. The U.S. government believed that if the Nicaraguan National Guard could handle security, the American marines could be withdrawn from the country. Under the agreement, a Conservative would serve as president of the country until the elections could be held.

The Liberals, including Somoza, accepted the American-brokered deal. There was only one holdout: Sandino. It is little-known that Sandino initially *demanded* that the United States military should take over the government until elections! The U.S. was unwilling to do this resulting in Sandino withdrawing into the hills from which his *Sandinistas* conducted a series of raids in what can be called a proto-insurgency for more than five years. From his base in remote Jinotega province Sandino reversed his previously held political position and refused to lay down his arms until the American marines left Nicaragua.[24]

By 1930 American political opinion had shifted decisively against intervention in Nicaragua, and the Hoover Administration was seeking a way to withdraw the marines without leaving a political vacuum. In 1932, with a second U.S.-supervised election now completed, newly elected Pres-

---

[23] Christian, p. 9.

[24] *ibid.* p. 10. Yet another irony is that in large part, the U.S. Marine Corps's celebrated *Small Wars Manual* was written based in part upon experiences gathered in chasing Sandino around the Nicaraguan hills.

ident Sacasa was in office, and Somoza was the new head of the National Guard. With the Nicaraguan government in apparently capable hands, American forces could come home.

Through his control of the National Guard, papa Anastasio, sometimes known as "Tacho" Somoza founded a political dynasty that would last almost half a century. Following patriarch Tacho's death in 1956 power passed to Luis Somoza Debayle, his eldest son, who governed Nicaragua for the next eleven years. When Luis died in 1967 yet another Somoza, Anastasio "Tachito" Somoza Debayle assumed the family throne until he was overthrown on 17 July 1979.

The lack of political space for Nicaraguans, other than those closely associated with the Somozas, caused dissent to grow over the years among the out group in the educated classes. Perhaps the spark that united members of all social classes into active opposition was the aftermath of the devastating earthquake of late 1972. International aid provided to relieve hunger and disease was shamelessly stolen by government officials and never reached those for whom it was intended. This thievery became widely known and was a major grievance unifying thousands of people against the Somoza regime.

In El Salvador, the worldwide depression after 1929 caused the collapse of coffee prices. While this affected everyone to some extent, the wealthier classes saw an opportunity to buy out the smaller coffee planters and add more land to their already extensive landholdings. The oligarchy also used its money and political power to dispossess many peasants and Indians from their land. Ultimately, the desperation of their abject poverty caused an uprising in the western part of the country that was composed mainly of Indians, who were called *chanchos* (pigs) by the city folk, and some landless mestizos. Some historians claim that the organizer of the massive uprising was Agustin Farabundo Marti, but it is possible that Marti was actually in jail when the unrest began.[25]

Regardless who was responsible for organizing or leading the Indians and peasants, the Salvadoran regime reacted savagely and massacred large numbers of the poor. This repression in the early 1930s came to be known

---

[25] Buckley, p. 82.

as *La Matanza* (The Massacre) and helped shape radical thinking in El Salvador over the next four decades.

> [President Hernandez Martinez] said that the uprising had been crushed and 4,800 traitors "liquidated." In the absence of adequate records, [Thomas P.] Anderson estimates the total of the dead at 8,000 to 10,000. The right usually accepts Hernandez Martinez's figure, while the left favors the official Communist version of 30,000. The rebels, according to the government, killed 35 civilians and 30 soldiers and police.[26]

Whatever the exact number of murders, it is clear that the Salvadoran government had blood on its hands. The peasants may have been repressed for the time being, but *La Matanza* was still being discussed sixty years later; the memory persisted.

But this was not the only political sin committed by the ruling elite in El Salvador. The 1940s and 1950s featured a series of coups and high-level assassinations, but somehow the tiny country prospered. Still, in the face of this prosperity new sociopolitical dysfunctions began to appear. These new challenges came from an emerging middle class.

> During the prosperity of the 1950's, the country's growing middle class became conscious of its lack of political power. The snubs of the oligarchs and the army were infuriating to physicians, lawyers, accountants, and engineers. As they saw it, the old system of exploitation and repression could not go on working indefinitely. If reforms were not made, there would eventually be rebellion, and it was likely to be more successful than the one of 1932. The oligarchs could leave, but the middle class did not have bank accounts in New York and Zurich and mansions in Miami.[27]

The answer to the demand of the rising middle class for a share of political power came with the foundation of the Christian Democratic Party (PDC) in 1960. One of its founders was Jose Napoleon Duarte who was educated as an engineer at Notre Dame University. The Christian

---

[26] *ibid.*, p. 83.
[27] *ibid.*, pp. 83–84.

Democrats, with help from Europe, advocated "land reform, better schools and health care, and equitable taxation."[28]

While some members of the emerging middle class were advocating reform there were others, many of whom were university-educated, who were organizing for social revolution. These Salvadorans became the founders of five Marxist parties that in late 1980 banded together as the Frente Farabundo Marti para Liberacion Nacional: the FMLN.[29]

I hope the reader has detected societal illnesses that gnawed at the people of both Nicaragua and El Salvador for many decades before eventually bursting forth as violent insurgencies. While festering over the years, it was only in the late 1970s that the invisible suddenly became highly visible.

True to form, the United States was caught flat-footed by both insurgencies. The relationship with the Somozas went back to the time of Secretary Henry L. Stimson in the 1920s. It comes as no surprise that the United States considered West Point-educated Tachito Somoza to be a pillar of stability and valued Nicaragua as a reliably friendly vote in international forums.

The U.S. relationship with El Salvador was not as intimate as the relationship with Somoza in Nicaragua. Nevertheless, the insurgency there was viewed through the prism of East-West conflict and the "Cuban hand" in promoting Communism. Certainly with the triumph of the Frente Sandinista para Liberacion Nacional (FSLN) in Nicaragua and its cordial relations with Havana, the threat of Cuban subversion in the 1980s in El Salvador and elsewhere in Central America seemed quite credible.

As we draw our examination of Nicaragua and El Salvador to a close, it is important to note that a significant difference existed between the two countries as their respective insurgencies developed.

In the case of Nicaragua—admittedly, a family dictatorship somewhat like the Ngos of South Vietnam, who owned much and controlled all in

---

[28] *ibid.*, p. 84.

[29] The FMLN was founded on 10 October 1980 and consisted of five Leftist groups that agreed to band together to take power. The groups are:

FPL = Fuerzas Populares de Liberacion Farabundo Marti
ERP = Ejercito Revolucionario del Pueblo
RN/FARN = Resistencia Nacional/Fuerzas Armadas de la Resistencia Nacional
PCS = Partido Comunista Salvadorena
PRTC = Partido Revolucionario de los Trabajadores Centroamericanos

the country—the FSLN was able to cut away the political foundations of the regime by flexibly reaching out to other groups, many of whom were not at all Marxist. The FSLN strategy was to build a broad coalition of all disaffected elements of society who desired to put an end to the Samozas. Even anti-Communist elements were welcome into the Front, though it must be admitted that the Ortega brothers and Tomas Borge had no intention of establishing a liberal democratic republic once power was seized.

And yet, the coalition approach robbed the Somoza government of virtually all support save the National Guard itself and the elites, who were branded as *somocistas*. Once popular opinion had swung decisively to the rebels, all the weapons of the Guard could not save the regime. The political foundations of the Somoza regime had dissolved and the Guard, which had created and sustained that regime, was isolated and defeated. Here we see a regime whose effectiveness was doubtful and its legitimacy irretrievably lost.[30]

In the case of El Salvador—an oligarchic government in partnership with the military—the situation was a bit different. The 1980 murder of Archbishop Romero, an outspoken critic of the regime, brought the regime near to collapse. Yet, remarkably, it didn't collapse; it survived. The reason that the Salvadoran government survived the FMLN's armed challenge is that, unlike the crony regime of the Somozas, *it was capable of change*. And indeed, slowly and painfully, the Salvadoran government did change. (See Annex A, San Salvador 2038, which reports in exquisite detail just how that government did reform itself).

The turning point possibly was the 1984 election in which the Christian Democrats (Partido Demócrata Cristiano, PDC), led by Jose Napoleon Duarte, won a genuinely free-and-fair election. The oligarchs and military chieftains were not pleased with this outcome, but they accepted it. The PDC, with quiet American advice and funding, and the support of junior officers in the army, set about correcting some of the ills that affected Salvadoran society. One of the most important reforms was carried out within the armed forces. By the late 1980s, the Salvadoran army (ESAF),) had become a major player in transforming rural society. Instead of preying upon *campesinos*, as in the past, the ESAF provided food and small neces-

[30] See Hammes, Chapter VII, op. cit., for an excellent detailed description of the FSLN's campaign.

sities, and went out of its way to bond with the peasantry. The civil government, now staffed by professionals who took their work seriously, began to implement rural programs aimed at agriculture and education.

It is also true that the collapse of the Soviet Union in 1991 and the moribund appeal of Castro-style Communism did much to undermine the FMLN politically.

Still, by 1991 the FMLN had lost the hearts-and-minds battle for the Salvadoran people. There was no longer a compelling need to *fight* the government for rights or services that it was now providing. Moreover, the Duarte and later the Cristiani administrations appeared to offer a better deal than the insurgents. It was clear that FMLN recruiting appeals were falling on deaf ears, and that the insurgents' old enemy, the ESAF, was now popular. *The coup de grace* for the FMLN as an armed force was probably the ESAF's peace rally in the capital city early in 1992 that mustered a crowd estimated at two hundred thousand people. A week later, the FMLN tried a counterdemonstration that marshaled only about thirteen thousand. The Salvadoran insurgency had run out of steam.

AND SO?

The eight selected cases are admittedly only a few of the more notable milestones in America's half-century confrontation with Communism within the framework of the containment policy. They are presented as a sampler of the more prominent efforts abroad during the period 1945–1993. Regretfully, there is no space to mention all instances of post-World War II U.S. assistance, which has been generous, to various foreign countries, such as that given to Greece, Colombia, Indonesia, Morocco, Yemen, and many others, to help them cope with internal instability. Likewise, U.S. assistance to insurgent movements in Afghanistan, Angola, and Sandinista-ruled Nicaragua, assistance given within the general context of containment, is not covered. Nor is comment made of continual and strenuous efforts through nine administrations to achieve a peaceful settlement between Israelis and Palestinians.

The lesson to be learned from the eight situations chosen for this chapter is that a policy that ignores the will of the people places in jeopardy any proposed counterinsurgency strategy.[31] *It is possible to defeat an army, but it*

[31] What matters is what the people of Wikitania want, not what we Americans think they should have.

is simply not possible to defeat a people. This is most certainly true when *that people* are committed to a collective goal, are inspired and led by intelligent leaders, and are willing to accept sacrifices and hardships that its enemies either cannot or will not accept.

Frederick the Great once said, "The prince is the first servant of his state." A regime's first duty is to secure the well-being of its people. Here we return once again to caring for the roots if there is to be any hope for the health of the tree. *The nation has its roots in the people.*

It cannot be overemphasized that the caliber of a nation's leadership, and its demonstrated concern for the welfare of the people, is the measure of a state's health. For if the people are prosperous, secure, and content, the state will be at peace.

Leaders who are self-serving, venal and corrupt, and who make themselves masters to be served rather than servants of the people, eventually bring about not only their own ruin, but that of the state as well. Sooner or later arrogance will become venality, and venality will result in exploitation. Exploitation results in brutality, squalor and degradation. Ultimately, degradation, squalor and brutality produce popular violence.

In these circumstances, the Mandate of Heaven is sure to change. For as Mencius once observed, "Heaven sees as the people see; heaven hears as the people hear."

CHAPTER 7

COUNTERINSURGENCY CONUNDRUM

In 1937 Mao Tse-tung said,
"Guerrilla hostilities are the university of war. . . . "[1]

Dr. John Nagl, Rhodes Scholar and counterinsurgency expert, similarly called insurgency "the graduate school of warfare." A practitioner of insurgency must not only have a keen grasp of military strategy and tactics as would his conventional arms colleague, but also grand strategy and political warfare, and in-depth understanding of the cultures, politics, economics, and much else concerning the area in which he must operate. An insurgency is typically very complex.

WAR OF THE PEOPLE

As we have seen, unlike war between nations, which has its roots in the decisions of cabinet ministers and general staffs, often egged on by expansionist or jingoist political parties, insurgency has its roots deep in the grievances of the people as a whole. It is a social war with religious, racial, class, and economic aspects.

This sociopolitical fact of insurgent warfare colors it in the fiber. Not for a minute can the interests of the people be considered apart from the

[1] Mao Tse-tung, *On Guerrilla Warfare*, Chapter V. FMFRP 12–18, p. 73. He goes on to say, "Without question, the fountainhead of guerrilla warfare is the masses of the people, who organize guerrilla units directly from themselves."

unfolding armed conflict around them: it is the people who are both the political prize sought and the means of resistance. Human factors of a broad sociopolitical spectrum must take center stage, relegating the technical factors of war to a subordinate position. And because human factors are infinitely more complex to comprehend, and even recognize, than are the quasi-Jominian technical aspects of war, insurgency fully justifies its categorization as being the university or "graduate school" for students of conflict, whether military or civilian.

INSURGENT VS. COUNTERINSURGENT

If we would understand the capabilities and limitations of counterinsurgency, it is first necessary to understand the many facets of insurgency. In previous chapters we have explored some of these. Each side has its strengths and its distinctive Achilles' heels. To best comprehend the advantages and disadvantages of the insurgent and counterinsurgent, they must be viewed comparatively, side-by-side.

On the military side Mao Tse-tung observed that guerrillas were by their nature creatures of offense. Guerrillas should not prolong their attacks, and most certainly they dare not attempt to fight a defensive positional battle. By extension, Mao could have been speaking of insurgents writ large, not merely the guerrilla component of an insurgency, but the semiregular units and political mobilization components as well.

On the political side, all insurgents are, by definition, agents of change, even if *change* means moving society backwards. They are therefore oriented toward the replacement of an existing order by a governmental system of their own choosing. There are two broad forms of insurgent political behavior: those movements aiming to *transform* society from old patterns of social structure, politics, and economy into something new; and those movements that strive to *preserve* or restore the way things used to be, and *ought* yet to be. Both types of insurgent groups strive for change, but whereas transformational groups wish to move society forward to some ideal New Society, reactionary insurgent groups would turn the clock backward in an attempt to return to some bygone and possibly imaginary Golden Age.

Insurgents fight to remedy perceived national or societal ills. Indeed, the master of insurgent warfare, Mao Tse-tung, has said that the value of guerrilla forces (and for that matter, even regular columns) was found more in their political mobilization abilities than in their tactical capabilities. This is not to belittle the role of guerrilla units in harassing the enemy, tying down regular forces of far greater size, and destroying isolated outposts and valuable enemy equipment and supplies. Nor is it appropriate to equate larger insurgent formations with Western brigades or divisions as Jomini might do. Insurgent forces are fundamentally different from Western conventional forces by virtue of their inherent political qualities and their key role in mobilizing the people.

Mao was clear on this point saying, "The Red Army fights not merely for the sake of fighting, but in order to conduct propaganda among the masses, organize them, arm them, and help them establish revolutionary political power."[2]

First and foremost, an insurgent, whether civilian or military, is of the people and for the people. Local citizens understand that their sons and daughters, cousins, and uncles and aunts comprise the guerrilla units. In political as well as military terms, a guerrilla unit is the home team and therefore deserves the community's support. After passing through intermediate stages some local units become *regular* units: mobile formations capable of operating in any part of the country. However, even these regular insurgent columns, despite their wider mission, must still remain tied closely to the people. This is normally accomplished through close liaison with local guerrilla units and the political leadership in the valleys and villages where they operate.

In contrast, the political goal of the majority of counterinsurgents is to maintain the *status quo*. In some countries, maintaining the *status quo* means *ipso facto* protecting the lands and wealth of the great landlords and social elites. In other lands, it means supporting an unpopular regime, whether that regime consists of foreign overseers or local despots. Whatever the specifics of each situation, this fundamental difference in the political outlook of insurgents and counterinsurgents necessarily shapes their respective strategies.

Because the counterinsurgent wishes to preserve "the way things are" he will find himself defending, or attempting to defend, what he believes

---

[2] Mao, "On Correcting Mistaken Ideas in the Party," *Selected Works*, I, p. 124.

he owns physically or politically. This defensive mentality, and the desire to protect his possessions, tends to make the counterinsurgent reactive, that is, he is compelled to wait for the insurgent to act and then try to fend off or counter the insurgent's moves. Even the occasional foray into insurgent held territory is basically defensive. Why? Because a counterinsurgent's offensive actions are tied to an overall strategy of trying to protect fixed points from which he operates, and which he must defend. The counterinsurgent withdraws to those fixed points after his operation and resumes a defensive posture.

The counterinsurgent usually is tied to population centers and economic assets: cities, fortifications, ports and airfields, factories, mines, and the list goes on. The counterinsurgent *owns* everything, therefore he must protect everything . . . *all the time*. This is both costly and exhausting. Insurgents typically have little to guard or defend. Protecting everything all the time is one of the key disadvantages borne by the counterinsurgent.

And yet, from the counterinsurgent's perspective, he has little choice but to assume the defensive. This is because it is politically imperative to protect everything all the time. If he does not defend what he holds, the insurgent will gain control over ever-wider sectors of the population along with territory and productive resources. Because insurgency is a zero-sum game, there are no win-win solutions; a gain by one side results in a corresponding loss to the other. The stronger the insurgent becomes, the weaker the target regime is. (And vice versa.)

And so, the counterinsurgent yields the initiative to the insurgent, usually politically as well as purely tactically; he must await the insurgent's next move. Unless he has superlative intelligence, or receives a lucky break, the counterinsurgent does not know where or when the insurgent will make that next move. Or even *what* that move will be.

Second only to the sympathy or active support of the people, the political and tactical initiative is the insurgent's greatest advantage.

What is immediately obvious is that by enjoying the initiative, the insurgent can choose to attack, withdraw, threaten, sabotage, or merely rest. He can opt for political mobilization in some areas, guerrilla action in others, and no activity whatsoever in still others. This latter option is significant because for an insurgent, non-activity is *still* activity . . . when you have the initiative. Not only is inactivity a kind of still-life activity, it is subtly offensive in nature. This is because the threat of activity remains even though it is merely a pause between operations. But the counterinsurgent must always remain on the alert. Everywhere. This is tiring and psychologically unsettling.

By choosing not to take action in a particular sector or at a particular time, the insurgent can concentrate or focus his available resources on activities of his choice at some other point: that is initiative. His opponent the counterinsurgent, however, must continue to defend or protect *all* areas and thus is compelled to spread himself thin to meet any possible challenge. It is therefore difficult for the counterinsurgent to shift military resources because, for the most part, these are held in prepared defensive positions. And if the counterinsurgent does move certain units from their positions to meet new insurgent threats, he risks leaving the population centers or his economic assets unprotected, which is politically unacceptable.

As most people are aware, in a classic insurgency there is neither a "front" nor a secure "rear area." The insurgents are everywhere and nowhere. As Clausewitz noted:

> By its very nature, such scattered resistance will not lend itself to major actions, closely compressed in time and space. Its effect is like that of the process of evaporation: it depends on how much surface is exposed. The greater the surface and the area of contact between it and the enemy [ed. foreign occupier or target regime] forces, the thinner the latter will be spread, the greater the effect of a general uprising. Like smoldering embers, it consumes the basic foundation of the enemy forces. Since it needs time to be effective, a state of tension will develop while the two elements interact. This tension will either gradually relax, if the insurgency is suppressed in some places and slowly burns itself out in others, or else it will build up to a crisis: a general conflagration closes in on the enemy, driving him out of the country before he is faced with total destruction.[3]

The counterinsurgent thus finds himself in a kind of dilemma. He can choose an enemy-centric strategy that focuses upon chasing armed insur-

---

[3] Clausewitz, Book VI, Chapter 26, "The People in Arms," p. 480

gent bands in the hills in the hope of killing or capturing his armed foes. Or, he can choose a population-centric strategy based upon occupying and holding major cities and populated areas. The former approach, although somewhat proactive, risks depleting and exhausting the counterinsurgent's forces while accomplishing little; guerrilla bands will soon reappear if the insurgent infrastructure among the people is not eliminated. This approach cannot establish security and governance in populated areas and may also incur high costs and many casualties. Moreover, it does nothing at all to correct the basic social ills that caused the insurgency. The latter approach has the disadvantage of tying down the counterinsurgent's forces in more or less fixed defenses around population centers. This approach does offer the possibility of establishing security and governance in populated areas, and the opportunity to dry up the covert infrastructure, but it requires extensive human resources and administrative expertise. It is also extremely costly to maintain over a prolonged period. Worst of all, it leaves the political and tactical initiative in the hands of the insurgents, who are free to dominate broad rural areas, and whose remote base areas remain undisturbed.

There is also a more subtle aspect to the question of initiative: the value of *time.*

TIME AND MONEY

Possession of the initiative determines the value of time. In a contest of endurance, the side that can make best use of its days, months, and years ("stamina" as Cypriot General Grivas would say) is the side most likely to win. If the insurgents have the initiative, then in relative terms they also have more time. This is because they may choose to delay the onset of their next campaign while threatening a variety of points held by the counterinsurgent.

Threats against a particular town, road or rail junction can be made with very small units. These units do not even have to attack, but simply appear. This is a classic deception intended to put the defender on full alert, increasing his costs while also fatiguing him. To quote Master Sun: "To appear far when near; to appear near when far away."

Meanwhile, the insurgent can rest and refit, or train new guerrillas or regulars; if strong or relatively unharried, he can do both. He can use his forces to concentrate suddenly against an isolated government unit or a target such as an airfield. Put another way, the insurgent *can* be everywhere and nowhere at very little effort or expense while his adversary cannot indefinitely sustain the defensive burden. As long as he holds the initiative, time will strengthen the insurgent while it gradually wears down and weakens the counterinsurgent. Time therefore has different values to contestants according to the overall strategies they pursue.

"Time is money" is an old American adage. This is certainly true when applied to insurgency. Differing values of time result in vastly differing material and financial costs to the competing forces.

An insurgent movement has a number of cost-saving advantages over its opponent. By making use of guerrillas and unarmed volunteers (porters, medics, farmers, etc.) who serve for "the Cause," often for subsistence or without pay, insurgent movements can usually keep their costs low. Guerrillas are, in effect, part-time soldiers who pursue ordinary occupations when not engaged in operations. They are a kind of militia. Their weaponry is often very simple, at least until foreign powers decide to intervene and provide material assistance. Many insurgents can live off the land, avoiding the necessity of a massive logistical tail. Because the insurgent is fighting on home turf, he can also make use of friendly local citizens, in some cases even family members, for housing, medical aid, and food. The locals may also deny same to the counterinsurgent.

The regime, or an occupying force, has a far greater burden. Regular battalions sent to foreign shores must be supported by logistical systems that often are thousands of miles long, highly sophisticated, and very costly. An item weighing ten pounds can be carried for a few pennies in a backpack or on a mule or bicycle to a guerrilla unit; that same ten-pound item may cost hundreds of dollars to ship from a foreign shore to a regular unit in the theater of operations.

Regular forces, even those of client states, are paid regular salaries and benefits. As we have noted, treasuries must find the money to pay their troops. If the target regime is bankrupt, the funds must come from friendly foreign governments. And ultimately, foreign aid comes from somewhere. In democracies, it comes from citizens who are taxpayers . . . and voters. In autocracies, aid comes at the expense of the overall state economy, and thus indirectly from citizens who must then do without.

Each day, each month, each year that passes finds an ever-greater disparity in the costs borne by the opposing sides. It is quite true that costs may differ from one insurgency to another. A day supporting counterinsurgency in Central America, for example, may be less costly for American taxpayers than a day supporting counterinsurgency in Iraq or Afghanistan. Likewise, advisory efforts are far less costly than are efforts involving the deployment of large expeditionary forces. This is only a matter of degree, however. Either way, dollars in considerable quantity must flow to the counterinsurgency combatant.

Counterinsurgents can greatly reduce costs if the campaign is conducted with a small body of advisors working with indigenous manpower. But the point remains that each day still costs more to the counterinsurgent than to the insurgent. It is therefore to the advantage of the insurgent to draw things out, to delay, to use constant threats and fear more than actual attacks, in order to ratchet up the costs to his enemy. A day of guerrilla feints and thrusts costs the insurgents a day's worth of provisions. But even if not a single shot is fired, the counterinsurgent's bill for that same day will be considerably greater.

And if shots *are* fired, the counterinsurgent's bill can become astronomical if the insurgent force inflicts casualties or captures or destroys weapons or supplies. We should be mindful of the January 1963 Battle of Ap Bac which cost us 3 dead and 8 wounded U.S. advisors along with the loss of five helicopters and three M113 armored personnel carriers destroyed. The 1,400 South Vietnamese suffered 83 dead and 100 wounded whereas the 300 *trapped* Viet Cong, all guerrillas with no heavy equipment, lost only 18 killed and 39 wounded. Yet, after inflicting a stinging defeat on their attackers, the VC managed to make good their escape. Using only Jominian calculations of manpower, firepower, and cost, I will let you figure out which side should win battles like that at Ap Bac.

Adding to the counterinsurgent's financial burden is the insurgent's propensity to obtain weapons and supplies at the counterinsurgent's expense. In Chapter V of *On Guerrilla Warfare*, Mao Tse-tung bluntly states: "Guerrillas must not depend too much on an armory. The enemy is the principal source of supply."[4]

Adding to the advantages that can be enjoyed by insurgents is that of

[4] Mao Tse-tung, *On Guerrilla Warfare*, Section V. FMFRP 12–18, p. 83.

relative size. Small forces are less costly than large forces; their logistical demands and direct personnel costs are lower if only because there are fewer of them to support. (That insurgents usually cost less on an individual basis only increases their advantage.) Smaller forces are also easier to hide and are often more mobile than road-bound conventional forces, and have a far smaller impact on local communities and rural populations. They are less likely to disrupt local patterns of life. Indeed, like the French GCMA units, they may be able to take their strength from the indigenous people.

On the face of it, the factors of size and cost would seem to argue for counterinsurgents to employ small, elite forces that are highly mobile, and that do not rely on large logistical tails. It would seem wise that in order to reduce cost while gaining time, the counterinsurgent should abandon both his defensive positions and his defensive mentality.

And yet, this is not so easy for the counterinsurgent to do.

Remember that the counterinsurgent represents the way things are. At least in part, the government-in-being claims its right to rule by virtue of its responsibility for protecting its people and institutions. Doubt about a regime's ability to protect its people results in doubts about the regime's legitimacy. The counterinsurgent thus normally requires a sizable military and security force even if the ruling regime is inclined to address the sociopolitical issues that sustain the insurgency.

Smaller forces are certainly less likely to disturb local people, but they also are less capable of establishing a real presence over a large area. Generally, small forces are capable of holding only the ground they occupy. They trade staying power for flexibility. While this is a tactical plus, it is decidedly disadvantageous politically to the ruling regime. It is virtually impossible to govern or to secure governmental personnel and facilities without a reliable, broad-based security presence.

It follows that if a counterinsurgent employs only small forces, no matter how good they are man for man they will be unable to establish population and resource control, which is vital in defeating an insurgency, or even to conduct meaningful programs of civic action and rural development. Small forces simply lack the muscle power to do this. The people will quickly realize that the target regime cannot protect them and from self-interest will consequently opt for neutrality or even side with the insurgents. Either outcome is a political defeat for the government-in-being and a victory in this zero-sum game for the government-in-waiting, the insurgents.

In sum, the issue of small versus large forces has mixed results for counterinsurgents. Small size reduces but does not eliminate cost as a factor weighing upon the treasury and ultimately on the political leadership of the counterinsurgents. Tactically, a small force can appear and disappear more rapidly, operate at a higher overall skill level, and be less disruptive of normal civilian life in towns or rural areas. The reader has probably noted that these are advantages enjoyed by insurgent forces. And so they are.

The price paid by a counterinsurgent using small forces is to render both the population and resource base vulnerable to subversion and attack as they cannot be adequately protected. Moreover, governmental stability will be undermined as civil servants and their activities are more subject to attack. Finally, the populace cannot depend on a reliable economy or administrative services if local government is in a constant state of turmoil and insecurity.

The bottom line to this conundrum, if there is one, is that a target regime and its counterinsurgent forces will necessarily be at a strategic disadvantage regardless of whether they use great numbers of troops and police. This is summarized in the following table:

CRITERIA	SMALL FORCES	LARGE FORCES
Time	More available	Less available
Public impact	Less disturbance	More disturbance
Logistics	Less dependent	Much more dependent
Cost	Less costly	Much higher cost
Mobility/Flexibility	Greater capability	Less capability, often static
Presence	Stretched thin, less able	Greater saturation of area
Civic Action/Development	Less able	Greater capability
Population/Resource Control	Less able	Greater capability

POLITICAL WARFARE

There is one absolutely vital component missing from the foregoing discussion. That is the central matter of politics and political warfare. From the standpoint of the Western strategists, political warfare is the invisible part of the insurgency, a blind spot that it seems we Americans invariably cannot see.

Insurgents instinctively understand the need to conduct hard-hitting political warfare campaigns to agitate the people and draw attention not merely to perceived ills in society, but to build popular support for the insurgent's proposed solution for those ills. Otherwise their insurgency will be short lived.

Typically, the government is slow off the mark. When target regimes finally recognize the need for a political warfare campaign to overcome the insurgents' effort, it is often an afterthought that is poorly crafted and executed as well as lacking credibility. Instead of promoting reforms and building popular support, the regime finds itself in its propaganda attempting to defend itself from insurgent charges or excusing its misdeeds. (If many of the charges weren't true it is unlikely an insurgency would have arisen in the first place.) Also, if the regime has no real intention of carrying out needed reforms, its propaganda effort will be *dead on arrival.*

Insurgents generally have an easier time at political warfare than do target regimes for several reasons.

First and foremost, the insurgent is essentially the challenger, the underdog, the Young Turk. He focuses the public's attention squarely on societal diseases that the people cannot ignore, cannot avoid, and apparently cannot cure. The insurgent presents himself and his ideology as *the solution*. Good propaganda, the ammunition of political warfare, is relevant to basic issues that affect people's lives. Good propaganda is credible and verifiable, and it always calls for action.

The insurgent can point to glaring failures laid at the feet of the regime itself. Indeed, corrupt and inept regimes are their own worst enemies: this is not a trivial point. How easy it is to tell the people the government is corrupt if, in fact, everyone *knows* it is corrupt. How easy it is for a skilled propagandist to pillory certain governmental figures for nepotism or stupidity if indeed, those individuals routinely practice nepotism and make stupid mistakes. How easy it is for a political warfare specialist to write pamphlets or make broadcasts or deliver ringing speeches to a public *already aware* that serious societal problems exist and that their current leaders are to blame.

Pseudo-leaders such as the Somoza and Ngo families, and dictators like Mobutu and Batista are veritable poster children for insurgent propagandists to fix upon. Usually, there are so many skeletons in a dictator's closet, and these are so widely known, that it is child's play for a skilled political activist or master propagandist to exploit as many of these skeletons as he wishes. This is also true of illegitimate and ineffective regimes.

It is not weaponry but political factors that weigh most heavily in deciding the success of insurgencies. And a regime would not be vulnerable to upheaval and bloodshed if all its societal roots were healthy and flourishing. Again, "the nation has its roots in the people."

Now we come to the nettlesome challenge of reform.

CAN A LEOPARD CHANGE HIS SPOTS?

The most potent weapon in the arsenal of the counterinsurgent is reform. And yet it is the *weapon of last choice* for many target regimes. In their attempt to defeat the rebels, corrupt and oligarchic regimes will try almost any expedient, with brute force being a favorite, to avoid swallowing the bitter pill of reform and begin treating their diseased societal roots.

Reform can take as many different forms as there are societal maladies. If the societal problem is concentration of too much land in too few hands, especially if that land was acquired by shady means, the cure may be land reform. If the main problem is rule by a tyrant or foreign occupier, especially if that regime also is exploitative, the cure may be home rule or independence. If access to political power is restricted to a tiny oligarchy or a ruling family, political reform, even if limited, is likely to prove curative. And if society grinds under lack of justice (corruption of justice and law enforcement), judicial and police reforms are recommended.

The nature of the cure depends upon the nature of the disease.

There is only one problem with all of this. It is easy to say that *reform* is the weapon of choice of the counterinsurgent. The fact remains, however, that reform is one of the most thorny and difficult undertakings facing any regime. Why should this be so? It is because reform strikes at the heart of the interests of those who benefit from society's ills. Reform implies fundamental change: redistribution of land and wealth, changes in social position, and ultimately redistribution of political power. And that is why so many threatened regimes are unwilling or unable to undertake reform. By undertaking reform those heading the target regime would also necessarily undercut their own perceived interests, economic and political.

Landed gentry, as in El Salvador or prewar China, are reluctant to give up even half an acre of their vast landholdings. For landlords the basis of their wealth and power is their land. Giving up their land to others reduces their wealth and power, and the high social status that goes with it.

Tyrants and occupiers find it hard to cede even a measure of independence to others. We have seen that the government of the French Fourth Republic in 1946, consisting of supposedly progressive French Socialists and Communists, refused to budge an inch on independence for Indochina. America's experience with British colonial officialdom combined with Parliament's high-handed declaration that it had the right to legislate for the colonies "in all matters whatsoever" demonstrated a similar political myopia.

It is inconceivable that ruling political dynasties like the Somozas or the Ngos would agree to hold internationally supervised elections and then gracefully abide by the results. And yet, a free and fair election, even if marred by irregularities, is better than prohibiting elections altogether.

Reform of justice and law enforcement means cutting off sources of *squeeze* that both judges and police depend on. In some countries applicants for positions will buy their jobs and then pay monthly fees to their bosses in order to keep them. The money funneled upstairs is ultimately squeezed from the little people who may have been arbitrarily arrested or threatened, or brought before corrupt courts. We may meditate on the evil consequences of such systematized shakedowns in South Vietnam, Afghanistan, and even closer to home in Mexico.

The core of this daunting challenge of reform amounts to this: is the regime *willing*, or even *able*, to reform itself?

In some cases, it is definitely possible. The examples of Ramon Magsaysay in the Philippines, and Jose Napoleon Duarte and Alfredo Cristiani in El Salvador are encouraging. Unfortunately, we also have the examples of Chiang Kai-shek's Nationalist Party in China, Ngo Dinh Diem and a parade of generals who succeeded him in Vietnam, and Anastasio "Tachito" Somoza in Nicaragua among many, many others of similar ilk.

The problem that has vexed a string of U.S. administrations of both political persuasions is how to encourage client regimes that are battling active insurgencies to undertake serious programs of political, economic, social, and military reform. Despite heavy diplomatic pressure and huge amounts of aid, some client regimes—the former government in South Vietnam is a good example—seemed impervious to real change. As President Dwight D. Eisenhower observed in his first Inaugural Address: "A people that values its privileges above its principles soon loses both."[5]

A workable system of incentives and disincentives that produce the desired changes in clients such as Wikitania has not yet been devised. Although the Wikitanians may pay lip service to America's suggested reforms, these may never materialize. After all, the Wikitanians know that we have little ability to monitor reforms. Moreover, they know that often we will take no punitive steps if U.S. aid is misused or our advice is ignored. While short-term measures can sometimes curb excesses, what is of greater importance is implementing longer-term reforms that bring about genuine social change. An educated, prosperous, socially stable middle class is the best bet for politically stable allied governments.[6]

The skeptical reader, especially a counterinsurgent practitioner who is more inclined to use weapons rather than ideas to solve political problems, may ask: "Why is the issue of reform so very important in defeating an insurgency?" This is a good question and, in fact, is part of the reason that I decided to write this book.

The answer is that *reform robs the insurgent of his greatest weapon: the support or sympathy of the people.* If the grievances experienced by wide sectors of the populace can be eliminated, or even ameliorated through government-sponsored reforms, it is likely that popular discontent will be significantly reduced. This, in turn, will make it much more difficult for anti-regime activists to mobilize the people against the government-in-being. If the government is actually on the side of the peasant, and is promoting reform of corrupt judicial and administrative functions, aiding in agricultural and economic development, encouraging primary education and health care, what can the insurgents offer that is a *better deal*? Nothing.

The central question of an insurgency may be reduced to its basic element: *a clear choice between promises and actual deeds has been put before the people.* Given such a choice, people will always support whichever side *does* things. But if there are no deeds forthcoming from the regime, the

[5] President Eisenhower, Inaugural speech, 20 January 1953.
[6] A view also held by Aristotle, see *Politics*, Book IV, chapter 11.

people have no other option than to hope for the fulfillment of the insurgent's promises. Shakespeare has an appropriate line in his play "Measure for Measure."

> The miserable have no other medicine
> But only hope. [7]

A supreme irony is the fact that insurgents of all stripes actually *fear* reform. While this seems not to square with insurgent claims of a better life or self-determination or almost any appeal you can name, the fact remains that an insurgent movement absolutely does not want the *government* leading the parade toward reform.[8] If the regime *captures* the revolution, the would-be revolutionaries are out of business. Indeed, their relevance, their very reason for being has vanished. With the government now ahead of the insurgent movement on all political fronts, the rebel movement will have no Cause that can be used to stir the enmity of the people against the regime. In a matter of weeks, the insurgents will be unable to recruit new members for their mass base or as replacements for their guerrilla and regular forces. Reform is lethal to revolution.

PLAYING A ZERO-SUM GAME

As noted earlier, insurgency is very much a zero-sum game. As one side gains advantages, these necessarily come at the expense of the opponent. Because the prize for either side is the support of the people, the greatest single game changer is reform, not numbers of troops or weaponry.

If the government-in-being is widely perceived as illegitimate, it is starting off at a distinct political disadvantage even though it may have a preponderant military advantage over its insurgent opponents. Thus, the counterinsurgency already is *down one* even before serious trouble begins.

General Sir Frank Kitson, former commander-in-chief of British land

---

[7] Shakespeare, *Measure for Measure*, III, i., 2. In the years immediately after World War II, the Germans joked that: "The Russians promise us everything, but do nothing. The Americans promise nothing, but do everything." People will always side with those who have their interests firmly in mind.

[8] Movements such as Sendero Luminoso, the Viet Cong, and the Taliban have not hesitated to murder officials, teachers, aid workers, and others who alleviate social ills precisely because these competent and dedicated people are viewed as mortal threats to the movement's prospects for taking power.

forces and an expert on low-intensity operations, once observed: "insurgents start with *nothing but a cause* [emphasis added] and grow to strength while the counter-insurgents start with everything but a cause and gradually decline in strength to the point of weakness."[9]

The particular constellation of social ills and the relationship of the governing regime to those ills gives the insurgent movement its political fuel. The insurgent must define a Cause that reverberates throughout society, or at least with key groups in society, and that touches upon the people's perceived interests. This Cause provides the policy program that the insurgent will pursue on his way to power. If the diagnosis of society's ills and their causes is clear and can be explained to the target audiences the insurgent hopes to win to his side, the result will be a groundswell of support. It is incorrect to assume that only peasants or the underclass can be rallied. If dysfunctions are widely felt, as for example in Somoza's Nicaragua in the 1960s and 1970s, the insurgents can build their power from many classes in society: professionals, educators, artisans, etc. The Chinese and Vietnamese did exactly the same thing.

The insurgent leadership will make a detailed analysis of the society that it seeks to capture politically. They will discern three broad groups: those who are disaffected from the regime, those who support the regime, and everyone else, the would-be neutrals.

Clearly, if the vast majority of a country's population is disaffected from their rulers, the game is over almost as soon as it begins. Insurgencies such as those in Ireland (1919) and Cyprus ran their courses rapidly.[10] Toppling Somoza and Batista also did not take long. Why? The political conditions were highly favorable to the insurgents.[11] Again, we may refer to Lipset's criteria of perceived legitimacy and regime effectiveness.

Normally, there is a fairly balanced breakdown of supporters, oppo-

---

[9] Kitson, p. 29.

[10] We may speculate that the rapid victory of Michael Collins's movement was facilitated by the fact that southern Ireland is overwhelmingly Roman Catholic and the Irish people regarded British rule as illegitimate. In contrast, Ulster (Northern Ireland) is predominantly Protestant, many of Scottish descent going back to the seventeenth century, and accepts royal rule as legitimate. Hence, the insurgency in the south progressed rapidly (1919–1921) whereas the IRA and Sinn Fein, having support only in the minority Catholic neighborhoods in Ulster, experienced virtual stalemate.

[11] The external political situation is an important factor that can make a difference, but as the example of Nationalist China (1949) makes clear, no amount of external help can save an inept regime from defeat.

nents, and neutrals. In the American Revolution, it must be remembered, a third or more of all colonists were ardent supporters of the Crown; they favored the *status quo*. Some historians believe that at the outset of the Revolutionary War, a third or so of the colonists advocated separation from Great Britain and the establishment of an independent government. It is possible, however, that the largest single group included Quakers, other pacifists, political fence-sitters, and those who simply wished to be left alone. However, from 1761 onward Parliament's actions caused many colonists to question the Crown's legitimacy in ruling the colonies. Even so, other colonists maintained what the French observer, Alexis De Tocqueville, called an "instinctive loyalty" to monarchy.

When the populace is relatively evenly divided, more political mobilization work has to be done to build a solid base of public support for the insurgent movement while eroding remaining sympathy for the existing government. This, of course, takes time, but it is a very necessary step.

Often, the target regime will help the insurgents through its implementation of ham-fisted or brutal policies. As we've noted, this was certainly the case in the Carolinas during the American Revolution, courtesy of Lord Cornwallis and his scourge, Lt. Col. Banastre Tarleton. Marshal Soult and his French troops had the same catalytic effect in Napoleonic Spain. Learning nothing from the past, we find the Emperor Maximilian signing the Black Decree in Mexico and Field Marshal Lord Harding overseeing mass arrests in Cyprus. We may speculate that the Somozas and the repressive Salvadoran military prior to 1980 were unwitting as *recruiters* for the FSLN and FMLN, respectively.[12]

Counterinsurgency expert David Kilcullen has devised a theoretical process he calls "the accidental guerrilla syndrome," positing that a local population will reject outside intervention and thus throw in its lot with the insurgents, in his example, Al-Qa'ida.[13]

I would take Kilcullen's theory half a step further. In my opinion, the greater the *cultural distance* between the local population and that of an

---

[12] The reader is invited to read Annex A in its entirety. The State Department cable cited describes how the Salvadoran army managed to change its character completely, becoming an agent of positive change and ultimately gaining widespread support among the Salvadoran people.

[13] Kilcullen, p. 35 (Figure 1.1).

intervening force, the greater will be the strength of its rejection. It follows that forces deployed to intervene to counter an insurgency should ideally be *home-grown*, of the same culture as the people involved in the conflict. There may still be a negative reaction by the people to intervention, but it should be of less intensity if those who are assigned that task are of the same "blood and belonging." Afghan forces, when properly trained and disciplined for counterinsurgency work, should be more effective with fellow Afghans than are American or European soldiers.

Because communication skills are vital to building political power, both the regime and the insurgents must compete for many of the same groups. This is no easy matter if large sectors of the population are illiterate. Yet, whichever side is effective at communicating its message is more likely to win the people to his side. In the case of China, Mao Tse-tung and his senior cadres spent years mobilizing millions of illiterate peasants. With the low rate of literacy then prevailing in China, the Chinese Communist Party found it necessary as an interim measure to conduct thousands of peasant literacy classes. This massive educational program, which had as its goal to teach every peasant one hundred basic Chinese characters, was the prelude to political education. If a peasant could read a minimum of one hundred characters, he could then read simple news bulletins and Big Character Posters[14] containing elements of the Party's program. In short, he could then be indoctrinated and incorporated into the insurgent movement. In the Islamic world, literacy similarly aids political mobilization.

SIZE OF THE FIGHT IN THE DOG

Not least, there is the question of relative degrees of motivation. Clausewitz might consider this to be one of his "imponderables." History is replete with examples of small, but very highly-motivated armies soundly thrashing much larger, but less-motivated units. How can this be since official Western strategic thinking, particularly Jomini, holds that "God is on the side of the *heaviest* battalions?"

Perhaps the answer lies in the strength of emotional attachment to the object desired. There is an old saying: "It's not the size of the dog in the

[14] Big Character Posters (or Da-dze-bao) were just that: large eye-catching wall posters conveying political messages and guidance intended for residents of a particular village or neighborhood. These formed a key part of a fully integrated campaign of propaganda and political mobilization during and after the war.

fight, it's the size of the fight in the dog." So it is with individuals; so it is with military forces.

It should be remembered that the French Indochina war involved Vietnamese units on both sides, the Viet Minh on one side, but with surprisingly large numbers of Vietnamese on the French side. And yet, it is hard to escape the conclusion that, with rare exceptions, the Viet Minh consistently outfought their pro-French countrymen.

Clearly, the Vietnamese on both sides spoke the same language, shared the same culture, and were similar in physical size and mental capacity.

The difference between the two, I believe, lay in the relative strengths of their desire to attain their competing political goals. The Viet Minh were totally committed to obtaining independence from the French whereas those who supported the French had a vague notion of loose autonomy under French suzerainty.

Returning to General Grivas's struggle for the independence of Cyprus: as he observed, the majority of Cypriots desired freedom whereas the British soldiers were in Cyprus simply because the Ministry of Defence had sent them there. This is not meant to detract from British military professionalism, but professionalism alone cannot equal the strength of motivation that comes from deep emotional commitment to a desired goal.

Grivas himself may have put his finger on the core of a people's motivation to resist an occupier: "the upper hand would be gained by the one whose moral stamina was higher and his will stronger," and "faith in the justice of our cause."[15] We might ask how the Jominians would calculate persistence, determination, and raw courage?

In our own revolution, strength of commitment to the cause of independence, raw tenacity despite grave hardships, ultimately resulted in victory despite repeated defeats inflicted by an army clearly superior to the Continentals in training, discipline, equipment, and logistics. Von Steuben marveled at the ragtag flotsam he observed at Valley Forge and stated that no European army could have survived such appalling conditions. A year earlier, at the crossing of the Delaware River shoeless men left a trail of blood in the snow as they marched at night to defeat the Hessians at Trenton. Can there be any doubt as to the outcome of a struggle in which men are prepared to go to any length to gain their desired goal?

---

[15] Grivas, op. cit., p.43.

NUMBERS, NUMBERS, NUMBERS

This brings us to the perennial question debated by counterinsurgency theorists: What is the proper ratio that must exist between counterinsurgents and insurgents in order for the former to achieve victory over the latter? We hear of one expert saying that a numerical advantage of ten-to-one is required; another says that it takes twenty-to-one to insure victory. Most of these theorists do not know what they are talking about. Seduced once again by the beguiling formulas of Antoine Jomini, they wallow in numbers, numbers, numbers.

The master insurgent, Mao Tse-tung, remarked that: "Numbers *by themselves* [emphasis added] confer no particular advantage." He should be heeded. Consider General Grivas, who succeeded in bringing Her Majesty's government to the negotiating table despite a breathtaking thirty-two-to-one British numerical advantage in soldiers and police over EOKA.

Why are force ratios or population ratios irrelevant? They are irrelevant because they are simplistic and measure only what can be seen and quantified, that is, the numbers of troops and capabilities of various weapons. This is the fallacy of Jomini. Clausewitz recognized that there is much more to a battle than mere numbers of troops or mathematical calculations of artillery trajectories. Liddell Hart grasped the idea that very small forces could achieve victory by indirect means. Still, the U.S. Army has yet to figure out that Jomini has no place in the *graduate school of warfare.*

Let's take a closer look at the fallacy of numbers and ratios.

We have already touched upon several factors that call into question the supposed value of ratios. A major factor is that of different levels of motivation. A man who is prepared to die for his beliefs is far more formidable than a man who doesn't particularly want to be on the battlefield in the first place. This was as true in Cyprus in 1956 as it was at Trenton in 1776. Consider the difference between a conscript drafted into service and a volunteer whose brother has been killed by the enemy. How do you quantify or measure motivation, especially commitment to a Cause? Can religious zeal or belief in a better life for one's children be counted? How does one measure resentment or hatred? How does one place a number on the desire for freedom or for revenge? Can courage, bitterness and determination be quantified? What about the capability of regime soldiers who have had their salaries stolen by their officers?

We also touched upon the "two kinds of time" that exist in an insurgency. Time usually is an ally for insurgents; it helps them conserve strength. Normally, time is a foe for counterinsurgents as it eats away not only at their supplies, armaments, and equipment, but at their morale. As time goes by, the insurgent gradually grows stronger while the counterinsurgent, by contrast, becomes slightly weaker. Can psychological or even physical exhaustion and uncertainty be quantified? Given a seemingly endless war, as the weeks and months pass by how does one quantify the capability of those men who are tired and hungry, miserable and homesick?

Even cost is a major factor calling into question the validity of ratios. One can argue that the greater the numerical ratio between the size of the counterinsurgent forces and the insurgents, the *weaker* the incumbent regime becomes! The reasoning for this counterintuitive thought is that as the size of the counterinsurgent force swells, cost is stacked upon cost especially if it is sustained from abroad and depends on high-tech weaponry. If it costs $32 for you to counter every single dollar I put down as the insurgent, I may eventually bankrupt you. Then what good is your massive conventional force? It is a liability, not an asset.

I feel very confident that insurgents are capable of inflicting financial losses far in excess of thirty-two to one on their adversaries. Here is what David Kilcullen has to say about the relative costs between Western conventional weaponry and Al-Qaida's asymmetrical style of war:

> Efforts of insurgents and terrorists since 9/11 may in fact have already put an end, through unconventional and asymmetric means, to the much-bruited military superiority of the United States, showing the way to all future adversaries and leaving Western powers with fabulously capable and appallingly expensive militaries that are precisely adapted to exactly the wrong kind of war.[16]

As numerical ratios increase conceivably to thirty- or forty- or more to one in favor of the counterinsurgent, the counterinsurgent security force becomes increasingly unsustainable; now that's ironic! There is a point at which the counterinsurgent eventually faces the dilemma noted by Clausewitz:

---

[16] Kilcullen, p. 24.

> Such an interaction could lead to a maximum effort if a maximum could be defined. But in that case, all proportion between action and political demands would be lost: means would cease to be commensurate with ends, and in most cases a policy of maximum exertion would fail because of the domestic problems it would raise.[17]

More simply: *is the game worth the candle?* Was the French gamble of nearly eleven billion dollars (at 1950 values) and the deaths of ninety-five thousand soldiers worth the payoff of retaining Indochina as a French dependency? What was the long-term impact of this disaster on France? Was Cyprus worth the British cost in trying to suppress Cypriot nationalism by force of arms?

Clearly the counterinsurgent faces a daunting challenge. Indeed, he faces a conundrum. First, he is caught in a trap whereby as a defender of the status quo he must maintain many of the social and political ills that caused the insurgency. Second, to *win* his only option is reform, yet the leaders of the target regime quite often are loath to make concessions because reform implies loss of political and economic power. Third, as he attempts to protect population centers and economic assets, the counterinsurgent must do so at the cost of hobbling his offensive capabilities, thereby yielding the initiative to the insurgent. Fourth, the larger his presence grows, the more likely it is that he will unwittingly stir up even more hatred and resistance, especially if the counterinsurgent is of a markedly different culture. And fifth, as he deploys ever more troops and equipment into the war zone, his costs spiral out of control, exceeding his means. The treasury faces the dilemma of cutting non-military programs to pay war costs or rolling the printing presses; both options are unattractive. His strategy is undone, because his political ends cannot be achieved within available means, or at any cost remotely commensurate with the value of his political goal.

This is the counterinsurgency conundrum.[18]

---

[17] Clausewitz, p. 585.

[18] Author does not mean to imply that conducting a counterinsurgency effort is a hopeless proposition. It is not. However, senior policymakers and generals must ponder imponderables and develop strategies that are far more sophisticated than those currently in use. Insurgency is a thinking-man's war.

CHAPTER 8

AMERICAN MYOPIA

"Do you not know, my son, with how little wisdom the world is governed?"

In 1648, with those words as encouragement, Chancellor of Sweden Axel Oxenstierna sent his son Michael, a rising diplomat, to represent his country at the negotiations that resulted in the Peace of Westphalia that ended the Thirty Years War. As prime minister to Gustavus Adolphus, the warrior king of Sweden, and his successor Queen Christina, Oxenstierna had witnessed the devastation of Europe as various armies crisscrossed the land burning cities, destroying farms and homes, and slaughtering people on a scale unknown until World War II.[1] Oxenstierna had more than ample justification for his statement.

THE WAGES OF UNWISDOM

The tragedy of the Thirty Years War was soon forgotten as French armies under Louis XIV ravaged Germany and its neighbors from 1670 to 1713. The eighteenth century saw Europe torn apart by the War of the Austrian Succession (1740-1748), the Seven Years' War (1756–1763), and after 1791 the wars of the French Revolution. Napoleon had conquered almost all of

[1] The population of Germany, where most of the combat and destruction had taken place, was halved. It took fifty years following the 1648 treaties for the population just to recover to prewar levels.

his neighbors until Europe finally united to defeat France in 1814.

Still, nineteenth century Europe learned nothing from these wars except how to build larger armies and better weapons. Twice in the twentieth century Europe came perilously close to committing suicide as massive armies clashed from 1914 to1918 and—after a pause to rest, refit, and recalibrate—resumed their lethal quarreling from 1939 to 1945. When disease and starvation are added to battlefield casualties, not to mention the incalculable moral, psychological, and economic damage, it is clear to any observer that the European world was governed with incredibly little wisdom for at least three centuries.

It may be that the end of World War II marked the beginning of a fundamentally new chapter in world history. The old empires were either gone or going. Subject peoples in Africa and Asia were asserting their independence from a Europe that had proved itself unworthy to continue colonial rule. While what became known as the Third World began its difficult transition to freedom, traditional enemies in Europe were moving toward a close economic, military, and political partnership, burying ancient animosities and the nationalist hatreds that had nearly destroyed European civilization. As the European Union became reality, and as Euro-Communism petered out, it became increasingly clear that wars would no longer scourge the European continent, nor plunge its lands and peoples into utter desolation. The scene of probable conflict now shifted to other regions of the globe, principally to the vast reaches of Asia and Africa.

But while sober appraisal of the war's effects brought Europe together under wiser minds, the effect in many former colonial lands was the opposite. The trauma of decolonization, complicated by problems of wrenching political and economic change, the spread of seductive ideologies and ethnic politics, and the glut of weapons left behind spawned a host of "small wars" in many remote places. While no single small war posed an existential threat to the United States or its European allies as did the war unleashed by Nazi Germany, when viewed cumulatively these "small wars" are capable of inflicting on the West what the ancient Chinese called "the death of a thousand cuts." Small wars are to be taken seriously.

As a cadet and young lieutenant in the mid-1960s I remember being trained for conventional operations on NATO's Central Front: our focus was the enemy ready to pounce on us from beyond the Fulda Gap in East

Germany. The Soviet Union's 1st Guards Tank Army and 3rd Shock Army are no longer in East Germany. Indeed, there is no longer an East Germany or a Soviet Union. The division of Europe into two camps is now history and the Iron Curtain has rusted away. Some might hold up a Chinese threat to East Asia as a replacement for the now-defunct Soviet threat, but my view is that, unlike the Soviets, the Chinese can gain their objectives without using their armed forces in combat, but simply by having them as a "force in being." The main thrust of China's post-Mao external policy has been and, to no one's surprise, will continue to be heavily economic and political.

A key change in the way the world is governed is the formation of what is now called the "Group of Twenty." This is a grouping of twenty of the world's leading economies from around the globe.[2] Together, the Group of Twenty comprises two-thirds of the world's population (roughly 4.7 billion people), conducts 80 percent of world trade, and claims fully 85 percent of gross global product. We may note with interest that Germany, Italy, and Japan, all three of our World War II Tripartite Pact enemies, are members, as are our more recent adversaries, Russia and China. The economic interests of these leading powers will hold the Group of Twenty together and make First World warfare highly unlikely.

Colonel T.X. Hammes makes the following point about the global economic power of what Thomas Friedman has dubbed the "Electronic Herd":

> Although on the surface the markets seem to be purely economic, their impact is that of a powerful political player. This player can dictate trade policies, influence elections, determine interest rates, place limits on national social policy, decide acceptable banking practices, and drive many other activities of nations.[3]

We can derive two points from this. The first is that a global market-

---

[2] The Group of Twenty [http://www.g20.org/] was established in Berlin in 1999 and has now replaced the Group of Eight. Its membership roster: Argentina, Australia, Brazil, Canada, China, France, European Union, Germany, India, Indonesia, Italy, Japan, Mexico, Russia, Saudi Arabia, South Africa, South Korea, Turkey, United Kingdom, United States.

[3] Hammes, p.37

place valued at some $20 trillion now places sharp limits on the former prerogatives of First-World nation states including that of making war. The second, unstated point is that much of the Third World, certainly non-state actors, lies outside the powerful gravitational force of the Electronic Herd and is much less subject to the restraints and limitations imposed by the marketplace on the wealthy countries.

So where does that leave us? What will be the likely challenges in the coming century? Germany? Russia? China? Japan? While we cannot rule out the possibility of limited conventional conflict on the Korean peninsula or in areas of the Middle East, it would appear that the focus of conflict for the next few decades is likely to be in poorer Asian and African lands for many of the reasons cited in Chapter 1. And these conflicts will be small wars, not high-intensity conventional warfare. But do our military and political leaders fully perceive where future challenges lie? I suspect not.

THE PILLARS OF CLAUSEWITZ

Clausewitz considered that war potential rested on three pillars: the army, the people, and the regime. Later thinkers have quibbled that Clausewitz's three-part conception is simplistic. Perhaps it is, but as a framework for analyzing the state of America's preparedness to meet the likely challenges of the coming century his conception is quite useful.

The Declaration of Independence states that a democratic system of government ultimately rests on the will of a sovereign people. It is the people whose "combined wisdom and folly" shape the government and thus its domestic and foreign policies. In its turn, in the name of the American people the Congress called into existence the armed forces of the United States. By Constitutional authority, the President of the United States commands those forces through his appointed officers. Thus, the military is a direct extension of the government and one of its several instruments for carrying out national policy. By further extension, the armed forces of the United States are, in Lincoln's words, "of the people and for the people." They exist to protect and serve the American people.

If we accept the foregoing as our basis for assessing our capability to wage war, especially protracted wars in remote parts of the world, we should examine for that task the people, the government, and finally the armed forces. Each of the three pillars must carry a critical element of the burden. Yet, as we will see, there are significant obstacles that limit our capabilities. Whether each pillar is up to carrying its responsibilities in a rapidly changing world is very much an open question.

The ancient Romans observed: *"Tempora mutantur, nos et mutamur in illis."* "The times indeed change, and we [must] change with them."

If the times are changing, and our enemies are not likely to be the Germans, Russians, Chinese, or Japanese, the question arises: *How well prepared are the American people to meet challenges in regions of the Third World?*

The answer, I am afraid, is *not very well.*

AMERICAN IGNORANCE

The American people are the bedrock upon which the government and armed forces rest. The effectiveness of our government and armed forces is shaped in substantial part by the American people. Unfortunately, numerous studies and findings have been published indicating that American students in general are woefully ignorant of even basic facts of history and geography, to say nothing of non-Western languages, cultures, or socioeconomic conditions.

In their book *The War*, authors Geoffrey Ward and Ken Burns made the following highly disturbing observation:

> The second statistic was just as troubling as the first. Among a number of demoralizing facts about the continuing crisis in our schools over what our children know (and don't know), one item stood out. It seems that an unacceptably large number of graduating high-school seniors think we fought *with* the Germans *against* the Russians in the Second World War.[4]

Every so often articles appear in the press about high school and even some college students who cannot correctly place Canada and Mexico on a blank map of North America. Many Americans are ignorant of such basic information as the geography of the United States, the U.S. Constitution and the structure of the U.S. government, and even major themes of American history. It is an embarrassing fact that many native-born U.S. citizens

---

[4] Ward and Burns, p. xvi.

could not pass the relatively simple examination required of foreign-born applicants for American citizenship. When the topic moves to knowledge of foreign history and geography, or foreign governmental structures, American ignorance is beyond pitiful. This woeful ignorance is clearly unacceptable for a nation that is the world's preeminent power and which professes the desire to exert global leadership.

This is an indisputable case where the public education system has failed the American public. It is beyond our scope to comment upon specific curricula or current educational policy, but the point must be made that if we hope to play a prominent role in world politics in the twenty-first century, we must immediately begin to build a robust educational program aimed at giving our younger citizens the requisite background on both U.S. and foreign history, geography, and government. It is imperative that we quadruple our efforts on foreign-language instruction, especially the languages of the non-European world.

Further evidence of mind-boggling ignorance of even basic facts concerning American history, especially the founding of the American Republic and the central role of George Washington, was recently published in *The SAR Magazine*, the official publication of the National Society of the Sons of the American Revolution:

> Surveys reveal that [George] Washington's achievements are little known [ed. among students.] And, surprisingly, one in four Americans cannot recognize whose portrait is featured on the $1 bill. In a report published in July 2009, only 3.5 percent of high school students in the state of Arizona were able to pass the test to become U.S. citizens, while only 26 percent could name the first president of the United States. In a survey of fourth-graders, only 7 percent could identify the "important event" that took place on July 4, 1776.
>
> Washington is shown even less respect at the university level. At the nation's top 55 colleges, students can graduate without enrolling in a single American history course. In one recent survey of Ivy League colleges, freshmen scored better on history aptitude tests than graduating seniors, suggesting that students' knowledge of history had declined during their university tenure.[5]

---

[5] See *The SAR Magazine*; p. 11.

Equally troubling is growing evidence that the breakdown in American education may be centered in our high schools. Elisa Crouch, staff writer for the *St. Louis Post-Dispatch*, cited the following information in her 2 January 2011 article titled "Colleges find area freshmen unready":

> Nationally, about 1.3 million students are taking remedial courses at public two-year and four-year institutions at a cost of at least $2.3 billion, according to a 2008 report by Strong American Schools, a nonprofit financed in part by the Bill and Melinda Gates Foundation. . . .
>
> In Missouri, state and college officials partly blame the increased demand for college remediation on high schools, where graduation standards don't always line up with what students must know to succeed in college. They also say the proportion reflects the fact that enrollments are up at two-year colleges—schools that typically accept all students no matter what their skill level. . . .
>
> The ACT tests skills in four areas: mathematics, reading, English and science. In Missouri, just 26 percent of students in 2010 met or exceeded benchmarks in all four areas. In Illinois, the proportion was 23 percent. Students who meet the ACT benchmarks have a 75 percent chance of earning a C or better in those college courses.[6]

We can get a glimpse of our nation's lack of expertise on African and Asian affairs from statistics compiled by the U.S. Department of Education on academic degrees awarded throughout the United States by degree-granting colleges and universities. Admittedly, the number of degrees awarded does not give us a complete picture of what expertise we have as a nation on Third World countries. Factors such as residence abroad, commercial contacts, and missionary work add to our pool of knowledge of foreign areas. The point remains, however, that Department of Education numbers give us a rough, but highly illuminating estimate of the expertise we as a nation have (or lack). The numbers are sobering.

For example, in the academic year 2008–2009, U.S. colleges and universities awarded more than 1.6 million baccalaureate degrees. Nationally, of that number only 251 were in Middle Eastern studies, 73 in African

---

[6] See Crouch; *St. Louis Post-Dispatch.*

studies, 14 in South Asian studies, and none were in Southeast Asian studies. Illustrative of our lack of foreign language fluency is the fact that only 85 baccalaureate degrees were awarded in Arabic, 3 degrees each in African and South Asian languages, and just 1 in Iranian/Persian languages. Put in perspective, just 430 baccalaureate degrees were awarded (0.00027 percent) in these studies from the June 2009 national total of 1.6 million.

Degrees awarded for East Asian area studies and languages (China, Japan, Korea) fare somewhat better at a combined total of just over 2,000 baccalaureates in 2009. This said, the fact remains that American universities are not training anywhere near our country's needs for the coming century.[7]

Graduate degrees awarded in 2009 in the aforementioned subjects are obviously on an order of magnitude lower than baccalaureate degrees. For example, thirty-five Ph.D. degrees were awarded in Near and Middle Eastern studies, seven in African studies, one in South Asian studies, and again zero in Southeast Asian studies. Twenty Ph.D. degrees were awarded in Middle/Near Eastern and Semitic languages, four in South Asian languages, and none in Iranian and Persian languages. One Ph.D. was awarded in 2009 in African languages.[8]

The grand total of Ph.D. degrees awarded in these studies across the nation was sixty-eight.

Despite America's pitiful ignorance of foreign conditions, the stunning irony is that we live in a global fishbowl where an enormous abundance of information is at our fingertips.[9] This includes information about powerful socioeconomic and religious forces noted in Chapter 1 of which we as a people are only vaguely aware. These are the forces that shape the political behaviors of peoples living half a world away.

I speculate that some of the following points may represent key short-

---

[7] Statistics compiled by the National Center for Educational Statistics, U.S. Department of Education, for Academic Year 2008-2009. See: nces.ed.gov/programs/digest/d09/tables/xls/tabn275.xls. NCES collects data from degree-granting Title IV post-secondary institutions throughout the United States.

[8] NCES data, op. cit.

[9] The irony is that decades of research by university scholars have amassed truly amazing amounts of data on even the remotest tribes and geographical areas. Yet, while our experts know more and more about these areas and peoples, the impression one gets is that the general American public knows less and less.

comings among the general citizenry—the American electorate—that hamper our ability to function effectively in often complex situations abroad:

- Ignorance of foreign geographical realities
- Ignorance of world history and world politics
- Weakness in understanding non-Western languages and cultures
- Persistent cultural and racial prejudices and stereotypes
- Difficulty in understanding the relevance of events abroad to conditions at home
- Misunderstanding of the nature of insurgency and its causes
- Desire for thumping, but normally unattainable, "total" military victories a la Erich Ludendorff or Henri Navarre

Recognizing the speculative nature of these shortcomings, let us briefly examine several of them and their consequences.

Knowledge of basic world geography is essential if voters (citizens) are to know where certain lands are and why they are important to the United States and other members of the world community. The fact that despite intensive press coverage most Americans have difficulty finding even such countries as Iraq and Afghanistan on a map is ample evidence of a serious failing of public education. If people are called upon to make choices at the polls between competing policies affecting our foreign relations, they absolutely must know what those choices are about. Sadly, many voters are clueless.

The same must be said about world history and politics. When students are so ignorant that they cannot even distinguish between the belligerents in World War II, it is clear that our educational system is producing citizens without a collective memory. One suspects that graduating seniors are more familiar with the lives and loves of Hollywood starlets than they are with matters of life and death in Afghanistan.

American weakness in mastery of non-Western languages and understanding of many non-Western cultures is embarrassing. If we did not have an influx of refugees and immigrants from African and Asian lands one might suspect that America would have no capability whatsoever in this area. Some high-school French, perhaps . . . ?

The consequence of lack of understanding of foreign tongues and cultures—ignorance—is frightful prejudice and cultural chauvinism. I remember only too well being on the replacement detachment bus heading to the 7th Division's old base at Tongduchon, Korea, and being embarrassed by the callous epithets our soldiers yelled at the local people through open bus windows. Even at age twenty-two, I realized that the support of the indigenous population was essential to our own safety and operational capability.

Alienating local inhabitants is unwise, yet the cultural ignorance of many young people leads in that very direction. As I learned later in life, this Korean example was not unique, or even out of the ordinary. Our deployed personnel have repeated this terrible mistake in Vietnam, in Iraq, and Afghanistan. This prejudice is not learned in the U.S. Army or Marine Corps: it is homegrown back in River City . . . and then carried abroad.

The American people are also impatient by nature and typically incapable of slow and steady perseverance. To be sure, the "I want it and I want it now" mentality manifests itself commercially in people buying on credit things they cannot afford. In the political world it shows its colors in demands for instant solutions that, in many cases, simply are not possible. Among these is the desire for short *decisive* wars. While I agree in principle that a short war is better than a long one (although best is no war at all), the enemy has a vote. Americans do not understand the dynamics of insurgency. Patience is required when dealing with insurgency, but the record indicates that patience is in short supply among the American people.

Yet another challenge for the policy community is the natural tendency of the American voter to ask: "Well, how does this relate to *me*?" It is a reasonable question. In the days of Louis XIV or Frederick the Great, such impertinence, had it occurred, would have been slapped down. But we are a democracy. If a citizen is asked to send his son to a foreign war, and to pay increased taxes for foreign adventures, he is more than entitled to a cogent answer from our elected leaders. But part of the burden should be on the citizen himself: reading, studying, asking questions. It is human nature, however, that most people will settle for pat answers supplied by television pundits in sound bytes. Reading and research takes too much time. Intellectual laziness therefore opens the door to fuzzy or wishful thinking, warped or superficial understanding of issues, and manipulation of public opinion.

The early nineteenth century philosopher and diplomat Joseph de Maistre once quipped: "Every nation has the government it deserves." We have already heard from James A. Garfield that "All free governments are managed by the combined wisdom and folly of the people."

It is time we took a peek at the capabilities of the American government, both its executive and legislative branches, in light of our preparedness for protracted *small* wars.

AMERICAN POLICYMAKERS

If we take Harry Truman at his word, the buck, so happily passed by one bureaucrat or congressman to another, stops at the desk of the chief executive. Many of America's blunders overseas must be laid squarely at the feet, not of our military commanders, but at those of our elected officials. True, the blame for failure is often shuffled off onto the backs of the defense and intelligence establishments when, in fact, the tar and feathers should be applied to members of the executive and legislative branches. Politicians are quick to claim credit for the successes of others, but slow to accept responsibility for failures of their own.

I think that many of our worst blunders overseas have been those of flawed policy. If policy is flawed it follows that any strategy based upon that flawed policy will fail. In Clausewitz's words:

> No one starts a war—or rather, no one in his senses ought to do so—without first being clear in his mind what he intends to achieve by that war and how he intends to conduct it. The former is its political purpose; the latter its operational objective. This is the governing principle which will set its course, prescribe the scale of means and effort which is required, and make its influence felt throughout down to the smallest operational detail.[10]

And yet, despite this sage advice, we often see administration after administration venturing forth in ignorance of what it intends to achieve and how it intends to conduct its war. We have also seen instances where commands went forth from the Oval Office stating one political objective, only to have the policy goalposts moved abruptly while the operational

[10] Clausewitz, Book VIII, Chapter 2, p. 579.

game was in progress. I perceive a temptation by occupants of the Oval Office to look first to our military forces to "solve the problem." This may be a contemporary version of the 1920s cry "Send in the Marines!" whenever some teapot tempest whistled in the Caribbean. Policymakers usually demand from their subordinates quick and clear-cut resolutions. They often "hip shoot" in their decision-making based more on feeling than on fact. Most disturbing, political leaders dealing with foreign events often tend to assume that money or high technology will solve any problem.

The American government in the first decade of the twenty-first century appears to suffer from several key shortcomings, some of which are inherent to the system, but others of which derive from the electorate that the American government is supposed to serve. Among them:

- Ignorance of foreign geographical realities
- Ignorance of world history and cultures
- No global grand strategy; a fire-brigade, respond-to-emergencies mentality versus thinking proactively
- Short term focus, that is two to four years out, nothing beyond the next election
- Constantly searching for *the* silver bullet, the easy quick fix
- Hubris and political posturing in place of careful thinking and quiet reflection
- All politics local: paying too much attention to noisy minority constituencies
- Capricious legislative intervention in foreign policy without careful thought regarding possible consequences
- Politicization of senior appointments
- Baleful influence of mavericks like Sen. Joseph McCarthy or the China Lobby

The executive and legislative branches share the tar and feathers equally. Let's direct our fire on the executives first; they are directly in charge of foreign policy and our armed forces, or are supposed to be. Military power is best used when it is least used. True, as the Romans stated centuries ago, we should build our strength in times of peace. But we should do so largely to ensure that peace is credibly maintained. The only problem is that, as we've already said, we are constantly building only our high-tech, equipment oriented capabilities, not our low-tech, people oriented capabilities. The late Director of Central Intelligence William Colby was quoted as saying: "There has got to be something between a diplomatic note and sending in the Marines."

The commander-in-chief has the Constitutional responsibility for directing our nation's armed forces and, for that matter, the immense capabilities of our civilian departments and agencies. The president has it within his power to urge his uniformed and civilian subordinates to come together to reach new and more intelligent methods for combining the many capabilities, civil and military, that we possess. Supposedly he has the authority to *order* his cabinet secretaries and other subordinates, but practically speaking the president has to depend on his people to respond to his leadership as opposed to following his orders.

While it is true that some halting half steps toward civil-military collaboration have recently taken place, it is equally true that these have been feeble and perhaps reluctant. For example, the Defense Department recently offered to partner with State and USAID more closely on Afghan projects and asked those departments to send sufficient numbers to fill the positions identified. As it happened, the response was much less than had been hoped. Only a relative handful of civilians stepped forward to fill these hazardous posts. Thus, the burden of carrying out many tasks that normally would fall to civilians had to be retained by the Defense Department.

The fact that this is so may be due to the innate "stovepiping" administrative structure of executive branch entities that tends to keep departments and agencies at arms' length from one another. Structurally they are vertically integrated, not horizontally integrated. While it is true that some rotational assignments do take place, it is usually at senior levels a few years before an officer retires. And, typically that officer receives only *one* rotation per career. Thus, a foreign service officer may serve an "embedded" tour with a military unit, or a military officer might serve in, say, State's Bureau of African Affairs. But the cross fertilization of *departments* is often pretty thin.[11]

---

[11] A hopeful sign of change is GAO's November 2010 publication of a 58-page study: *National Security: An Overview of Professional Development Activities Intended to Improve Interagency Collaboration.* [GAO-11-08]. GAO identified 225 opportunities open to federal government officials for familiarization "across agency lines" ranging from one-year

Worse, talented civil and military officers can be reluctant to spend a year on rotation fearing, and often rightly so, that they will fall behind their contemporaries for promotion. Hence, many qualified officers avoid or turn down assignments in other departments. Then, when the next crisis arises, the cost to the American people is that the administration throws together a jumble of senior officials in a task force to solve the problem. These senior officials often do not know one another, are unacquainted with the cultures (or even charters) of other departments, and are nearly clueless about each other's strengths and weaknesses.

Moreover, "stovepiping" maintains a vertical career track in one department or even a subunit of a department, thereby producing officers who might be highly skilled or knowledgeable in some narrow field, but virtually ignorant of what lies outside the stovepipe. Consider the fate of specialists who spent their entire careers gaining expertise on aspects of Soviet defense policy only to watch those specialties become virtually superfluous following the demise of the Soviet Union. Yet the federal career management system tends to penalize "generalists" having broad experience in many areas. This is particular true of uniformed personnel in the Defense Department who are "tracked" for almost formulaic assignments. Officers risk non-selection for promotion if they deviate from the prescribed path.

On top of this, there are further complications regarding budgets and staffing, "turf" (responsibilities for various functions), personal ambitions and animosities, and the all-too-human desire to be a prima donna rather than simply a loyal member of the choir. The Roman historian Tacitus mused that: "The desire for glory clings even to the best men longer than any other passion."

But there are also serious flaws on the Legislative side of the ledger.

Perhaps the most serious flaw is the obvious one enunciated so clearly by former House Speaker, Tip O'Neill: "All politics is local."

Congressmen and women, senators and representatives alike, but especially members of the House of Representatives with their generally small districts and two-year election cycle, are captives of their electorates. While this is *good* theoretically and the way the Founding Fathers intended for

---

rotational assignments to thirty-minute online courses. Author warmly welcomes this excellent initiative but nonetheless remains skeptical of its success. The Federal "culture" of promotions and career advancement tends to hinder or discourage individuals from seeking out-of-home office rotational assignments, however broadening they may be.

the people's representatives to act, this legislative *localism* in Congress tends to have deleterious consequences in the realms of foreign and defense policy. Congressmen are surprisingly often capable of turning their local constituents' wishes into national law.

The most obvious consequence is the tendency of congressmen of both persuasions to push hard for special-interest legislation that ends up in defense spending directed toward certain states and districts. From time to time we read about Congress approving expensive weapon systems that the Pentagon itself has neither requested nor can effectively use.

Apart from being a waste of Americans' tax dollars (to the advantage of a certain congressman, his district, and its voters) this type of legislation casts doubt on the integrity of the American political system and introduces distortions into both military thinking and policy planning. This is analogous to a carpenter who asks for a saw to cut a board, but instead he is given an expensive hammer and then told he must figure out how to cut wood with a tool that is inappropriate for the job. Lots of money has been spent, but whether the carpenter can saw the board remains an open question.

Congress commits other transgressions, as well. One of the most egregious is its habit of weighing in with legislation that is overly restrictive not only on foreign policy, but even on conduct of minor tactical operations. More often than not, such meddling is at the behest of a small, but noisy group of constituents. A good example of this was the lobbying by CISPES (Committee in Solidarity with the People of El Salvador) set up in the United States by the brother of Salvadoran Communist Party chief Shafik Handal and affiliated with the Soviet-controlled World Peace Council. In effect, CISPES was a political action arm of the FMLN operating openly throughout the United States to raise funds and support, and openly lobbying on Capitol Hill.

Congress has frequently passed legislation, often in ignorance of its consequences, that controls U.S. policy toward countries like Wikitania. A hypothetical example of this would be Congressional support for a somewhat uncooperative Wikitanian regime based upon pressure brought by a relatively small vocal group of U.S. voters of Wikitanian heritage. The legislation might require the administration to provide aid to Wikitania with "no strings attached" despite the fact that the government of Wikitania is quite friendly with a larger power having interests inimical to those of the United States. Bound by this restrictive legislation, the administration has no choice but to modify both its policy and strategy *in the entire region* to ensure compliance with Congressional mandates. The author is well acquainted with a real-world case like this from the 1990s.

There are even times when Congress will pass legislation demanding immediate social or political changes in lands like Wikitania that are at sharp variance with local cultural practices. (Never mind that such legislation, however well intended by its sponsors, smacks of imperialism in the eyes of the Wikitanians . . . and much of the rest of the world.) While couched as promoting reform, these measures merely stir resentment and actually retard changes that are more likely to come about over time through education and economic change. Yet Congress, in its infinite wisdom, has to have a law on the books, probably to placate some noisy domestic pressure group.

On one hand, Congress is right to set limits and ensure that public monies are spent wisely. On the other hand, it has no business interfering in the administration of foreign policy or prescribing to military commanders how to execute their duties. Article I of the Constitution specifically gives power to the Congress to declare war (often violated by the executive) and gives the Senate the power to ratify treaties. However, the *conduct* of foreign policy and military duties are executive branch duties. Prudent oversight is one thing; interference is quite another.

And yet, during the 1950s we regularly heard braying from senators and representatives influenced by the China Lobby, a disparate collection of people, Chinese and American, who worked to influence the United States to favor the Nationalist regime of Chiang Kai-shek and in opposition to the Chinese communists. The "Who Lost China" syndrome hamstrung American policy for nearly two decades, and ruined many lives and careers along the way. When backed by zealots such as Senator Joseph McCarthy all sense of balance and rationality was lost in political Washington. Some congressmen sought to blame defeatists and Communists in the State Department, pilloried "Old China Hands" who had sacrificed their careers trying to educate Congress to reality, and even impugned the character of George C. Marshall. As we have seen in an earlier chapter, the fact of the matter is that despite U.S. advice to pursue meaningful reform it was the

Chinese Nationalist Party that *lost* China, not Communists in the State or Defense departments. Yet for years irresponsible outbursts on Capitol Hill made it difficult if not impossible to formulate a rational China policy.

We may ruminate about whether our present elected representatives have been any more thoughtful and moderate than some of their Cold War predecessors in their pronouncements on contemporary foreign affairs.

Some of the very same senators and representatives who place local constituent interests above those of the nation as a whole rise to very senior positions through longevity. These denizens then have power to pigeonhole requested legislation or speedily pass bills inimical to national interests. Moreover, Article I of the Constitution requires confirmation by the Senate of senior presidential appointments, including all ambassadors, cabinet-level appointees, generals and admirals. This check on executive-branch power is wise. However, the danger in this check is that it presents the very real possibility that appointments may go to those who curry favor in the Hart or Russell Senate Office Buildings, rather than those who might be better qualified for top-level appointive positions. One wonders whether today our Senate would confirm such politically "checkered" officers as George Patton, Billy Mitchell, or Ulysses Grant.

It should be noted that much of the day-to-day work on Capitol Hill is done by members of a congressman's personal staff. Although there are some talented and knowledgeable staff members, especially on the House and Senate permanent staffs, the majority of personal staff members are young college graduates, often from the Member's home district, who can be woefully deficient in their basic knowledge of history and geography, and even the basic functioning of the federal government. And yet, these staffers—on Capitol Hill for a year or two to build their resumes—often are responsible for gathering research materials on foreign issues, preparing a member's remarks, and for carrying the member's views to executive branch departments and agencies. If Hill staffers lack basic knowledge of geography and world history, it follows that their advice and staff work will reflect that ignorance.

One great tragedy of the contemporary American political scene is the trend toward polarization. This polarized atmosphere prizes heated slogans and strident, empty rhetoric over thoughtful study, and desire to reach consensus on tough problems. Both sides of the aisle are guilty of this tendency.

It appears as though playing political gotcha is more important to our legislators than reaching sensible, practical solutions to problems overseas, or, for that matter, domestic problems. The American voter is reacting to this empty posturing either by dropping out of the electoral system entirely or by casting protest ballots for contrarian politicians.

We are also periodically treated to *forgetful* congressmen, especially those who were the authors of foolish policies, now discredited, or those who find themselves in court on felony charges. There is no excuse for a legislator to suffer a case of *political amnesia* when called to account for his actions on any public matter, nor does any government official have the right to be wrong in his facts or his conduct. Public officials who use unsupportable assumptions to *prove* foregone conclusions, or the power of their position for personal advancement should be removed. Honor and integrity should be the unquestioned hallmarks of public service.

From the sidelines it is painful to watch the world's premier democracy put its bombast, foolishness, and prejudices on global display.

And now we come to military myopia, a condition that only grows worse with seniority.

MILITARY MYOPIA

There is an old joke in military circles that has probably been around for centuries: We are always preparing to fight the *last* war.

Unfortunately, this joke is not purely jest. There is a tendency among the world's militaries to study the most recent successful campaigns in the expectation that future campaigns will merely be iterations of the recent past.

While it is useful to study past conflicts to gather useful insights into what factors or actions led to victory or defeat in particular campaigns, the danger is in attempting to superimpose past models uncritically on present situations. And yet, this is often how we develop our doctrine and train our new lieutenants. In our military schooling system, we pay almost reverential respect to advanced technology while ignoring the "soft power" elements noted by Liddell Hart, Delbrueck, and even Clausewitz. Perhaps this is because our military, especially the U.S. Navy and Air Force, believes that technology was central to victory in World War II and will therefore be central to winning any future campaign.

There is always the danger of learning the wrong lesson from the past. The experience of trench warfare of World War I convinced the French (and perhaps to some extent the British, as well) that strong defensive lines were required: hence, the ponderous and very expensive Maginot Line. As every lieutenant knows, in 1940 the Germans outflanked this military white elephant, sliced through the British and French forces in Belgium, and achieved the defeat of France and the expulsion of the British from the European continent in a matter of weeks. Thus, the *lessons learned* by the World War I victors had undone the French army and republic, and shattered British strategic plans in the opening phases of World War II.

The Department of Defense has its own share of shortcomings, some hidden, others fully acknowledged, as it gropes forward into the twenty-first century. Some of these are products of the American people, on whom it draws for officer and enlisted personnel, and some may be laid at the feet of the legislative and the executive branches. But sadly, other problems are of the Pentagon's own making:[12]

- An overly Jominian focus in its training and doctrine (Jominian ideas may apply to naval and air forces, but do not apply to ground forces, especially in dealing with insurgency, as Jomini himself would freely admit).
- No real understanding of insurgency in more than a narrow military sense, usually emphasizing particular weapons and tactics.
- Professional military education lax in terms of understanding global politics, foreign languages, and cultural issues.
- Failure to understand a changing world and the military's place in it, especially the advantages to be gained by anticipating problem areas and developing means to prevent them from becoming crises.
- Wedded to ultra-costly high tech weapons as the ultimate solution to all problems.

[12] Former Defense Secretary Robert M. Gates himself touches on many of these issues in his *Foreign Affairs* articles titled "A Balanced Strategy" and "Helping Others Defend Themselves." Author applauds these insights but holds the opinion that they do not go far enough toward rooting out basic problems.

- Sharply divided at the top (and downward) in officer ranks over doctrine.
- Unprepared to comprehend or deal with political or political-military issues, and often unfamiliar with the charters and "culture" of other government agencies.

John Nagl, in his insightful book *Learning to Eat Soup with a Knife*, raised the question of whether the U.S. Army is a learning institution or if past successes and established doctrine had made it a sclerotic bureaucracy. The jury may still be out on this question, though I must confess my personal doubts about the Army's willingness or ability to learn from its own mistakes, much less from the mistakes of others.

Although from time to time in history, the "tried and true" has carried the day militarily, more often than not it was an unconventional thinker, using an unconventional approach, who swept his enemies before him and won new empires as the reward of his boldness.

Nobel laureate economist Friedrich von Hayek observed that "Never will a man penetrate deeper into error than when he is continuing on a road that has led him to great success."[13] There is wisdom here for both our political and military leaders. Certainly there is a message here for the formulators of U.S. Army doctrine. Let the record show that the United States had never lost a war until it foolishly attempted to apply conventional doctrine to an unconventional war in Vietnam. Of course, blame also lies with the policy community for its decision to order the military to intervene.

There are glimmers of hope. Acting together, the U.S. Army and Marine Corps created and published *Counterinsurgency* (FM 3-24) . We have a handful of brilliant scholars such as Dr. Nagl and a few others to thank for this field manual. But the existence of the FM does not by any means indicate that the army has had a Damascus Road-like doctrinal conversion. Many generals wedded to the old doctrine of firepower, massive force, and high technology still think these are essential keys to victory in any war. This group of Jominians scornfully brands advocates of a "soft power" approach to likely future conflicts as "COINdinistas." It is clear to

---

[13] Hayek, p. 175.

me from this pejorative term that the U.S. Army is, regrettably, not a learning institution.

There is another disturbing tendency that retards learning. It is often the case that higher-level military officers flail about looking for any sign of *reportable* success. This results in a bad habit of trumpeting the positive while muting the negative. *We have to show progress!* insist most senior commanders and staff officers. Only a few officers have the moral and intellectual courage to own up forthrightly to failure or tell their policy-community bosses that the emperor is naked, that their strategy is unrealistic and unattainable. After all, such effrontery may reflect adversely on an individual's next performance appraisal . . . and prove lethal to his career. The Chinese have a saying for this all-too-human failing: *Success has a hundred fathers, but Failure is an orphan.*

The Pentagon's seeming addiction to buying high-tech weaponry keeps the Defense Department budget growing, which is good news for manufacturers of costly new weapon systems, but not necessarily good news for our boots on the ground. A relative pittance is put aside for training and development in the field of low intensity conflict or for the training of foreign militaries from Africa and Asia who are the first responders in dealing with local disturbances.[14] (We have yet to lose a soldier or marine to enemies employing state-of-the-art weaponry such as F-35s, but we seem to be losing a lot of courageous young Americans to low-tech roadside bombs and indirect fire weapons used by fighters whom the shock-and-awe crowd contemptuously regard as "rag heads"). Let us be mindful that Lt. Todd Weaver, to whose memory this volume is dedicated, was killed by a jerry-rigged roadside bomb put down by hand, not a laser-guided missile fired by a computer algorithm.

To the extent we are able to keep our secrets secret, technology will continue to aid our deterrent of technologically advanced countries where that is needed. But are technologically-advanced nations our real, current threats? I would venture to say that the Russians and Chinese are respectable regional military powers, but neither poses an existential threat to the United States. Rather, the Russians are more interested in peddling oil and gas to the West, and the Chinese are now so rich that they could buy con-

[14] See Robert M. Gates, op. cit.

trolling shares in half the corporations in America if they wished to do so. What would be the point for the Chinese of attacking a country that they hold heavily in their debt?[15] Why would the Russians attack Western Europe, the main source of their hard currency income?

The Pentagon would be wiser to plan for small wars in the Third World than for a bolt from the blue from a G-20 country that will never come. What is the point of wearing a suit of armor if the threat is likely to be fire ants crawling up your pants leg?

WARS OF BELIEF

Apart from the three pillars of people, governments, and armies there is a fourth key issue that was new when Clausewitz was a young officer in the Prussian army: the role of ideology in battle. Although Jomini was completely oblivious to ideology, Clausewitz perceived it but arguably did not comprehend its enormous power. Only in the past century have ideology and influence operations in armed conflict come into their own. Unfortunately, the American people appear not to take seriously the importance of this new factor, even in conventional military operations, and one suspects that the Congress and Defense Department are still not paying close attention to ideology's powerful role in insurgencies.

Ideology and influence are at the core of insurgency. We ignore these factors at our peril.

In the early twenty-first century we live in an information age where real-time news from around the globe is at our fingertips. We live in an age in which millions of people even in the poorer nations are literate and many are at least somewhat politically aware. We live in an age in which millions of people routinely carry cell phones and many have laptop computers. Events taking place half a world away can be flashed in minutes to hundreds of millions of these listeners and viewers in all parts of the globe.

Today we also live in an age of ideology, buttressed by the telecommunications revolution, in which large masses of humanity are manipulated

---

[15] According to data released on 16 November 2010 by the Federal Reserve Board and U.S. Treasury, the People's Republic of China held $883.5 billion of Treasury bonds and notes of various kinds. If PRC-controlled Hong Kong, which holds a further $135.9 billion in U.S. government securities, is added the total amount of U.S. government paper held is $1.019 trillion. These figures do not include U.S. private investment in China or private debt. See http://www.ustreas.gov/tic/mfh.txt for complete statistics.

and motivated by carefully packaged, systematized beliefs. Strictly speaking, this is not new, but what is new concerning ideology is that mass media make it possible to mobilize and direct human effort on a scale without historical precedent.

Because the times are different, so too are the issues . . . and the politics that follow from them. As we discussed in Chapter 1, today part of the planet is blessed with highly advanced societies with high living standards and complex economies. At the same time, the other half remains either at the level of traditional agrarian societies or somewhere along the line in the painful process of modernization. In these lands societies have one foot in the Age of Information and the other squarely planted in illiteracy. As we discussed, these *torn* countries—split by ethnic divisions, disparities in wealth and poverty, differences in social advancement, and many other divisive factors—are the settings for the warfare of the coming century. These will increasingly be "wars of belief."

Wars of the eighteenth century were fought almost exclusively by professional soldiers who were recruited, trained, and maintained by monarchs for the express purpose of fighting against other professional soldiers. Somewhat like the gladiators of ancient Rome, these fighting men were set against one another in contests that were decided on the basis of the relative physical strengths of the contenders, the nature of their armament, and their comparative skill at employing strength and weaponry to overwhelm the foe. Ideology played little, if any, role among the soldiers fighting for the Duke of Marlborough, Conde, Prince Eugene of Savoy, Turenne, or Frederick the Great.[16] Indeed, many professional military officers "changed employers" based on salary and benefits, not ideology. It was nothing personal, just business.

Only in the second half of the 1700s was the new factor of ideology introduced into warfare. The American Revolution with its Minutemen morphing into Continentals, followed by the Wars of the French Revolution, marked a departure from the old paradigm. For the first time, civilians motivated by ideology battled military professionals. And, in France, they were drafted civilians. The French *levee en masse* brought in hundreds of

---

[16] It is easy to understand how Jomini reached many of his conclusions about the nature of war if he drew his principles of war from observing or studying the campaigns of marionette armies of the eighteenth century.

men of varying physical strength and skill at arms who were thrown against the armies of Prussia, Austria, Holland, and several German states such as Brunswick and Hanover. The old armies were far better trained and equipped than were the revolutionary French. But the men of the French armies under Lazare Carnot were fired by the strength of their belief in the ideals of the French Revolution.

> A peculiar mixture of patriotism and terror was transforming armed mobs into soldiers. What had happened was mainly due to the incessant efforts of one man: Lazare Carnot, a stern, uncompromising soldier of the old regime, who amalgamated the raw conscripts with the remnants of the old professional army, and brought discipline to enthusiastic hordes of Frenchmen filled with the valor of ignorance.—DuPuy and DuPuy, *Encyclopedia of Military History*

Without overdrawing the point about the "valor of ignorance," the fact remains that the new French armies had a weapon that the old European armies lacked: belief in a *cause* that carried them forward despite inadequacies of training or equipment. This was clearly a joining of political ideals and goals with military means. Perhaps it was this spectacle that caused Karl von Clausewitz to begin his speculations about the psychology of battle.

Twenty years earlier, the American rebels had experienced something similar in the way that public opinion had been drawn into the conflict and ultimately proved decisive. There are striking parallels between what Carnot did for the French and what Baron von Steuben did for the American insurgents. Certainly both men brought discipline and basic military training to a rabble in arms. But there are also striking parallels between the psychological power of the American Declaration of Independence and the French Declaration of the Rights of Man that inspired and motivated ordinary men to achieve extraordinary things against far more powerful enemies. American Patriot foot soldiers often fought without pay for an idea they thought valuable whereas their professional British opponents fought for three pence a day.

The preindustrial societies, at least those before the *levee en masse*, produced smaller, more professional armies and navies of longer-term soldiers and sailors, commanded by a professional officer class. Logistics shaped capabilities as they always do, but public opinion made citizen armies possible during the American and French revolutions. Arguably, when the Declaration of Independence was first read to the proto-citizens of a new republic struggling to free itself of royal and colonial rule, public opinion entered the battlefield: *the population was mobilized.* There can be no doubt that French public opinion—fired by *Liberte, Egalite, Fraternite*—marched with Napoleon's army as it trounced the professional armies of Europe.[17]

Napoleon himself observed that: "Power is based on opinion. What is a government not supported by opinion? Nothing."[18]

Ideology, that is, systematized beliefs, continued to play a role in the European and American conflicts of the later nineteenth century. Clearly, the Union Armies of the American Civil War were motivated by the Cause and political message of "Preserving the Union" and, following the Emancipation Proclamation of late 1862, that of "Freeing the Slaves." These goals were reinforced by books such as *Uncle Tom's Cabin* and songs like "The Battle Hymn of the Republic."[19] True, blood and iron also were required to realize American political goals in 1865. But beliefs moved the public and its armies.

Likewise, *Blut und Eisen* were required to realize the popular German goal of national unification in 1871. Blood and iron were *not* unrelated to the political and psychological forces that moved the armies of the industrial age. Rather, they were merely the physical manifestations and tools of ideology.

---

[17] In this regard, it is interesting to note that Napoleon's Grande Armee—a polyglot army made up only partly of French soldiers, but in large part by levies from subject peoples—was turned back in 1812 by a peasant army under Alexander I, though admittedly with great help from Generals Snow and Mud and Napoleon's flawed strategy. Man for man, the French were better equipped, better trained, and better led than their Tsarist opponents. It is telling that Hitler and his generals learned nothing from this tragic example and ended up repeating it.

[18] Quoted in Ellul, p. 123.

[19] The Emancipation Proclamation was welcomed by many thousands of Northerners, especially in New England and, to a lesser extent, in the Middle Atlantic states as a holy cause worthy of dying for. Indeed, the words of "The Battle Hymn of the Republic" (one of the most masterful pieces of political propaganda ever written) caused Northern congregations and Union battalions alike to sing: "as He died to make men holy, let us die to make men free . . . " After all, who beyond the occasional atheist could argue against fighting for a holy cause?

In his speech before the House of Commons in May 1901, Winston Churchill forecast the scope of the wars to come in the twentieth century and the role that ideology would play:

> I have frequently been astonished since I have been in this House to hear with what composure and how glibly Members, and even Ministers, talk of a European war. I will not expatiate on the horrors of war, but there has been a great change which the House should not omit to notice. In former days, when wars arose from individual causes, from the policy of a Minister or the passion of a King, when they were fought by small regular armies of professional soldiers, and when their course was retarded by the difficulties of communication and supply, and often suspended by the winter season, it was possible to limit the liabilities of the combatants. But now, when mighty populations are impelled on each other, each individual severally embittered and inflamed—when the resources of science and civilization sweep away everything that might mitigate their fury—a European war can only end in the ruin of the vanquished and the scarcely less fatal commercial dislocation and exhaustion of the conquerors.
>
> Democracy is more vindictive than Cabinets. The wars of peoples will be more terrible than those of kings.[20]

The role of ideology in battle reached new proportions with the rise of fascism in Italy and Germany, and Communism in the Soviet Union during the twentieth century. While students of World War II give much attention to comparisons of tanks, aircraft, artillery, and other weapons, the power of ideology and politics goes almost unnoticed. To be sure, the two world wars were fought with massive, fully industrialized armies along conventional Clausewitzian lines. But they nonetheless were also *people's wars* in the sense that millions of citizens of all belligerent nations were engaged through the power of ideology in industrial production, agriculture, scientific research, and a host of other vital supporting functions in addition to mortal combat on the battlefield. To a great extent, this stupendous activity was made possible because of belief in a *Cause*.

The landings at Normandy and the defeat of the German Reich could

[20] Churchill, Speech on Army Reform before the House of Commons, 15 May 1901.

not have taken place had it not been for factories, forests, and farmlands in the Allied countries: the material elements of strategy. But of greater importance were the people who had a burning desire to destroy Nazism and Hitler. Let us not forget that George C. Marshall himself asked filmmaker Frank Capra to produce the *Why We Fight* series of motion pictures as a means of mobilizing millions of Americans. This was the vital moral element of strategy.

Our allies and enemies also used the mass media of film to mobilize huge masses of people. Hitler had a superb propagandist in Leni Riefenstahl. Josef Stalin had Sergei Eisenstein, another master filmmaker. We also must be mindful of the soaring speeches of Winston Churchill, whose words time and again rallied the British people to fight on. We should never ignore or belittle the power of the spoken word or the stark image to mobilize millions of people to act in desperate times. They continue to do so today.

We tend to forget that varieties of ideology also played roles, not only in a number of wartime resistance movements in Nazi-occupied Europe, but in stirring the colonial world as well. Communist ideology motivated millions of Chinese and Vietnamese to take up arms not only against Japanese aggressors, but in the cause of national self-determination. Nationalist ideology swept through Algeria, Cyprus, and other lands such as India. The point is that belief systems of varying types brought about political change.

From the late-1960s a new ideology has taken its place among the old: extremist, reactionary Islam. Again, strictly speaking, this extremist brand of Islam is not new. Religious thinkers such as Ibn Taymiyya (AD 1263–1328) provided the theological underpinnings of what emerged in the twentieth century in the writing of Said Qutb and others as a coherent ideology possessing both an intellectual structure and an operational plan. It should be understood clearly by policymakers and military officers that so-called radical Islam[21] is a powerful ideology capable of motivating populations. It is not a journalist's fanciful description of a few misguided religious fanatics acting in an uncoordinated manner.[22]

---

[21] Reader is invited to read Annex B on Islam.

[22] Author notes that the term "radical" Islam is a gross misnomer, probably fostered by journalists. In point of fact, the ideology of the extremists is *reactionary*, not radical, as it strives to restore society to a "Golden Age" of the distant past, not to destroy old religious

It is a fatal mistake for America and the West to underestimate the power of this old-new ideology. The reason for this is that increasing numbers of Muslims, disenchanted with the failure of secular Arab socialism, and alienated by Western cultural and political models, look to Islam for guidance and material help. Kaplan mentions the following stark example:

> Egypt could be where climactic upheaval—to say nothing of the more immediate threat of increasing population—will incite religious upheaval in truly biblical fashion. Natural catastrophes, such as the October 1992, Cairo earthquake, in which the government failed to deliver relief aid and slum residents were in many instances helped by their local mosques, can only strengthen the position of Islamic factions.[23]

What gives ideology of any stripe its power is the Age of Information. No other age has offered near instantaneous communication with the entire globe. The internet has even greater revolutionary potential than did Gutenberg's printing press of five centuries ago. Like the printing press, used to influence and motivate American colonists and French revolutionaries in the eighteenth century, and radio and film, widely exploited by German Nazis and Russian Communists in the twentieth, the internet is being skillfully used by Islamic extremists to promote their ideology to audiences worldwide today in the twenty-first.

Dr. John LeBeau observed that: "Modern communications will permit geographically distant insurgencies to feel somehow united, and may eventually develop into a means of coordinating diverse groups and individuals."[24]

Of special interest is the role that modern communications have come to play in bringing together what are called "flash mobs." While these mobs can be criminal as well as frivolous in their intent and their actions, it is only a matter of time before flash mobs assume distinctly political roles

---

beliefs and practices. The sooner that the extremists' true reactionary political coloration is recognized, the sooner it will be that the policy community in Western and Islamic countries can respond appropriately.

[23] Kaplan, p. 75.

[24] LeBeau, p. 162.

and contribute to a vulnerable regime's overthrow. The Egyptians in Tahrir Square can be considered a particularly persistent flash mob.

The question arises how any ideology can influence masses of people. Certainly it is reasonable to ask what relevance reactionary Islamic extremism (or Communism, for that matter) has with the matter of instability and insurgency. Decades ago, the answer to this question was offered by V. I. Lenin when he observed:

> The art of any propagandist and agitator consists in his ability to find the best means of influencing any given audience, by presenting a definite truth, in such a way as to make it most convincing, most easy to digest, most graphic, and most strongly impressive.[25]

An ideology influences the people to act because it offers an explanation for the political, social and economic ills that exist, and a prescription for correcting those ills. Jacques Ellul, a former Marxist who became a French Catholic intellectual, states that propaganda "succeeds primarily because it corresponds exactly to a need of the masses." [26] Put a negative way, if the target audiences addressed by a propagandist had no perception of political or social inequities in need of change, it is unlikely that violent prescriptions aimed at changing the social order will find a hearing. Imams who are agents of change, however, will be sure to focus the attention of the faithful on their societies' most serious and widespread problems. And they will not hesitate to prescribe a cure for those ills.

The implication in this is that peoples who are striving for change will readily find at hand an ideology that provides both the justification for change, and the means. The writings of Marx and Lenin provided the political and operational roadmap for social change for much of the twentieth century, just as Enlightenment ideas served as guideposts in the eighteenth and early nineteenth centuries. Perhaps extremist Islamic theory has replaced Marxism as the talisman for change in the twenty-first century.

It is ironic that whereas Marx and earlier thinkers put forward a vision of radical change of society from something old to something *new*, the Islamists offer a vision of change hearkening back to something *centuries*

---

[25] Lenin as translated by Dora Cox in *Lenin Collected Works*, p. 41.

[26] Ellul, p. 146.

old. What the extremists actually offer is a sterile pathway to a Golden Past that probably never existed and, in any case, offers the people only a political dead end; a reactionary's ticket to nowhere.[27]

Our ignorance and myopia prevent us from seeing the reality that is before us.

People grasping for a better life, or the redress of perceived ills, look to ideology to find 'something practical that works' to achieve their goals.

At one time Marxism-Leninism and its variants appeared to millions of people to be the practical means to national self-determination and material progress until that ideology proved itself a dead end in the 1980s. In the Arabic speaking world, secular ideologies loosely based on Arab socialism attracted supporters for decades after Nasser's overthrow of King Farouk in 1952. Secular non-Communist socialist ideologies covered with a thin veneer of Islam have now been discredited. Today, the new compass for social and political change in the Islamic world appears to be a shrill, violent reactionary ideology based upon Sunni Islam. At this writing, neither the West nor its allies in the Islamic world have any response, much less a credible theological alternative to this virulent ideology.

And yet, in false economy the U.S. Government has shut down a once robust effort to reach out and influence millions of people in other lands. Although the Voice of America continues to broadcast, the U.S. Information Agency (USIA) was shut down in 1999, ostensibly as a cost cutting measure. USIA libraries in foreign capitals and other major cities were closed and public diplomacy is just another additional duty for overworked embassy staffers. We can imagine how much time and effort is devoted to influencing foreign audiences by harried foreign service officers who already have a full plate of duties and little training in public relations. Around the world America has left the grass-roots ideological debates to its extremist opponents.

At the very time when Islamist extremist ideology is gaining credibility in many parts of the world, the United States stands virtually mute. Not only has no serious thought been given to presenting a credible alternative

---

[27] Colonel Newsham observes (correctly in author's view) that where Islamist extremists have actually held power and governed for a time as in Iraq's Anbar province, Buner and Swat in Pakistan, or Afghanistan under the Taliban, they invariably alienate the people through their harsh, dogmatic, regressive rule.

view, or set of alternatives, but we now lack the means to project any views at all to a world grown skeptical of American political goals and doubtful even of our willingness or capability to carry out the policies we profess to hold.

It is time now for us to revisit the Third World.

THE COMPASS

Recently, a friend of mine visited Ethiopia. While seeing the sights and meeting with many people in that country, my friend reported the following:

> President Obama is immensely popular in Ethiopia and Kenya, maybe elsewhere in Africa as well. But I heard one dissenting opinion: "He said he was going to help Africa! He said he would send aid to Ethiopia! Where is the aid?" The truth is that he [President Obama] probably never specifically promised increased aid to Ethiopia. But what many Ethiopians don't seem to know is that tons of U.S. foreign aid ARE coming into Ethiopia. An American importer that we met said that the problem is allocation and distribution once the stuff is unloaded inside Ethiopia. Because of politics and corruption, mountains of it are stockpiled in one area while another area is starving. And furthermore, the information about U.S. aid doesn't seem to get out to the public very well.[28]

Not only has the United States failed to educate its own people about what it is doing in Asia or Africa, it has virtually no capability to publicize to Africans and Asians the nature and scope of aid that we provide. By so doing, we set ourselves up for antiforeign resentment at home and anti-American frustration abroad, both of which result from ignorance. In effect, American taxpayers are being asked to pay for millions of dollars' worth of aid for which the United States does not receive credit that is rightly due, but instead sometimes earns the rage of foreign populations believing that somehow Uncle Sam has hoodwinked them.

It is an old and tragic song that millions of dollars' worth of food and

---

[28] Note to author from Alan Bunner, 5 October 2010.

other aid has been stolen by corrupt officials and sold to the poor on the black market. It is also true that other U.S. aid has been wasted, lost to spoilage and other damage. On some occasions American aid has been false-flagged by Communists or Islamic extremists and then distributed as if this critical material had come from them, not from the American people.

What is required is a more tightly controlled program of foreign aid assistance that is restricted to governments and agencies that administer U.S. assistance with minimal corruption and waste. We must also have robust, carefully targeted aid campaigns that leave no doubt in local minds about the nature and scope of American assistance. Where local administrative structures cannot guarantee that U.S. aid will go unhindered to those for whom it is intended, our assistance should be coldly and abruptly terminated. We should be mindful of Theodore Roosevelt's advice a century ago: "There is only one quality worse than hardness of heart, and that is softness of head."

While terminating assistance may be draconian, and I would be the first to admit that unhappy citizens already victimized by corrupt regimes will suffer, it must also be clear that to provide aid that merely fuels corruption and repression actually works against American interests. It perpetuates injustice.

There are those who hold the view that America *has no choice* but to tolerate theft and corruption for geopolitical reasons. If Wikitanian officials are diverting our aid into their own pockets, it does no good to soft-pedal their knavery in the vain hope that these same officials will aid their own people, or even support us when we need it. This is pure wishful thinking. Indeed, I would go so far as to say that uncontrolled humanitarian assistance is not only feckless expense and wasted effort on our part, but *inhumane.* Such assistance does not substantially help the neediest people, though it can prop up corrupt elites who *rightly* should be overthrown. If we are to be true to the ideals of our Founding Fathers, we must always be on the side of the people. We should not help thugs in evening dress keep themselves in power at the expense of the misery of their own people.

Our compass must always be our ideals, not reliance on our wealth or upon our great military power. The simple truth of our ideals is enshrined in the Declaration itself:

> We hold these truths to be self-evident, that all men are created equal; that they are endowed by their Creator with certain unalienable rights; that among these, are life, liberty, and the pursuit of happiness. *That, to secure these rights, governments are instituted among men, deriving their just powers from the consent of the governed; that, whenever any form of government becomes destructive of these ends, it is the right of the people to alter or abolish it, and to institute a new government*[emphasis added] laying its foundation on such principles, and organizing its powers in such form, as to them shall seem most likely to effect their safety and happiness.

Have we forgotten our core beliefs and somehow lost our way?

THE PRICE OF IGNORANCE

The brilliant former president of Harvard, Derek Bok, once responded to a critic by saying, "If you think education is expensive, try ignorance."

We might take Bok's observation a step further. When education is teamed with real world experience and turned to good purpose, it brings great reward to the individual and his nation. It continually produces handsome dividends on its "investment." However, the price of ignorance is beyond all calculation. Its cost has no limits. Far from yielding a handsome return, ignorance in our thoughts, words, and especially deeds, brings only infinite loss. Moreover, the terrible consequences of acting in ignorance remain with us, and our descendents, for all recorded history. For ignorance combined with arrogance is a sure recipe for catastrophe.

The German philosopher, Johann Wolfgang von Goethe, observed that: "There is nothing more frightening than to see ignorance in action." Active ignorance manifests itself in arrogance, stupidity, blundering, and injury. Better that the ignorant do nothing.

What we observed abroad in bygone decades was ignorance that begged for solutions that fascism and later Communism pretended to supply. In today's world, it may be that extremist ideologies offer similar pseudo-solutions to problems faced by millions of the world's people, whether or not those people are Muslims. Bigotry, vengeance, and ultimately extremism are the products of ignorant people goaded by tyrants.

The security of a country having a democratic political structure rests on the people's views expressed in open and reasonably intelligent, informed discussion; thoughtful and far-seeing legislation; and ultimately wise choices at the ballot box. Without an educated and mentally alert electorate, wise choices are impossible. If the voters are ignorant, if they are unsure of even the geographical locations of Canada or Mexico, if they are goaded more by passions and slogans than by reflection and thought, it follows that those placed in office will be pretty much the same kind of people as the ignorant voters. The door then will be opened to the same kind of bread-and-circuses charades of the declining Roman republic . . . and worse.

As matters stand, many of the people's elected representatives may be expected only to promote narrow, often self-serving interests. Through legislative processes involving log-rolling and back-scratching they are capable of transforming petty sectarian interests into federal law. Passion, prejudice, and partisanship too often combine to frame or limit flexibility in American policy and strategy. This is another form of ignorance in action.

More than 130 years ago, James A. Garfield observed that it is the American people who are responsible for the quality and character of our legislators:

> Now more than ever before the people are responsible for the character of their Congress. If that body be ignorant, reckless, and corrupt, it is because the people tolerate ignorance, recklessness, and corruption. If it be intelligent, brave, and pure, it is because the people demand these high qualities to represent them in the national legislature. If the next centennial does not find us a great nation it will be because those who represent the enterprise, the culture, and the morality of the nation do not aid in controlling the political forces.[29]

We have examined aspects of Clausewitz's three pillars: the people, government, and military forces, and the factor of ideology. I believe the case has been made that we as a nation are not well prepared for a world that is likely to witness further violent upheavals and small wars as the social and

---

[29] Garfield, pp. 486, 489.

economic conditions mentioned in earlier chapters grow steadily worse. Time will not stand still for us. If we dither at home, we do so at our peril abroad. Shakespeare's King Richard II captured the problem succinctly when he said: "I wasted Time, and now doth Time waste me."[30]

What I hope has been achieved is to call attention to systemic failures at home that contribute to disasters abroad. These failures begin in our school system that generally speaking places little emphasis on subjects once taught as *standards*: geography and world history. As we have seen, our skills base in non-Western languages is paper thin; the number of young people going into programs to study foreign areas and non-Western cultures is relatively small; and public comprehension of global political, economic, and social conditions is sketchy at best. Our citizens are nearly blind when it comes to perceiving our interests abroad.

There is much that needs improvement and correction if we are to maintain leadership of our global community. If we Americans are unwilling or unable to change with the times, and instead show ourselves unworthy of thoughtful and compassionate global leadership, we may rest assured that leadership will pass to others who will gladly fill the vacuum. But there is no guarantee that our rivals will show either much thoughtfulness or compassion.

Or wisdom.

---

[30] Shakespeare, *Richard II*, Act V.

CHAPTER 9

WISE COUNSELS AT HOME

Slightly more than two thousand years ago, the Roman orator Marcus Tullius Cicero observed: "For arms are of little value in the field unless there is wise counsel at home."

The United States today finds itself, quite possibly, with the most powerful armed forces in history. And yet, as events have shown in Vietnam a generation ago, in Somalia two decades ago, and most recently in attempting to defeat insurgencies in Afghanistan and Iraq, America's incredibly powerful armed forces have proved less than entirely useful and, in some respects, flatly counterproductive in achieving desired policy objectives. Without wise counsels at home they are of little value to us abroad.

QUO VADIS

American administrations and probably the American people, as well, feel frustrated and bewildered by the fact that the American defense establishment, having consumed hundreds of billions of tax dollars, cannot quickly vanquish "primitive" enemies who have no air force or navy, and who use only infantry weapons and ancient techniques. Despite the astronomical investment by the American people in national security, the defense establishment has shown itself less than fully competent at dealing with low intensity conflict: insurgency.

The answer to this failure is fairly straightforward: the policy community and the defense establishment have forgotten the very heart of warfare.

It was simply stated long ago by Clausewitz: war is the *continuation* of political relations "by other means." The seduction of high technology has brought about a decidedly Jominian tilt in our thinking about military problems. From our military journals and other publications, it appears that we think about war as a challenge that can be solved through ever more advanced technology, ever more accurate and lethal firepower, not as a political problem having both a political cause and a political resolution.[1]

It is clear that as far as insurgency is concerned the Pentagon and policy community will fail again in the future if they refuse to come to grips with the reality of the Third World.[2] Insurgencies are fought because the aspirations of ordinary people have been frustrated; this is "down in the weeds" politics. Instead of thinking hard about this reality, Pentagon chiefs have spent trillions of dollars—truly mind-boggling sums—preparing for computerized wars that likely will never take place. In theoretical warfare, far removed from the harsh realities of the real world, space age weapons technology sweeps aside all enemies and techno-victories are registered on computer screens. The political roots of war have been forgotten.

In his obituary, William J. Lederer, career naval officer, author of *The Ugly American*, and American patriot, was quoted as follows:

> It pains me to say this: Our military leaders and CIA agents and diplomats are still ignorant about the countries they're assigned to. We're still fighting poor, hungry, angry people with bombs and tanks when what they would really respond to is food and water, good roads, health care, and a little respect for their religion and culture.[3]

---

[1] It is all too easy to conclude that administrations of both persuasions view defense spending not as a means of achieving viable political goals abroad, but as the means to keep defense industries humming in congressional districts at home, engineers and technicians employed, shareholders happy, and incumbents in office. From the perspective of the Pentagon's inner circle, the problem of defense has become a matter of winning interservice competitions over budgets and turf, creation of new flag-officer billets, and developing *new* programs that ensure lucrative postretirement jobs within the galaxy of defense contractors.

[2] Again, the reader is referred to Secretary Gates's essays, op. cit.

[3] William J. Lederer, quoted in his *Washington Post*, obituary, 10 January 2010, p. C-6

While food and water, good roads, health care, and especially genuine respect for the culture and beliefs of others are vital to success, there is one thing more. That is the need for America to reassess its role in the world and determine what will be required in the coming century if we are to have the kind of world we'd like our children to inherit.

WHAT IS TO BE DONE

As we address the future, the first and most fundamental step is for policymakers to step back from business as usual and take a very hard, very detailed look at that other half of the world that lives in squalor and tyranny, and that yearns for a better life. It is only by doing serious in-depth analytical work on countries in the Lower Half that the policy and military communities have even a chance of anticipating trouble spots well before they become trouble spots. If we are blind to the dimensions of the developing crises in many lands of the other half, it follows that we will constantly be taken by surprise by upheavals in faraway places, not even understanding what the issues are. As we've seen, by the time that social ills manifest themselves in massive disturbances and acts of terrorism and insurgency, it is usually too late to apply preventive measures that would have earlier forestalled the violence at relatively little cost in blood or treasure.

If U.S. policy aims at a safer, more humane world—and I believe it does—then it follows that we must use our enormous economic and political power wisely to bring about reforms that will ensure that countries now living on the brink evolve peacefully and with a minimum of social upheaval. Frederick W. Lewis, a U.S. Army brigadier general in the early twentieth century, was quoted as saying that: "the time to win a fight is before it starts." A wise man, indeed. We can and should be taking a greater interest in the needs of broad masses of people who, through the worldwide growth of telecommunications, are now well aware of the social ills they suffer and are actively seeking means to redress their grievances. The people and government of the United States must always be on the side of the people, not necessarily on the side of their rulers. Rulers come and go, but the people will always remain.

American policymakers would do well to promote economic and social measures aimed at slowly, but steadily raising the socioeconomic standards of people in Third World lands. The people living in these lands must know, and know clearly, that we Americans are their allies, even if their own rapacious and despotic leaders tempt us with alliances. We do not need clingy, inherently unstable client states run by a handful of plutocrats. They will suck us dry . . . and ultimately collapse. Instead, we need stable, socially progressive and self-sufficient allies like our sister democracies in Asia and Europe.

Clear-headed reasoning, constantly asking ourselves two questions, will keep us on the right track: *What are we trying to do?* and *Are our goals beyond our means?* I admit that sometimes it is difficult for our senior leaders to do what is reasonable rather than what is expedient, but it is imperative that we take a longer view, a more pragmatic view, of our national and global interests.

It is very hard to help downtrodden people lift themselves out of the mire if bombs are going off. This assertion is proven by the difficulties that our governmental agencies, those of our allies, and many nongovernmental agencies experience on a daily basis in Afghanistan. Much better then, that we do what needs to be done well before an insurgent movement supported by angry people begins shooting. If we are unable or unwilling to help effect change peacefully, they will do so violently.

Noted *New York Times* columnist Thomas L. Friedman had it right when he stated: "The only way to even begin to manage this new world is by focusing on . . . nation building . . . helping others restructure their economies and put in place decent non-corrupt government." Detractors might argue that Friedman's view is too idealistic, it's pie in the sky. But my rejoinder is: Have we really tried to pursue this strategy? Apart from Europe and the Far East, have we really given this approach a fair try? You be the judge.

Do I call for vast give-away programs? By no means. George C. Marshall achieved a monumental, world-changing feat through his European Recovery Plan. His plan not only sparked the recovery of Europe's economies that had been flattened and ruined by war, but rekindled hope and optimism, and engendered profound respect for the United States even among vanquished enemies. It paved the way for the triumph of democratic rule even in those countries whose experience of democracy was minimal. What might have been the alternative had we stood by smugly and done nothing? I fear to think what a Soviet-ruled Europe would have meant for the United States or the world.

So, should our strategy be one of waiting for an insurgency to appear and then sending in our massive conventional forces? Or, is it wiser to anticipate an incipient insurgency and, by means of helping build effective national and local governments in time of peace that actually serve the people, preempt the agendas of those who cynically offer promises to the people while fixing chains on their legs?

There is, however, a catch: *the United States must never agree to work with any regime anywhere at any time that adamantly refuses to put its own house in order.* Only when a government steps up to the plate and courageously does what is required, as in the Philippines under Magsaysay or El Salvador under Duarte and Cristiani, can American assistance be of lasting value.

There is great danger if the United States government tries to get out in front of a regime unwilling to take ownership of its own future and conduct *meaningful* programs of reform and development. The temptation of "clientitis," where regime officials happily step to one side and let Uncle Sam do it, is too great. This robs the regime of what remaining nationalist credentials it might claim and it opens the door to corruption and escalation of violence. As the situation worsens, as it inevitably will if the regime does little or nothing for its own people, and we Americans try, in effect, to govern, the United States opens itself to charges of neocolonialism, and risks alienating the people. Also, such an approach has a high probability of costing the American taxpayer dearly, with the result still being the eventual collapse of the client regime.

If armed force is involved and there is nothing but a shadow *pretend* government that is the target of a popular insurgent movement, U.S. intervention will only result in prolonging the illegitimate regime while costing American and local combat deaths. Victory through force of arms alone, absent a realistic political program that appeals to the broad masses of the people, is simply impossible.

It follows, then, that for a counterinsurgency program to have any prospect for success, that program must:

1. Support a government respectful of the people that is commit-

ted to leading serious programs of reform;
2. Base itself squarely on the aspirations of the people and aimed at helping them achieve their desired political goals or reforms;
3. Focus upon providing assistance through training of government officials and civil servants at all levels, with ample attention paid to the vital aspect of public accountability and effectiveness;
4. Promote education and small business—the development of *civil* society—independent societies and guilds, consistent with the cultural norms of that society; and, above all,
5. Capture the political initiative from the insurgents by correcting the basic ills that gave rise to the insurgency.

Preempting the insurgents' political program—indeed, leading the effort toward genuine political and social reform—is the surest way to defeat his strategy. Sending in massive ground forces to hunt guerrillas does nothing to capture the political initiative from the insurgents, nor is such an approach likely to secure the active support of the people. Indeed, as mentioned, it is quite possible for the introduction of forces on a large scale to have the opposite effect: creating more insurgents from people who otherwise would remain neutral, or even supportive of the existing order.

The path forward is for policy planners and military professionals to take a fresh look at the role of American military power in the twenty-first century. We are no longer living in the historical period of the Cold War when the world was divided between American and Soviet spheres of influence that involved a strategic triad of land and submarine-based missiles and manned bombers. Neither is the appropriate paradigm that of mobilizing ninety infantry and armored divisions to meet the *Wehrmacht* head-on in France. Memories of old confrontations may have blinded us to the challenge of political instability in many parts of the Third World, and to the steady growth of Islamic extremism that provides a new political language of upheaval to frustrated peoples in many parts of the Muslim world. As I have labored to make plain, the enemies of the future will not oppose us with manned bombers or armored divisions, but with powerful ideas. We must be more skilled in dealing with political and ideological issues.

If the agony we experienced in Iraq and Afghanistan—due to our inability to grasp the nature and scope of those wars—has taught us nothing else, it should have taught us to pay attention to the aspirations of the local people and thereby avoid inflicting pain on ourselves and others. It should have taught us that insurgents fight on their terms, not on ours. Above all, it should have taught us to formulate a thoughtful policy and then develop an *integrated civil-military strategy* appropriate to that policy.

LOOK BEFORE YOU LEAP

Now almost forgotten, Major General Fox Conner served as the informal mentor to Colonel George Marshall in World War I and to Captain Dwight Eisenhower in Panama in the 1920s. Fox Conner was perhaps the Army's only true intellectual and theoretician of his day. Eisenhower credits his mentor as having predicted the outbreak of World War II as early as 1921 based on General Conner's careful analysis of the Treaty of Versailles and postwar political conditions in Europe.

General Conner put forward three principles to Eisenhower and Marshall as guidelines for a democracy attempting to fight a war:

- Never fight unless you have to;
- Never fight alone; and
- Never fight for long.

Although Conner was speaking in terms of the Great War in Europe, his observations can be applied to U.S. involvement in low intensity conflicts in non-European areas. His principles serve as a kind of litmus test for judging the wisdom of military deployments in unstable areas.

Let's examine his three principles in turn. Over the last half century the United States has committed its land, air, and naval forces (in varying sizes) more than twenty times in different areas of the globe, ostensibly in support of various client allies. Some of these deployments, such as that to Lebanon in 1983, served no apparent purpose and resulted ultimately in 241 Marine deaths and the humiliating withdrawal of the remnants of the force. We have already mentioned the Somalia debacle and the Vietnam War. Were he alive today, Fox Conner might ask these questions:

Is this proposed deployment to Wikitania made to defend our vital interests?

Is there a responsible government in place that is both legitimate and effective to serve as our partner and host?

How long do we anticipate our involvement in Wikitania to last?

Put another way, Conner would wish to know the purpose, or political objective, of the involvement, the character and quality of our ally, and the nature and length of our commitment.

Military power is best used when it is least used. It is all too easy for a chief executive to order the deployment of U.S. forces to politically unstable lands; it is infinitely harder to extricate ourselves once we are there. As we have seen, countries having little or no governance are strong candidates for the outbreak of insurgency since neither legitimacy nor effectiveness is present. If we go in absent a responsible government, we are in effect going in alone; there is no partner or host. Not least, administrations of both persuasions either have no idea of the nature and length of some of our commitments or they are astonished to find that they had vastly underestimated what would be required. In other words, they unwittingly had made an open-ended commitment, signed a blank check.

General Conner probably would say that it is wiser to ask many hard questions well before undertaking a deployment than it is to ask those hard questions afterward.

In an insurgency, our main military role relative to the host nation should be in order of priority: advising, training, and equipping. Our combat role should always be limited and only done in concert with local government forces. By assuming the brunt of the fighting, we not only incur the bulk of the casualties, but rob the host government's military of their nationalist credentials while tempting them to let us do their fighting, as well.

Fox Conner's last point bears some additional thought. We considered the differing values of time in Chapter 7. A nation attempting to use conventional means to oppose an insurgent movement will quickly run out of time as its costs and casualties mount exponentially in comparison with those of the insurgents. This was clearly shown in French Indochina and Cyprus. But a nation committed to genuine reform and wise enough to employ methods basically comparable to those of the insurgent, methods that address the fundamental political issues thereby robbing the insurgent of his Cause, will suddenly find the insurgent's time advantage has been neutralized. We have earlier noted the Viet Minh concerns regarding the French GCMA forces. *And, if the counterinsurgent has successfully regained the political initiative from the insurgents, time will now work against the insurgent movement.*

With a tip of the hat to Albert Einstein, time *is* relative for the war fighter just as it is for the physicist. Time can be *curved* to advantage, but only under the right conditions. And those conditions are political, not military.

Consider how time might be curved to the counterinsurgent's advantage if the right combination of reforms is undertaken promptly; the right mix of security, intelligence, and influence operations is set in motion; vigorous steps taken to train disciplined and effective police and armed forces; and above all, the trump card of political legitimacy is maintained by wise and inspiring local leaders. Which side now has the initiative?

Will these measures prolong the armed struggle . . . or shorten it?

Time is not merely something to be measured; it is to be used. Wisely. The point of buying as much time as possible is to use it to expand effective local governance and reform. This must be done gradually and methodically. It is a building block process in which expansion is to adjacent districts, not to isolated bases distant from secure areas.

As discussed earlier, at its core insurgency is political competition with arms. Put another way, military operations are conducted to support effective local administration. Special operations veteran General Stanley McChrystal stated his military goal concisely: "The point of security is to enable governance. . . . My metric is not the enemy killed, not the ground taken: it's how much governance we've got." [4] Precisely.

GAINING THE INITIATIVE

Let us return to the first of the five points that should be used as our criteria for assisting an embattled government in which the ills of the roots have now manifested themselves in open conflict among the branches and trunk of the tree of the local society.

For a government to command the support of the bulk of its people, it must first earn their respect, then their loyalty, and finally and most

---

[4] General Stanley A. McChrystal, commander's guidance.

importantly their affection. *The love of the people is the king's protection* goes an old proverb. A regime made up of plutocrats, cronies, goons, thugs, or praetorians (in any combination) is unlikely to gain much respect, and its chances of being loved by the people are virtually nil. Given an alert embassy staff, the U.S. government should be under no illusions concerning the relationship of the regime and the people. A government lacking popular support is a dead horse. Do we really want to bet on a dead horse?

The quality of a government's leadership is a key factor, *perhaps the key factor*, in an insurgency. For if there is no inspiring leadership around which the people can rally—leadership that proves its zeal for reaching the people, leadership willing to take firm hold of the nettlesome problem of reform—the key elements of political legitimacy and administrative effectiveness are fatally compromised.

To get a colorful idea of what leadership is all about, we should take a leaf from Steven Pressfield's *Gates of Fire*, a novel about Thermopylae:

> I will tell His Majesty what a king is. A king does not abide within his tent while his men bleed and die upon the field. A king does not dine while his men go hungry, nor sleep when they stand at watch upon the wall. A king does not command his men's loyalty through fear nor purchase it with gold; he earns their love by the sweat of his own back and the pains he endures for their sake. That which comprises the harshest burden, a king lifts first and sets down last. A king does not require service of those he leads but provides it to them. He serves them, not they him.[5]

Eloquent. Let us take Pressfield's marvelous description and apply it to the kings we know of. Would the above description apply to George Washington? Winston Churchill? Mohandas Gandhi? Nelson Mandela?

Would the above description apply to Anastasio Somoza? Fulgencio Batista? Ngo Dinh Diem?

Perhaps there is a lesson here, a yardstick we might use as we coldly assess the Kabilas (Democratic Republic of Congo) and Chalabis (Iraq) who flit across the American policy screen. Perhaps we might understand

---

[5] Pressfield, p. 361.

more clearly where our interests lie and where success is more likely to be found. It is found in character and courage, not in gold and guns.

Around Washington, D.C., much policymaker bleating is heard in these words: *What does success look like?* People from beyond the Beltway would be amazed at the degree of thrashing about that goes on amongst scholars, policy wonks, and generals over this question. And yet, the answer is simple. The answer is, in fact, another question: *What was the political objective of the effort?* In the absence of a clearly defined political objective, it is impossible to define victory or any other outcome, save defeat.

Here we have come full circle as we recognize how important it is for the policymaker and his general to carefully and precisely define the war aim and the scope of the effort. As he often does, Clausewitz has an answer to this challenge:

> The first, the supreme, the most far-reaching act of judgment that the statesman and commander have to make is to establish by that test [ie. the political aim] the kind of war on which they are embarking; neither mistaking it for, nor trying to turn it into, something that is alien to its nature. This is the first of all strategic questions and the most comprehensive.[6]

It is this requirement, based not on empty slogans, petty domestic issues, hubris, or false promises that will shape the outcome of the war. All our blood and treasure will either be used wisely or wasted foolishly depending upon the cold, hard assessment of the situation in the land requesting our assistance.

KNOW THE ENEMY

There is also the requirement to know the nature of the enemy and the land in which operations are contemplated. Commenting upon a point in the *Sun Tzu Ping Fa*, the Sung Dynasty general Ho Yen-hsi detailed the pitfalls of operating in hostile and unfamiliar lands centuries before General Henri Navarre learned these lessons the hard way:

---

[6] Clausewitz, Book I, Chapter 1, pp. 88–89.

> Now, if having received instructions to launch a campaign, we hasten to unfamiliar land where cultural influence has not penetrated and communications are cut, and rush into its defiles, is it not difficult? If I go with a solitary army the enemy awaits me vigilantly. For the situations of an attacker and a defender are vastly different. How much more so when the enemy concentrates on deception and uses many misleading devices! If we have made no plans we plunge in headlong. By braving the dangers and entering perilous places we face the calamity of being trapped or inundated [overrun] Marching as if drunk, we may run into an unexpected fight. When we stop at night we are worried by false alarms; if we hasten along unprepared we fall into ambushes. This is to plunge an army of bears and tigers into the land of death. How can we cope with the rebels' fortifications, or sweep him out of his deceptive dens?[7]

We may pause to ask ourselves how well we knew Vietnam, or Somalia, or Iraq, or Afghanistan before sending in our armies? Certainly we had maps and perhaps some overhead photography (for what those are worth in an insurgency), but did we have even so much as a clue about the political and cultural aspects of these lands, to say nothing of the nature of our potential enemies or the terrain, their home turf ? Or, did we merely plunge into these lands, supremely confident that our military might, technological advantages and American ingenuity were sufficient to guarantee victory?

Before committing even one advisor, trainer, or soldier to support a country battling an insurgency, it is imperative that we become expert about that country, its topography, ethnic groups, languages and religions, economy, local government, attitudes of the people, political issues (especially those that weaken the government's hand) and comparative strengths and weaknesses of the two competing sides.

This requirement highlights the need for brainpower more so than firepower. What is essential is to have in-depth expertise, especially skilled linguists and trained advisors who are thoroughly familiar with the land

---

[7] Sun Tzu, p. 105.

and its people. It takes years to develop such expertise. Therefore, it is important to begin today to promote language and area studies of non-Western regions. When a decision is made to deploy forces to an Asian or African land, it is too late at that point to begin language and area training. But this is the catch-up reaction so typical of American responses to overseas crises. Surely we can be smart enough to anticipate where most of our challenges are likely to appear.

It should be noted that the U.S. Army does have a foreign area officer (FAO) program, and it does train a limited number of personnel in various languages and in various countries and cultures. There are only two criticisms of this otherwise excellent program: first, there are far too few FAOs; second, this field is not viewed as being career enhancing, which tends to discourage promising young people from applying. Promotions are slow and the "stovepiped" personnel system tends to value command of platoons and companies over fluency in Amharic or Sinhalese. And, on occasion FAOs are placed in billets where their skills are not used by commanders who neither understand nor value their expertise.

THE NEW VITAL LINK

When the Greatest Generation went to war to defeat the mightiest war machines ever known to that date—the Axis armies, fleets, and air forces—the American people on the home front were marching alongside. We are all familiar with Rosie the Riveter and other anonymous heroes who grew the crops, mined the ores, fabricated the metals and materials, launched the ships, and equipped the soldiers, sailors, and marines. We might also take a moment to bow in humble respect to America's great academic community: its thinkers. Most often we remember the brilliant physicists, chemists, engineers, and other scientific personnel. But we should not neglect the social science scholars whose research on foreign areas or on critical operational skills such as influence operations helped make victory possible.

It is possible that the bond forged during World War II between America's scholarly community and its armed forces was broken by the Vietnam War. For more than a decade, this estrangement denied policymakers and military professionals the skills and knowledge of America's brightest academic stars, its best thinkers.

It is hard to say whether the current struggles in Asia have threatened yet another breach. Let us hope this is not the case.[8] But the fact remains that it is vital for the political leadership to serve as a bridge to rebuild the close working ties that existed between the campus and the encampment. The American people must face the challenges of instability and insurgency together; we cannot afford to be divided against ourselves.

There is no country on Earth blessed with more in-depth expertise than the United States. Somewhere in America, perhaps hidden away in some corner out of the limelight, there is someone who knows something—perhaps a great deal—about almost any subject you can name. The great trick is finding that person and persuading him or her to pitch in and help in our country's national effort. In World War II that proved fairly easy. Since that time, finding the individual and winning his cooperation has been more difficult. Even so, it is essential that America win and hold the support of our nation's multitalented brainpower.

DECISION AT DAWN

In late spring 1954, as the situation at Dien Bien Phu became ever more perilous, the American policy community gave serious consideration to massively intervening in French Indochina to help stave off defeat. There were those who strongly advocated intervention despite the findings in the National Intelligence Estimate indicating that the situation in Indochina was beyond redemption. The collision at that time was between those committed to stopping the spread of Communism at any price and those who based their judgment on careful appraisal of the likelihood of success of military intervention.

The history of this decision is that we did not go to war that May. Dien Bien Phu was overrun, and within a few months a ceasefire was arranged at Geneva. The decision not to intervene did not come easily, and it certainly was far from unanimous. But as events were to prove twenty years later at the close of the Second Indochina War, our decision not to commit forces in Vietnam in 1954 was wise.

---

[8] The "Af-Pak Federation Forum" sponsored by the Organization of the Joint Chiefs of Staff (OJCS) is a very promising indicator of the support of the war effort by some of the best brains in America.

We may also take note of our decision in the 1980s to send a limited number of advisors to El Salvador with the proviso that genuine political and social reforms take place. This decision proved successful. A few years later, regular forces were dispatched to the failed state of Somalia: this decision proved disastrous. In El Salvador there was a government that was prepared to carry out the reforms that it pledged it would make. In Somalia, there was no government worthy of the name, only gangster warlords. We certainly had no political strategy in mind. Admittedly, comparing the failure in Somalia with the ultimate success in El Salvador is a bit unfair. The social and political factors in both countries were and are very different. But the question raised is this: When is American help *wise* and when is it not? Under what conditions can we expect to achieve our policy aims? And when is it highly doubtful that our aims, if we can *even* define them, can be achieved at any cost?

How can we arrive at wise decisions here at home that make possible the effective use of our power abroad with a greater likelihood of success?

The President of the United States has at his disposal an array of advisors who are there to provide all manner of details needed when a decision must be made. Some are substantive experts and others are political appointees knowledgeable of Peoria, but ignorant of Peshawar. As we witnessed in both the Johnson and Nixon administrations, some are temperamentally hawks while others are doves. Pity the poor commander in chief besieged by such a phalanx, hit not merely by two conflicting views, but by a kaleidoscope of conflicting opinions. One suspects that President Johnson had as many opinions offered to him as he had advisors. We are mindful of the words of Chancellor Oxenstierna to his son.

So, how can an American chief executive pick his way through such a tangled maze?

Perhaps the answer is that the commander in chief must structure his questions to his advisors in such a way that he starts with the basics, rather than leaping immediately to considering options. By this I mean directing his advisors and staff to start with this basic request: *Tell me everything you know about the government of Wikitania, to include how it is perceived by its people and whether it is viewed as legitimate and effective.* Simplistic? Perhaps. But if you were sick, would you prefer that the doctor immediately prescribe medicines for you without first making a thorough diagnosis of your illness?

A basic request of this kind is one that can be answered with fact, not value judgments or opinions. Equally important, the request will table for the moment that terrible question: *What are we going to do?* Instead it addresses the fundamentals. No discussion should take place on policy recommendations until every tiny aspect of the Wikitanian political reality is laid bare. Once the fundamentals are clear to all, and the assessment of hard facts agreed to, there is a firm starting point. We are on track for a potentially wise decision.

The next stage should be directed at the Wikitanian government itself, to gauge its ability and willingness *to take the lead* in reforms that bring the regime closer to the people. If the Wikitanian government is unwilling or unable to make the tough decisions required to clean its own house, there is nothing that the United States can do or *should do* on Wikitania's behalf, other than perhaps offer asylum to selected refugees.

You may object that this is not how policy is decided in the real world! You are absolutely correct; it isn't. In fact, policy is shaped by injections from zealous Congressmen, insistence of paid lobbyists, and the advocacy of domestic and foreign groups or individuals.[9]

This is to say nothing of congressional hearings and endless carping and Monday quarterbacking from pundits in the press. Think tanks and scholarly journals will weigh in. Even the Wikitanians themselves will enter the U.S. policy debate through their embassy, through high-level officials, and even celebrities and well-known Wikitanians, especially expats living in the United States.

It is not merely "All the President's Men" inside and outside State and the National Security Council who help shape policy, but dozens, even hundreds of others, inside and outside the government. Some of these people warp rational and methodical policy formulation. Their chirps and belches must be curbed, tactfully if possible, but rudely if necessary.

I hope we have learned from hard experience with charlatans like Chalabi of Iraq or the shrill members of the old China Lobby. Our ability to

---

[9] To include political action organizations that are funded from abroad, even from hostile governments and insurgent or terrorist groups. An example of such a group is the Committee in Solidarity with the People of El Salvador (CISPES), which was founded in the 1980s in opposition to U.S. policy and continues today.

think clearly is deformed when we allow hucksters to influence our judgment. Because of our folly in listening to people who will never go near the front lines or be in the slightest danger, young Americans will die or be crippled for life by roadside bombs. That is criminal negligence. Those who prefer to abide safely in their tents have no right to shape policies for others who, as a result, must bleed and die on the battlefield. Let us remember Lt. Todd Weaver as we consider the use of armed force.

Hucksterism leads to flawed reasoning and, as we have seen, flawed reasoning leads to fatally flawed policy and strategy.

DENOUEMENT

As we approach the end of our survey of insurgency, it is vital to note that history is filled with the debris of human folly. Barbara Tuchman has done a marvelous job capturing several different historical examples of persistent stupidity in her book *The March of Folly: From Troy to Vietnam*. Tuchman defines folly as being a decision taken when (a) a clear, sensible alternative was available, (b) ample evidence indicated that the course chosen was contrary to one's own interests, and (c) the foolishness of the decision was recognized by many at the time it was made. And yet the rulers profiled by Tuchman—the King of Troy, several Renaissance popes, Lord North and his cabinet of American Revolution times, and the Johnson-Nixon policy crowd—pursued foolish policies based upon preconceived notions and wishful thinking, and refused to change course even when the inanity of their policies became obvious.

If folly is defined as *a costly undertaking having an absurd or ruinous outcome* and if it springs from *lack of good sense, understanding, or foresight*, then wise courses of action would be pretty much the opposite: *exhibiting common sense, prudent* and *having understanding or discernment of what is true, right, or lasting. . . .*[10]

Now we must apply those definitions as we assess American policy formulation as it has been conducted in the recent past. It is from this last reflection that we will hope to glean an understanding of what constitutes wise counsels at home.

Making errors of judgment is a fact of life. At one time or another, all

[10] The American Heritage College Dictionary, p. 529 (folly) and p. 1548 (wisdom).

of us have made poor choices. Ideally, we learned from our mistakes. But persistence in error after it has been revealed requires commitment and determination, real woodenheadedness. In the epilogue to her book, Tuchman states that:

> If pursuing disadvantage after the disadvantage has become obvious is irrational, then rejection of reason is the prime characteristic of folly. According to the Stoics, reason was the "thinking fire" that directs the affairs of the world, and the emperor or ruler of the state was considered to be "the servant of divine reason [appointed] to maintain order on earth." The theory was comforting, but then as now "divine reason" was more often than not overpowered by non-rational human frailties—ambition, anxiety, status-seeking, face-saving, illusions, self-delusions, fixed prejudices. Although the structure of human thought is based on logical procedure from premise to conclusion, it is not proof against the frailties and the passions.[11]

If our decisions and actions are to be wise, we must guard against hasty, ill-considered policies founded more on wishful thinking than on sober hard fact. Every effort must be made to avoid being sucked in to a violent whirlpool due to false pride or pious hope, yielding to small noisy groups, or by deluding ourselves that somehow we will muddle through. Our campaign must be founded on a clear political objective that is anchored on the bedrock of reform. Clever slogans that attempt to justify political expediency have no place in policy. No crime is greater than for a president to send a young soldier or marine off to die in defense of a protection racket passing itself off as a "friendly government."

Let us hope that we Americans have not lost faith that we can—and should—make a positive difference in the world. We cannot turn a blind eye when a client state flagrantly and brutally mistreats its own people, nor can it be business as usual at State and the White House when foreign regimes use open repression to suppress dissent and squelch the demand for reform and accountability. If American aid continues to flow from

---

[11] Tuchman, p. 380.

our coffers irrespective of the conduct of those we are supporting, our hypocrisy is on display and we have made a mockery of our principles.

When true wisdom guides political greatness, folly and evil are avoided, and the nation and its people will dwell in peace and security.[12] As Euripides noted: *"Cleverness is not wisdom."*

SALUS POPULI
SUPREMA LEX ESTO

[12] Inspired by Plato's comment in *The Republic*, Book V.

ANNEX A

SAN SALVADOR 2038

San Salvador 2038, a remarkable State Department cable reproduced verbatim below, is a masterpiece of analysis of the crisis in El Salvador in early 1980. Not only does the cable dissect the Salvadoran political situation but it presents a proposed Country Team strategy consistent with U.S. policy. The reader should be aware that a key figure in Salvadoran politics, Archbishop Romero, was assassinated only five days after this cable was released. Ambassador Robert E. White faced an explosive situation as extremists of both the left and right tried to polarize the political situation and bring about a general insurrection.

As the cable will make clear, the goal of U.S. policy was *broad reform* intended to support the political center and *achieve democratization* of the government. Although American liberals are unaware of the fact, it was younger Salvadoran army officers who spearheaded the reform programs with quiet U.S. assistance.

Experts like RAND analyst Ben Connable classify the outcome of the Salvadoran insurgency (ending in 1992) as mixed according to his criteria because neither the FMLN nor the Salvadoran government was victorious, and a negotiated peace was arranged. Author offers an alternative viewpoint that the outcome of the ten-year war in El Salvador was in fact an American success, precisely because it resulted in a centrist coalition government respectful of the people's rights and committed to democratic reform. That was the object of U.S. policy. Ambassador White should be commended for his clear thinking and great vision.

A glossary is provided following the cable to help the reader decode the abbreviations.

SAN SALVADOR 2038 (19 March 1980)
NODIS [DECLASSIFIED]

Subject: Preliminary Assessment of Situation in El Salvador

2. [paragraph 1 is understood to be the subject line] Summary: The analysis and recommendations which follow do not pretend to be final or definitive. But they are the only policies which make sense to me right now. I am convinced that El Salvador is not in imminent danger of being lost. If we use our power correctly I believe the chances of success are very good.

3. In El Salvador the rich and powerful have systematically defrauded the poor and denied eighty percent of the people any voice in the affairs of their country. A revolution is now underway and we are one of the principal actors. There is no stopping this revolution; no going back. We can influence the course of events, however, and try to guide it into channels which will benefit the Salvadoran people, provide an alternative to the Nicaraguan model for Guatemala and Honduras and safeguard our security interests in Central America and the Caribbean.

4. The main players in this revolution are:

- The extreme or ultra-Right, made up largely of rich landowners, their private armies and certain high military officers;
- The regular army and the security forces, National Guard, National Police, and Treasury Police;
- The Christian Democratic Party, the only party represented in the government;
- The United States Government and its visible symbol, the American Embassy;
- The Church, Archbishop Romero and the Jesuits; conservative forces in the Church exist but wield no measurable influence;
- The popular organizations, the three action-oriented pressure groups ranging from the leftist but responsible FAPU to the wild-eyed, lunging LP-28 which occupies embassies and public buildings;
- The three far Left guerrilla groups, underground mirrors of the

popular fronts, ranging from the relatively disciplined FARN to the murderous ERP.

5. There are two potential players which are not now taking an active role:

- Other parties of the center-left; without much popular support but with some competent leaders;
- Businessmen's organizations such as ANEP (entrepreneurs but big landlords as well) and ASI (industrialists and exporters) which could influence the moderate, sensible elements of the private sector to cooperate with the government, especially by encouraging investment, reopening factories, etc.

6. The government is beleaguered, attacked by extremists and moderates on both the left and the right. Without our constant and visible support the government would fall in a matter of days.

7. The major, immediate threat to the existence of the government is the Right-wing violence. In the City of San Salvador, the hired thugs of the extreme Right, some of them well-trained Cuban and Nicaraguan terrorists, kill moderate Left leaders and blow up government buildings. In the countryside, elements of the security forces torture and kill the campesinos, shoot up their houses and burn their crops. At least two hundred refugees from the countryside arrive daily in the capital city. This campaign of terror is radicalizing the rural areas just as surely as Somoza's National Guard did in Nicaragua.

8. Unfortunately, the command structure of the army and the security forces either tolerates or encourages this activity. These senior officers believe or pretend to believe that they are eliminating the guerrillas.

9. But the younger officers of the army, represented by junta member Colonel Majano, are unhappy with the way things have gone since they overthrew the former dictatorship. They are determined to finish the revolution they started by reasserting their power. In my judgment this is the sector that will decide whether we will win or lose the war. And this is political warfare, nothing short, and the only way to avert civil war. If old guard officers in crucial positions can be eased out and the younger officers can reassert their power, then the Salvadoran military can survive as an institution and this government will succeed.

10. If this does not happen and if the systematic violation of human rights in the countryside does not cease, all the agrarian and banking reforms in the world will not help. Sometime over the course of the next six months, the civilian members of the junta and Colonel Majano will have to insist on the ouster of those in the army and security forces who permit and encourage torturing and killing innocent civilians in a brutal effort to end political action. The extreme Right will keep on trying to convince the conservative officers to return to their natural alliance with the rich and, if they can engineer a coup to oust Majano and the PDC, we will have a new military government of the Right. At this point the whole civilian leadership, including the Christian Democrats and the Church, will link up with the popular forces. Many of the younger army officers will either be purged or will voluntarily join the guerrillas of the far Left. Then we will be only a few steps away from the People's Republic of El Salvador.

11. What can we do to avoid this calamity and bring our resources to bear in such a way that this government can succeed? First, it is vital to understand that no moderate government can succeed without the support of Archbishop Romero and the Church.

Bringing in the moderate elements within the popular organizations is also important. Therefore we must avoid any action that will alienate them irretrievably or drive them further to the Left. It is in this context that military assistance becomes such a problem. The MTTs will be interpreted by all sectors as support for the armed forces as currently constituted and as approval for the campaign of repression. If it is true, as I have postulated, that an end to officially-sponsored and tolerated violence is crucial to the success of the government, then we should use all our influence to bring this to an end including withholding military assistance, particularly the MTTs, to gain our objective. I have already told Colonel Garcia how difficult it would be to bring in the MTTs under current conditions and he understood and accepted the point. Dr. Morales Ehrlich, the key civilian member of the junta, explicitly asked me yesterday not to send MTTs at this juncture, arguing that this would strengthen the baleful influence of Colonels Garcia and Carranza, the Minister and Vice-Minister of Defense. Regarding the argument that MTTs will assist the army and not the repressive security forces, this is a distinction made by very few people. It is true that there are various branches of the armed forces but all are led by army officers. There is only one officer corps and its members are routinely assigned to any of the various branches.

12. Given the high visibility of helicopters, the need for an accompanying MTT and their obvious utility in carrying out missions, I am forced by the logic of my own position to urge that these too be held up until the worst of the right-wing violence is brought to an end.

13. What can we do:

- Make clear that a move to the Right is unacceptable to us;
- Pressure the leadership of the army and the security forces to crack down on Right-wing violence;
- Encourage the security forces to go after the Left-wing guerrillas and stop torturing and killing any youth between 14 and 25 because he may be involved with labor unions, church organizations, etc.
- Encourage the younger officers to build and consolidate their support to the point that they can take over command of the armed forces;
- Do nothing that would strengthen the hand of the older officers against the reform elements within the military (again this brings up the problem of our military assistance). It is vital not to send mixed signals.
- Encourage the Christian Democrats to hang on and gradually explore possibilities of bringing in center-Left leaders into the government;
- Convince the archbishop and Catholic activists of our good faith in wanting to end the violence;
- Work to get the sensible people in the private sector to accept the government, support the reforms, and get back to work;
- Begin soon to split off certain elements of the popular blocs from the extreme Left;
- As soon as we have some semblance of a united and strong government, begin seriously to eliminate the terrorists of the Left.

14. Above all we must rid ourselves of the notion that the Cubans are playing an important role here. I do not doubt the reality of Cuban training for guerrillas plus weapons and other materiel via Honduras and Costa Rica. It exists. But it is marginal. El Salvador will be won or lost by the interplay of forces and actors previously described.

15. Thus a major U.S. effort will be needed if this government or a mutant thereof is to survive and succeed. Unless we move fast and effectively with people and resources, the agrarian reform will bog down and the Right will step up its attacks aimed at radicalizing the Left, disheartening the JRG and undermining its reforms. The far Left will do the same, insisting that reforms were never anything but a cover for repression designed to restore full power to the oligarchy. Ultimately we will face a Leftist takeover, probably ushered in by civil war.

16. Remember, we have to be realistic about this government. The PDC is a truncated version of the European species whose leaders have been out of touch with the people for many years and who cannot make the proper political moves because they lack the power to end officially sponsored, encouraged or tolerated violence.

17. The military is the key here but it is an open question whether the younger officers can muster sufficient leadership, conviction and force to reform the military, rid it of reactionary elements tied to the ultra-Right and eliminate the torture and killing of young people sympathetic to the Left which is radicalizing the Salvadoran campesinos towards insurrection.

18. The only way I see this whole crisis coming out in an acceptable fashion over the months ahead is as follows: Col. Majano succeeds in building up a corps of progressive officers who gradually acquire enough power to force out the commanders of the security forces, either into powerless retirement or prestigious posts abroad. At that point, the government would become acceptable not only to the Left-leaning Christian Democrats (who quit last week) but to others of the moderate and non-violent Left. Meanwhile, this junta of progressive officers and broad-based civilians might succeed in bringing home to the private sector that the Good Old Days of plantation life are gone forever and their future lies in cooperating with the new leaders to build a just society.

19. If something like the foregoing does not happen, I can see the security forces, impelled by the logic of their brutality against the poor, joining forces with the reactionary Right, their traditional home. The army, which prizes unity, would in all probability be dragged along by the National Guard and (Treasury) Police. A great deal of unselective Phoenix-type killing would follow over the next four to six months, providing the ultra-

Left a field-day for stirring up popular indignation and securing foreign (read Nicaraguan/Cuban) training and arms. Then the fight would be on. I honestly do not believe there is any doubt about the outcome of that scenario. The Left would win and carry out savage reprisals against the Right. It might take time to play out to its macabre conclusion and would require heavy Cuban and other assistance but, as in Nicaragua, there is no way that a few thousand soldiers siding with the extreme Right could hold off the combined forces of the Left, fueled by a popular insurrection with new recruits from the army, the security forces, the moderate politicians, and the oppressed peasantry.

20. This telegram only begins the work of how we must bring our resources to bear if we are to succeed. But it is a beginning. And it is necessary for me to understand the situation before I begin to prescribe remedies that will, if followed, require the allocation of important resources. Meanwhile, I cannot stress too much the importance of Washington deciding where El Salvador fits on our worldwide list of priorities so that all of us can have some idea of the share of the resource pie available to this mission. We must apply the resources that will work and not put in the wrong kind of resources simply because they are available. End Summary.

21. Dept [State Department] has requested a general assessment of the situation in El Salvador at the end of my first week on the job. This will be of necessity a preliminary and perhaps inconclusive effort but I will offer my best guess about where things stand, where they can go, and what we have to do to affect the outcome. In order to arrange these views in some coherent fashion, I have imposed a somewhat arbitrary outline, as follows.

Why does El Salvador face a Marxist revolution?

22. That it does is the main reason for our intense concern; why it does must underlie any plan of action we develop. An extremist Communist takeover here, and by that I mean something just this side of the Pol Pot episode, is unfortunately a real possibility due mainly to the intense hatred that has been created in this country among the masses by the insensitivity, blindness and brutality of the ruling elite, usually designated "the oligarchy." It is hard to describe the injustice that permeates this society. Let me offer a few examples: magnificent suburbs full of villas right out of Beverly Hills are flanked by miserable slums right out of Jakarta where families have to walk two blocks to the only water spigot. The traditionally stark contrast between rich and poor has been intensified dramatically in recent years by the immense riches that have accrued to the land-owning class as a result of high prices for export crops—coffee, sugar, and cotton—produced on their vast plantations staffed by impoverished and largely illiterate day laborers.

Meanwhile, the cities have been flooded with the poorest and most depressed campesinos who are fleeing overpopulation and rural poverty in search of work. A new element in this explosive equation is the growth of foreign-financed light industry, concentrated in marginal assembly operations where minimum wages are paid to young and otherwise unemployable slum dwellers and where unions are rigorously prohibited. Another growth sector has been banking in which enormous sums of money were concentrated in the hands of cadet branches of the "14 Families" and thereafter funneled into oligarchy operations in agriculture, industry and construction. One of the principal bankrollers of the ultra-right at the moment is Roberto Hill, who boasts that most of his banking fortune came not from his family's coffee plantations but from USAID low-cost housing loans in the era of the Alliance for Progress. Much of the sumptuous housing in the exclusive suburbs has been built with three percent mortgages from the oligarchy-controlled banks. All in all, this country is a social bomb that has been ticking way for a number of years and is only now at the point of explosion.

Why has change failed to occur?

23. Very simply, because the oligarchy and its lieutenants have stifled all forms of political expression for decades and relied on military force and ultimately torture and summary executions to maintain an oppressive system against all challengers. The conduct of the wealthy upper classes and the actions of the armed forces have created a deep reservoir of hatred and frustration among large sectors of the rural and urban poor. Fear of what the masses might do to them has in turn induced a high degree of paranoia in the upper classes. One of the maddest incidents in recent months was a generalized shootout in the wealthy suburbs on January 19 when all the householders were invited to go out in their front yards and fire off simultaneously all the guns they had on hand: the result was said to resemble World War II and was intended to terrify and intimidate the nearby slum dwellers and ultra-leftists who are working to organize them for revolution.

24. It should be well understood in Washington, given this background, that pressure for change in El Salvador is irresistible. Nor is it Cuban infiltrators or Russian arms shipments that have created this threat of violent revolution but rather decades of oppression and a studied refusal on the part of the elite to make any concessions to the masses. Archbishop Romero, who is openly sympathetic to the Left, makes the point that change can only come about here through pressure from below and while he deplores violence he recognizes at least tacitly that there would be no hope for reform nor any possibility of U.S. backing for social change without the constant threat of Marxist revolution. He and other moderates who believe profound structural change must come to El Salvador know that our role here will be central, that far from being a powerless observer the United States has traditionally called the tune in El Salvador and will continue to do so unless the most violent Leftist groups take power.

25. Whether Archbishop Romero likes it or not, the other most powerful actor in El Salvador is the armed forces, made up of the 8,000 man army; the 3,000 man National Guard, the 4,000 man National Police, the 2,000 man Treasury Police, and the tiny Air Force and Navy.

The security forces, the National Guard and Police, have been closely identified with the oligarchy for generations. The National Guard in particular has been a kind of landlords' militia in the countryside. All three security services have a very bad human rights record, most of it well deserved. The watershed date in El Salvador's recent history was October 15, 1979, when elements of the armed forces acted alone and essentially without civilian allies to throw out President Romero and the most corrupt colonels and generals in his entourage. Younger officers among the military were mainly responsible for the coup and inspired its revolutionary message that promised sweeping social reform, respect for human rights and establishment of a democratic form of government. Important sectors of the armed forces, especially the high command and the leaders of the National Guard and National Police, have gone along with the younger officers with considerable reluctance and have grudgingly accepted the need for social reform. It was these military sectors who planned a right-wing coup in mid-February when prospects for implementation began to become a reality. The threat of a split in the armed forces between the traditional oppressive elements and the younger more progressive officers is real. Maintaining the coherence of the military will be difficult because of the dichotomy in philosophy between the two main tendencies in the officer corps. It is a fact, nevertheless, that the Salvadoran Armed Forces are the most important ingredient in the search for a moderate solution. If the armed forces disintegrate, the only other army in the country belongs to the most militant and radical Marxist revolutionaries. Thus, military unity is an important desiderata but cannot be pursued at all costs if a political solution, which is the only one possible, is to be found for El Salvador's political crisis.

26. The far Left is the second most powerful military force in the country. Debate rages about how big its guerrilla force is but something like three to five thousand armed and rudimentarily trained leftists are distributed among the three major terrorist armies, the ERP, FPL and FARN. Among them are disciplined, armed and foreign-influenced elements who are probably considerably to the Left of any of the Sandinista units. They are adept at exploiting mass hatred in this hate-filled society but they have lost strength in the last few months and especially in the last few weeks as the JRG has begun to implement a serious reform program that threatens in the long run to dry up the reservoirs of terrorist recruitment in the countryside. One of their major sources of their funds, ransoms for kidnapped oligarchs, has evaporated in recent months with the flight of the big rich to Guatemala and Miami.

What are the chances for a moderate solution?

27. The role of the United States is central but cannot be played without domestic allies, civilian as well as military. If we are truly resolved that an ultra-Left victory is unacceptable to the United States, then we must pursue a political solution that will bring about a sharp drop in the country's social tensions. We should be clear that an ultra-Right victory is not a possibility because it is certain to bring civil war and, as in Nicaragua, end in the victory of the ultra-Left by acclamation. Here there is no doubt that the structure of a Western non-Communist society would be quickly swept away with no significant domestic opposition, once the army and owning classes had been destroyed in a civil war against the mass of the population. I can hardly overemphasize this point: there is no solution on the Right. The constant blandishments to the USG from the oligarchy and its allies among the cashiered officers of General Romero's regime must be resisted with utmost vigor or we will find ourselves in a cataclysmic civil war that will usher in the ultra-Left.

What can we do to strengthen the JRG and widen its political base?

28. Again, a political solution depends in great measure on our allies among the civilians and military in the present junta. The reform program has now begun. Agrarian reform has been a great success in its first two weeks and can ultimately provide land to 75 percent of the formerly landless peasants of the interior. Banking reform has broken the stranglehold of the oligarchy on national finance. Labor reform will result in the enforcement of Salvador's long ignored labor codes and bring to an end sweatshop conditions in the industrial sector. The screams of indignation from the landowners and bankers will soon be joined by the owners of assembly plants where 30 percent return on capital is standard and three dollars a day was considered an ample wage. Many of the last group are American citizens and will be heard from in Washington.

29. This raises an important question, what does the USG consider a moderate solution? The reforms proposed by the JRG and already underway will restructure Salvadoran society in fundamental ways but toward U.S. or European-style welfare capitalism, not toward Scandinavian socialism and very far from Cuban or East European Marxism. The day of baronial estates, million dollar fortified suburbs and vastly profitable sweated labor operations will soon end in El Salvador. This is essential if Marxist revolution is to be foreclosed. But to broaden the base of the JRG it will be necessary to move both Right and Left from the knife-thin edge which the government is presently poised upon. That means accommodating what we refer to as the acceptable elements of the Right and the accessible elements of the Left. The JRG's effort to open a dialogue with the industrial sector and the chastened former landowners seems to be proceeding very successfully. At least some of the private sector owners profess willingness to accept the reforms to date and say they will stop their bitter opposition to the junta. The non-violent Left is very unhappy with what it sees as a decided turn toward the Right and accommodation of the private sector. They see the JRG's toleration or at least inability to stop Right-wing terrorism and its accommodation of the private sector as the last straw that caused the Left-wing of the Christian Democratic Party to resign in protest last week. These relatively moderate Leftist elements have been victims of a well-financed and vicious campaign of political assassination and bombings that seems designed to radicalize the Left irretrievably and foreclose any movement in this direction on the part of the JRG.

30. The immediate threat to the junta is from the ultra-Right. Backed by the great fortunes of at least some members of the oligarchy, and abetted by the acquiescence and participation of some members of the armed forces, a wave of violence against moderates has been underway for several weeks and is reaching the decisive stage. The junta must end Right-wing terrorism if it is to win international support and lure away from the ultra-Left those moderates who want to see structural change and an end to oppression.

31. Archbishop Romero in particular continues to denounce repression, the term used by everyone on the Left to describe three distinct but interrelated categories: (1) ultra-Right terrorism, (2) security forces participation in these operations and (3) excessive use of violence by the military in responding to provocations from the Left, possibly engineered by the ultra-Left to produce evidence of massacre.

32. The daily total of dead, many of them teenagers bearing marks of brutal torture, result from Right-wing terrorism but they are easily confused with victims of undisciplined or purposely brutal security operations. Whatever the role of the high command in this mixture of terrorism and indiscipline, the reputation of the JRG is being blackened and the most serious doubts are being raised as to its *bona fides* here and abroad. For the ultra-Right, it seems clear that these acts of terror are designed to eliminate or radicalize the relatively moderate elements on the Left and preclude a moderate solution. For the ultra-Left, the goal is to provoke Rightist assassinations or a wholesale massacre that will outrage the population and kick off a national insurrection. Probably the most serious threat to a moderate solution would be assassination, whether by the ultra-Left or by the ultra-Right of Archbishop Romero, the most important political figure in El Salvador and a symbol of a better life to the poor.

33. A right-wing coup, followed by an intensive campaign of assassination, or even an isolated incident of terrorism against Archbishop Romero, for which the Right would be blamed, is likely to provoke a civil war that would almost certainly end in a rout of the Right and a radicalized Leftist takeover. Hence, for the moment, the principal enemy of a moderate solution is the ultra-Right and its allies within the high command who are permitting the current campaign of torture and murder to continue.

What do we have to do to prevail?

34. The most urgent priority for the USG and its civilian/military allies in the JRG is to eliminate Rightist atrocities. We are using every measure of influence at our disposal to convince the military authorities that these acts must end and the perpetrators be punished. Senior military officers do not excuse the Rightist campaign but they do profess a suspect ignorance of its operations that is far from reassuring. Several recent bombings, especially that at the Archbishop's radio station and the one Sunday night against the Ministry of Agriculture, bear all the earmarks of a highly trained professional terrorist organization. The Minister of Defense told me that anti-Castro Cubans may be operating here as hired mercenaries of the oligarchy. Every resource we possess must be used to stop Rightist terrorism because it is the proximate cause of civil war in El Salvador.

35. Our next priority is to convince the more intelligent and far-sighted among the private sector that there is no hope for them in blind reaction and that they must cooperate with the JRG in its reform program if a non-Communist El Salvador is to survive. We see encouraging signs that this realization is dawning on some of the entrepreneurs and even a few of the former landowners and bankers. It is among these people and the small middle-class now siding with the oligarchy out of fear of Communism that all the expertise is located. Together they will be crucial to future economic development here. Thus, it is important that the JRG begin to co-opt these entrepreneurs and technicians. Now that the main reform measures are in place, and the Right has been presented with a *fait accompli*, it is possible to open a dialogue with them without compromising the chances for progress or alienating the moderate left. The time has come, therefore, to approach the business and industrial classes to seek their cooperation. The U.S. Embassy can be a useful broker in this process because of its long identification with them.

36. Our role will be considerably more difficult in the effort to open up a dialogue between the junta and the non-violent sectors on the Left. These are made up largely of the Left-wing of the PDC, the socialist MNR, the traditional Communist UDN and the mass organization of the lower middle classes and the intelligentsia, FAPU. The key to a dialogue with this important grouping is Archbishop Romero. The PDC has sought his help in this endeavor but the withdrawal of the Left-wing of the party will severely complicate a move toward the more moderate Left. Before anything can be accomplished on this score, however, an end to the worst violence on the Right and among the security forces is essential.

37. What we are talking about is a complex and delicate role of social engineering for the U.S. and its allies in the JRG. Our objective must be to restructure this feudal society along Western lines, that is to say along lines of modernizing Third World countries where a moderate solution has been found by compromise and political sagacity: Portugal, Greece, Malaysia, and Singapore are possible role models. The alternative is not, as the Right and ultra-Right argue, some military-dominated conservative dictatorship like Chile, Argentina or Uruguay. Radicalization and mobilization of the masses has gone too far here for repressive machinery to succeed in doing anything except provoke an insurrection. The only real alternative to westernized political and economic life in El Salvador is a Marxist dictatorship along Cuban lines. We have said repeatedly that such an outcome would be unacceptable to us. Our only option, therefore, is to work for a moderate solution and have the patience to follow our policy to its ultimate conclusion, attacks from Right or Left notwithstanding.

What is the result for Central America if we prevail?

38. El Salvador's emergence as a just and rapidly modernizing society will have a crucial impact on the neighboring countries, not least among them Nicaragua. The disorder and confusion that has followed the Sandinista victory has been a source of profound discouragement to the moderate Left in this country and the success of a reformist non-Marxist government here might be decisive to the outcome there. The Rightist military government of Guatemala is already quite concerned that the "contagion of social change" (read land reform) in El Salvador might spread north, shaking another retrograde structure to its foundations. A successful outcome in El Salvador would thus reverse the trend toward Marxist revolution and turn this country from an example of societal dissolution into a model of structured political change. Our role in such an outcome can only be decisive.

What support will Washington give to this strategy?

39. It should be clear from this discussion that it is impossible to stop the revolutionary process underway in El Salvador. Our only hope for protecting our interests in Central America is to harness the massive pressure for change and guide it into channels that will produce a just, equitable, responsible and democratic system. This can only be done by broadening the moderate base and excluding the terrorist extremes on both Left and Right. The answer is here in El Salvador, not in Panama or Caracas and certainly not in Miami or Havana. What must be found is a political accommodation that will end violence by drying up support for the professional revolutionists on the Left and eliminating professional terrorists on the Right. We have to learn to work closely and faithfully with the only government El Salvador has had in 50 years that has tried to bring social justice to the people. We must avoid sudden shifts in direction that can disillusion and ultimately destroy our Salvadoran allies. As Bill Colby has said, *"There has got to be something between a diplomatic note and sending in the Marines."* There is: it is a tough-minded embassy speaking with one voice and enjoying the full backing of the government in Washington.

40. Full backing means sufficient resources to do the job. In order to strengthen the JRG and to penetrate and neutralize the ultra-Left and ultra-Right, we must have the diplomatic and developmental tools required to do the job. Above all, we need personnel to do the reporting and analysis. It is also important to provide the JRG with highly visible backing such as major economic assistance programs in support of agrarian reform. A broad foreign-financed assault on joblessness is required on the scale of the Depression-era WPA and CCC. Small-scale food aid is also needed but we must be careful not to undermine local agriculture and marketing by creating a dependency on outside food shipments. We are sending a cable today on PL-480 and how it can contribute to a moderate solution.

41. What to do about U.S. military assistance is the most delicate issue we face. I believe we should cooperate with the JRG by supplying non-lethal FMS and IMET to the armed forces but that the MTTs should be withheld at least until the worst violence on the Right is brought to an end. We must work carefully to strengthen the civilians and younger officers and do nothing to strengthen the traditionalist military in its tolerance for, or even encouragement of, Right-wing terrorism and brutal abuse of human rights. We can lose here fast if the Right has its way. That must be blocked.

WHITE

GLOSSARY

ANEP: Asociacion Nacional de la Empresa Privada—National Association of Private Enterprise.

ASI: Asociacion Salvadorena Industriales—Salvadoran Industries Association.

ERP: Ejercito Revolucionario del Pueblo—People's Revolutionary Army, one of the five armed groups that coalesced in October 1980 into the FMLN.

FAPU: Frente de Accion Popular Unificada—Unified Popular Action Group, a mass organization linked to the FARN.

FARN: Fuerza Armada de la Resistencia Nacional, one of five armed groups forming the FMLN.

FMS: Foreign Military Sales—a Department of Defense assistance program.

FPL: Fuerzas Populares de Liberacion Farabundo Marti, one of five armed groups forming the FMLN.

IMET: International Military Education and Training—a DOD training assistance program.

JRG: Junta Revolucionaria de Gobierno—the governing junta of El Salvador from 15 October 1979 to 2 May 1982 consisting primarily of young military officers and PDC members.

LP-28: Ligas Populares 28 de Febrero—a violent leftist organization of the streets.

MNR: Movimiento Nacional Revolucionaria—leftist political group under Guillermo Ungo that competed in elections in 1988.
MTT: Mobile Training Team—a DOD entity that could travel abroad to train foreign soldiers.
NODIS: "No Dissem"—cable term for dissemination to a select group of addressees.
PDC: Partido Cristiano Democratico—center-left party of Jose Napoleon Duarte which governed El Salvador from 1982 to 1989.
UDN: Union Democratica Nacionalista—a legal political front group for the Communist Party.
USG: United States government.

ANNEX **B**

SO-CALLED ISLAMIC "RADICALISM" PLACED IN ITS HISTORIC AND THEOLOGICAL CONTEXT

OVERVIEW

As it enters the twenty-first century C.E., Islam claims more than one billion adherents worldwide. At least forty countries are Muslim-majority states, and several dozen more have sizable Muslim minorities. Beyond a common profession of faith: *There is no God but Allah, and Muhammad is his Messenger*; the acceptance of the Holy Qur'an as God's Revealed Word to Man; and certain ritual obligations, there is actually little that unifies this enormous mass of humanity.

From the Muslim perspective, the True Religion was revealed to Man in stages during the early years of the seventh century C.E. The Prophet Muhammad was born to the Hashim clan of the Qureish tribe of Arabs about 570 C.E. in the Arabian province of Hejaz, bordering on the Red Sea. An orphan, Muhammad was brought up by his uncle, Abu Talib. A skilled camel drover, Muhammad emerged as a successful merchant and caravan leader who is thought to have made numerous trips northward into what was then the Byzantine province of Syria. His wife, and his first convert to Islam, was Khadija, who had been a wealthy widow who employed Muhammad to oversee her caravans prior to their marriage.

At that time Mecca was an important trading center, but it was also a religious center that boasted the Black Stone (in the Ka'aba) and various idols, especially of the Moon Goddess. Pockets of Jews and some Christians lived in Hejaz and Yemen. Across the Red Sea, Abyssinia was a Christianized empire, but for the Arab communities, whether city dwellers or Bedouin, the period was one of internal disunion, foreign invasion, and social dislocation. This condition was called *Jahiliyya* which means ignorance or spiritual darkness.

The angel Gabriel appeared to Muhammad about 610 C.E. and commanded him to "recite." By this means, God revealed His Will for Mankind through Muhammad who thereafter became known as Allah's Messenger. Muslims hold that the Qur'an was not created, nor was it a product of Muhammad's thought or literary prowess, but literally dictated by God. (Having been dictated by God through Gabriel to Muhammad means that the Qur'an is accurate and valid only in Arabic.) Muslims also hold the Torah and the Bible as divine Books—revelation—but not having the same absolute authority as the Qur'an. From the Muslim perspective, the Holy Books of the Jews and Christians are "inspired," and reflect God's Will, but are incomplete and, in any case, were falsified or misused by Jewish rabbis and Christian apostles and priests.

Barely thirty years after the Prophet's death, Islam divided into two major sects, the Sunni (taken from *Sunnah* or tradition) and the Shi'ite (from *Shi'a* or party of Ali). The cause of the split was a dispute over the succession to the Prophet between the heirs of the Caliph Uthman and the Prophet's son-in-law, Ali. Ali was murdered in 661 C.E. Ali's supporters believed that rightful succession should follow the bloodline of the Prophet. Details of this struggle lie outside the scope of this discussion, but it is important to know that both Shi'ites and Sunnis regard each other with certain hostility as apostates. Sunnis constitute perhaps 85 percent of the world Muslim community, and although use of violence is not unknown to Shi'ite groups such as Hezbollah, it was largely the majority Sunni Muslims who developed the theology of violence that gave rise to Al-Qaida and similar groups.

THEOLOGY OF ISLAM

Islam simply means "submission to God's Will" and is best understood as totally accepting the Deity's revealed guidance in all matters, personal or professional, and uncomplaining acceptance of Allah's sovereign Will, whatever it should be. In this view, there is no room for deviation from what God prescribes, nor exercise of one's personal will or desires. Acceptance by a Believer is total. A simplistic formulation of this faith might be: God said it; I believe it; that settles it. A modern Muslim scholar, the Maulana Sayyid Abul Al'a Maududi (1903–1979 C.E.) put it this way: "A Muslim who believes in the Qur'an as the Word of Allah cannot dare to differ with the Qur'an." [Maududi, *Fallacy of Rationalism*]

Of course, it isn't that simple. Like other holy texts, the Qur'an is often abstruse, vague and even contradictory in places. Because this is the case, Islamic scholars have debated the meanings of Qur'anic passages for centuries. Complicating the religious picture was the rapid growth of a body of Traditions (*hadith*) of what the Prophet was believed to have said or done in specific situations. Many items of the *hadith* were of doubtful origin and crafted centuries after the Prophet's death.

As the Islamic Empire expanded, first under the Omayyads (661-750 C.E.) and later the Abbasids (750–1258 C.E.) these debates became more intense due to two factors. First, the Muslims came to rule over many provinces of the Byzantine Empire; they conquered the Sassanid Empire (the final pre-Islamic Persian empire) in its entirety; and invaded other principalities from Spain to India. Many of the subject peoples had cultures, religions, and legal practices centuries old that in some fashion had to be accommodated into the Islamic Caliphate. Second, by absorbing non-Arab cultures and their advanced science and technology, a modernization of the traditional Arab way of life began to take place. Certainly the cosmopolitan Arab world of the Abbasid Caliph Haroun ar-Rashid (ca 800 C.E.) was not the limited, tribal world of the Prophet in Medina just two hundred years earlier. In theological terms, "innovation" (*bid'a*) began to creep into Islam with the spread of the faith into new lands.

The most significant fundamentalist challenge to this cosmopolitan Islam came from the thirteenth century scholar Ibn Taymiyya (1263–1328 C.E.) who lived in Syria at the time of the Mongol invasions. Mongol armies destroyed the Abbasid Caliphate in 1258 C.E. amid much slaughter and devastation. Albeit simplistically put, Ibn Taymiyya's view was that these calamities were God's judgment on His people for straying far from His Word. Muslims were being punished for their religious laxity and deviation from God's Revelation in the Qur'an.

Ibn Taymiyya, a member of the Hanbali School, held that the *shari'a*

(Islamic law) was complete in and of itself and, if followed faithfully, would keep the Believers from all harm. He attacked all practices and beliefs that he felt undermined or detracted from God's Word.

THE WORD OF GOD AS LAW

It was in the time of the Abbasids that the four principal schools of Sunni Islamic jurisprudence, of which the Hanbali School was one, came into existence, codifying what is called *shari'a* or religious law. These Schools were attempts by scholars to interpret the Qur'an and *hadith* for the people of that time. From least to most restrictive, these are: Shafi'i, Maliki, Hanafi, Hanbali. While discussion of the differences between these Four Schools is beyond our scope here, what is important is the fact that nearly every Sunni Muslim subscribes to one of these schools of thought. It is the most severe school, the Hanbali, accepted in Saudi Arabia, which gave rise to the fundamentalist tradition of Muhammad ibn Abd al-Wahhab (ca 1706–1792 C.E.) Next most severe is the Hanafi school, dominant in Central Asia, Pakistan, and India, that gave rise to the Deobandis.

What must be understood about the Qur'an is the fact that it prescribes not just a system of "right beliefs," but an entire way of life. It sets guidelines for one's daily practices, diet, relations with family and community, law and politics, manner of speech and dress, and many other topics.

All Muslims hold that the Word of God as revealed in the Qur'an is universal for all of Mankind, is timeless, and is total and complete. Put another way, God's Word knows no national or ethnic borders, and lays out everything one needs to know—*and do*—to lead a Godly life in this world and to prepare for entry into Paradise in the next. Since it is total, there can be no equivocation by Believers. Either one accepts the Qur'an as is, and is therefore considered a Muslim, or one must reject Scripture. There is no middle way of accepting some parts of the Qur'an, but not others. Of course, as with other faith systems, rejection can only mean one is a *kafir*: an unbeliever, sinful, and unclean. Fundamentalist Believers hold that only the strictest adherence to Holy Scripture can save Man (and the community) from disaster and spiritual death.

WHAT SALAFISM REALLY MEANS

The term *Salafi* is often used incorrectly to denote violent extremists. In point of fact, it is a reference to the *al-Salaf-al-Salih* or the righteous ancestors or companions of God's Messenger. Figuratively, a Salafist refers to one who lives according to the core beliefs of Islam, and seeks to rejuvenate or renew the original form of the faith. The great majority of Salafists, while certainly pious, are neither extremist nor inclined to violence. They are, however, divided into progressive and fundamentalist groups.

Salafism originated among Sunnis in the nineteenth century C.E. in reaction to colonialism and contact with the technology and advanced scientific thinking of the West. In that day, thoughtful and progressive Muslim scholars attempted to understand how and why the Christian West had achieved technological and political supremacy over the Muslim world. Some thought that if Western science and rational, scientific thinking could be integrated into Islam it would strengthen the faith. Anglophiles such as Sir Sayyid Ahmad Khan (1819–1898 C.E.) believed that Western liberal education was the pathway to Muslim advances. Today the progressives make up a sizable portion of Salafi ranks. These Salafists are still committed to incorporating what is best from Western science and thought, provided that it not conflict with core Islamic belief.

In many ways, the attempt to introduce modern, rational thinking into nineteenth century Muslim society had the same impact as did the introduction of Copernican astronomy to fifteenth century Europeans. Western rational thinking caused great conflict between old and new, and between secular thought and a deeply religious worldview. This posed a challenge to Muslim dogma and thinking styles that had stood for centuries.

As the twentieth century opened, some Muslims began to turn away from attempts to harmonize Western rational thought with Qur'anic traditions. Many secularists abandoned hope of modernizing Islam *per se* and opted to maintain only the outward trappings of the faith. Some leaders adopted a form of Muslim nationalism based on Western secular models. Examples of this approach include Nasser in Egypt, the Ba'ath Party in Iraq and Syria, and Ataturk's reform of Turkey. Islam became merely a veneer for them to justify what were essentially secular policies.

But for others—those who perceived a dire threat to core Islamic beliefs—the only option was to reject altogether Western ideals, Western rationalism, and Western education. They viewed Western intellectual penetration as a new form of *Jahiliyya*, separating Man from God and creating new gods in the form of capitalism, secularization, and agnosticism. The implication for these traditionalist thinkers was that Islam would be subverted, and that the *Ummah*, the community of Believers, would follow materialistic idols and melt away to nothing.

Here it is important to understand that there are five filters through which objects, techniques, and practices are viewed by Muslims. At polar opposites are those things that are Obligatory (that must be performed, such as prayer or profession of faith) and Prohibited (forbidden by Allah). Just short of Obligatory are things that are Recommended. These are not mandatory, but are highly suggested. Short of Prohibited stand those things that are Reproved. While not forbidden, Reproved activities are not considered especially worthy or acceptable conduct. However, in the middle stands the Neutral category. Here may be placed all other activities and things not mentioned in the Qur'an, assuming they do not violate Islamic principles.

The dividing line between progressive Salafists and those of a fundamentalist persuasion concerns what is Neutral. Fundamentalists hold that *if a thing is not specifically permitted or recommended* in the Qur'an, it cannot be in accord with God's wishes. The progressives, on the other hand, hold that *if a thing is not specifically prohibited*—for example, driving cars, eating ice cream, or studying physical science—then these activities are perfectly permissible for Muslims. In this way Salafists are divided into two groups, one of which favors absorbing certain Western ideas and methods, and the more conservative group rejecting all modern things as abhorrent innovations.

The fundamentalist Salafists—moving in a direction completely opposite to that of Sir Sayyid Ahmad Khan and the progressives—believe that salvation of the *Ummah* and of individual Believers lies only in a return to the strict practice of the True Religion. And the True Religion is that practiced by the Messenger and his Companions in the seventh century C.E.

Typifying this fundamentalist thinking were those like the Maulana Maududi and his intellectual heir Sayyid Qutb (1906–1966 C.E.) In their view, the common man had virtually abandoned true Islam for a mentality that was essentially Western and rational, and that all societies had reverted to a state of *Jahiliyya*. They hold further that Western pragmatism leads inevitably to rampant materialism where morals cease to govern behavior, and all that matters is material gain and self-aggrandizement. Fundamentalists believe that all material goods and property are owned by God alone, not by individuals, and are to be held for the good of society as a whole. At best, an individual is a temporary steward of God's possessions and must use these only as God dictates.

As mentioned, fundamentalist Salafists view innovation (*bid'a*) as any practice or cultural modification not specified by the Qur'an or the *hadith*. (As the *hadith* is made up of traditions stemming from what Muslims *believe* the Prophet did or said, it can be a source of substantial friction between different "schools" of Islam.) Departures from the perfect Revelation of God could only result in a return to *Jahiliyya*. Thus, the fundamentalist also is convinced that to save Man from himself *Jahiliyya* must be confronted and opposed wherever it is found. Since *Jahiliyya* applies to regimes that are deemed un-Islamic, the clear implication is that such "Others than God" must be struck down. However, it is important to note that only a fraction of even the fundamentalist thinkers believe that violence is the correct means to this end.

THE CONCEPT OF "SEPARATION FROM GOD'S WILL"

Jahiliyya is a key concept in Islam, and is of central importance to most contemporary fundamentalist Salafist thinkers like Sayyid Qutb, the Egyptian scholar whose work *Milestones* may be the most significant theoretical work on which so-called Islamic "radicalism" rests. Understood theologically, *Jahiliyya* signifies ignorance, spiritual darkness, and separation from God. Muslims, and certainly Salafist thinkers, view a state in which darkness, barbarity, and evil prevail as *Jahiliyya*. It was precisely such a world that existed in Arabia before God revealed the Qur'an to His Messenger.

In Qutb's view, *Jahiliyya* is caused by Man's allegiance to the rule of Others than God. This might well be enslavement to ungodly habits caused by ignorance and spiritual darkness, but it could also mean one's submission to ungodly governments. The point is that only by removal of the Others than God can a right relationship be restored between Man and his sovereign: Allah. *It is in the sense of removal of regimes or powers thought to interpose their will over that of God that Islam takes on a political character.* From a theological viewpoint, whatever stands in the way of Man's total submission to God must be removed; nothing and no one must separate Man from God. The Jew or Christian understands this idea as the first of the Ten Commandments: "Thou shalt have no other gods before me." In Islam the term gods does not mean merely idols, but all allegiances, interests and ties to any Others than God.

Contemporary Islamic thinkers view the True Religion as liberation from slavery to *Jahiliyya*. In a social and political context these scholars hold that because of Man's willfulness, greed and self-importance, he usurps God's rightful authority in every age. In political life, this means the establishment of kingdoms, republics, and dictatorships and the imposition of man-made laws, whether by elected parliaments, a king's ministers, or a dictator's party. Earthly powers crowd out God's voice, substituting men's own, and thus turn Man away from his rightful submission to God. God's laws are forgotten and Man then goes astray.

Sayyid Qutb held that there were three causes of *Jahiliyya* in the present era. The first of these is the ungodly (*kafir*) governments of the Islamic world; in his view, all of them are apostates and traitors. Of interest is that his second target is the *Ulema*, the scholars of Islam, who he considers have gone off the track spiritually and are leading the *Ummah* astray. Only third does he list the secular West which he regards as godless and materialist. What is important to understand is that for Qutb and his followers, the main target for violence is not the West, but Muslim regimes and clerics.

THE PROPHET OF VIOLENCE

In 1964, in his book *Milestones*, fundamentalist Salafist Qutb in his work postulated two methods of attacking *Jahiliyya*. These he called preaching and movement. They are to be used in tandem not only to restore purity in Islam, but also to advance Islam's banners into *kufr* (disbelief as opposed to *kafir*, disbeliever or unbeliever) territory. Preaching or *da'wa* is recruitment of new Believers by proselytizing. Movement is a euphemism for using religiously sanctioned force: *jihad*. It is of little consequence whether force is applied by a single terrorist acting alone or insurgents as a team so long as the goal remains destroying the institution or the *kufr* practice that intervenes between wayward Man and his God. Qutb is careful to say that movement is directed not at people, but at *institutions* that prevent a truly Islamic social order from arising.

The concept of *jihad* is as old as the Qur'an itself. Taken literally the word means striving or perhaps struggle. However, Muslim scholars differentiate between a greater and a lesser *jihad.* The greater *jihad* is a striving within oneself against one's own sinful and willful ways. In a sense, it is a spiritual struggle against Others than God that dwell inside each Believer. The lesser *jihad,* which is more familiar to the man in the street, is armed struggle against an enemy. The majority of Sunni muftis would place emphasis on the greater *jihad* as vital for Believers. The lesser *jihad* is deemed legitimate only if Muslim territory is attacked or when *da'wa* (preaching) is prevented. Since *da'wa* is God's Call to all mankind to take up the True Religion, those who impede God's preaching are in fact opposing God. However, a true *jihad* cannot be waged without the command of an imam—at its simplest, the prayer leader of a mosque—who is the legitimate leader of the Islamic community.

In the Prophet's day, the tiny Muslim community was surrounded by enemies and the Believers were often forced into battle. In theory, all able-bodied Muslim males constituted a militia and were called upon to defend the community. During the period of Islamic expansion, regular armies were created, and these in fact often included non-Muslim components. But the calling of *jihad* was carefully limited to certain conditions and called only by certain authorities. As God's Messenger, Muhammad certainly possessed the authority to call for *jihad* when so commanded by God.

Sayyid Qutb states that all Muslim regimes are *kuffar* (ungodly) and have forfeited all Islamic legitimacy. Since there is no extant Islamic government, there is no rightly guided leader. However, since the entire world has slipped into *Jahiliyya* (spiritual darkness), it is incumbent on all Muslims to act. As mentioned, this takes the dual form of preaching and fighting (movement). But Qutb takes *jihad* further. He brands all *Ulema* and other Muslims who do not share his vision of fire and sword to be *kuffar* (plural of *kafir*): ungodly ones. To declare someone a *kafir* is to hold that person as an atheist, an enemy of Islam. Put simply, one who is *kafir* is by definition an enemy of God and must therefore be destroyed. Second, Qutb holds that all Believers must participate in violent *jihad.* If they do not do so, they will be cursed by God. This theology leaves no wiggle room to Muslims. According to Qutb, they must either join the movement and wage war, or they will be eternally damned. Qutb holds that *jihad* is an obligation on all Muslims, and that it is only by waging total war on non-Islamic institutions and practices that the faith can be restored.

Although Qutb was executed by the Egyptian government in 1966 at the age of fifty-nine, his ideas passed to Islamic scholars who were invited to teach in Saudi Arabia in the 1970s. These included his brother, Mohammed Qutb, and others holding theologically conservative views. In Saudi Arabia a kind of intellectual mating took place between the state-sponsored Unitarian (Wahhabist) theology and that of the Qutbists. It may be that contemporary extremism resulted from this fusion, and partly in reaction to three traumatic events of 1979: the overthrow of the Shah in Iran, the seizure of the Grand Mosque in Mecca, and the Soviet invasion of Afghanistan. Perhaps these events served as accelerators to transform what heretofore had been merely fundamentalist theory into violent extremist action.

It can be seen at once that Qutb's violent fundamentalist Salafist view of Man and society is not only irreconcilable with contemporary Western rationalist thinking, but also with progressive Muslim thought and even the majority of nonviolent fundamentalists. Given that Qutb and the extremist Salafists have made an analysis of the ills of modern society and the threat to Islam as they perceive it, their prescription for change is a violent form of *jihad* or struggle. In a way, the Qutbist view of the world resembles Soviet cultural czar of the 1940s Andrei Zhdanov's "Two Camp" theory of Marxism and capitalism in which one inevitably must prevail over the other. Basing his core philosophy on a passage in the Qur'an—"Let those then fight in the cause of Allah who would exchange the present life with the Hereafter. Whoso fights in the cause of Allah, be he slain or be he victorious, We shall soon give him a great reward." [*Al Nisa* 4:74-75]—Qutb states the objective is to establish God's order and way of life in the world. This is clearly a millenarian viewpoint, here again somewhat akin to the Marxist-Leninist view that communism must eventually triumph throughout the world, whether spread peaceably or by the sword.

Sayyid Qutb's severe, but cogent theology and extremist theory influenced many of the current senior leaders of Al-Qaida, most notably Ayman al-Zawahiri and, indirectly, Osama bin-Laden. Zawahiri was a junior member of the Muslim Brotherhood when fellow member Qutb was hanged in 1966 by the Nasser regime. A decade later, Qutb's brother, Mohammed, taught a young bin-Laden at the Abd-al-Aziz University in Saudi Arabia.

Although car bombs and guerrilla attacks receive glaring attention by the media, it is in fact the slow, inexorable work of extremist recruitment and indoctrination of a new generation of extremists that is the greater threat to Middle Eastern regimes and the West. The preaching of the extremist Qutbist ideology to young men and women and their psychological shaping ensures that the doctrines of jihadist violence will pass to new generations and spread to ever-greater areas geographically.

"RADICALISM" SEEN IN PERSPECTIVE

As noted, the global Islamic community, or *Ummah*, consists of more than one billion Believers. What must be kept in mind, however, is the fact that hundreds of millions of Muslims are not Arabs. Indeed, the world's most populous Muslim country is Indonesia. Arabs of all countries constitute only about one fifth of the *Ummah*. Although in theory all Believers are One in Faith, Muslims in western China, the African republic of Mali, Albania, or Bangladesh are separated from the Arabs and each other by vast differences of language, culture, and history. Indeed, an Arab Believer visiting Indonesian islands might be as shocked by the way Islam is practiced there, as would be a Papal Nuncio visiting South American Indian tribes practicing Catholicism in the Amazon basin. The point is that the world community of Islam, including the majority of Arabs, is by no means united or in lockstep with Al-Qaida or supportive of terrorism.

In point of fact, Islamic extremists constitute a tiny percentage of Islam's adherents, and the majority of the true extremists may be found among the members of certain schools of Islamic jurisprudence, and in certain countries. As mentioned, the two legal schools of Sunni jurisprudence that produce the bulk of the extremist thinkers are the Hanbali and Hanafi schools.

In closing this brief study, one must always keep in mind three things. First, compared to the size of the world Muslim community, the number of active extremists is very small. That said, their numbers may well grow since the extremist movement has a solid theological underpinning and a message that is attractive to many Muslims. Should the West mishandle the situation, and especially if we prove unable to defeat the extremists' ideological challenge, the Qutbist movement could grow rapidly and spread into areas presently unaffected by extremist thinking. Second, we must always remember that there are hundreds of millions of Muslims who oppose both the theology and the methods of the followers of Ibn Taymiyya, Maududi and Qutb. It is incumbent on the West to engage as many of these natural allies as possible in the fight against extremism, especially since these Believers could pose credible theological arguments for a nonviolent course that would undercut the extremists.

But perhaps the third thing is most important. The sobriquet "radical Islam" is inappropriate. Partisans of the extremist way are hardly radicals. In point of fact, these men are unapologetic *reactionaries*. Their promise is that of spiritual renewal and the vague hope of a utopian society under God where life will be perfect simply by returning to the strict Islamic practices of the seventh century C.E. Beyond that, they have little to offer by way of practical means for improving men's lives. It would be a mistake to denigrate the obviously high moral and spiritual principles presented by the extremists, but the fact that the West and its allies in the Muslim world can offer tangible betterment of people's conditions is a powerful magnet that the reactionaries cannot match. A viable strategy is therefore to meet the extremists' ideological challenge, mobilize as many allies as possible in the Muslim world, and in concert with progressive Salafists and other Muslim allies, offer the *Ummah* an attractive alternative to violent extremism.

ANNEX **C**

UNDERSTANDING FANATICISM

Once you call something evil, it's easy to justify anything you might do to harm that evil. Evil has no rights, it has no human dignity, it has to be destroyed.—Ramsey Clark, U.S. Attorney General 1967–1969

The true believer is defined against the 'other', the non-Muslim, the heretic, the blasphemer or even the follower of another sect or a Westernized non-practising [sic] Muslim. Jason Burke, *Al-Qaeda*

Fanaticism: excessive and unreasonable enthusiasm or zeal

The psychological roots of extremism are to be found in a quest for the ideal, the perfect, and in the assurance of Certainty. An extremist cannot live with, or accept, anything less. Perfection may be defined as the quality or condition of being perfect, of being without flaw. Indeed, definitions of the word perfect include the following:

- complete in all respects; without defect or omission; sound; flawless . . .
- completely correct or accurate; exact; precise . . .
- without reserve or qualification; pure; utter; sheer; complete . . .

The theory of perfection is that it cannot possibly be improved upon.

Indeed, even a slight deviation or innovative change destroys The Perfect. One cannot make The Perfect better, and there is nothing about The Perfect that needs completing or correcting.

The Perfect *is* and needs no explanation or justification for being perfect. It is complete, pure, without blemish or defect, and completely correct as it stands. Its companion is Certainty, which is the complete absence of doubt, the acceptance without question that what one believes is absolutely true and correct. What is certain is by definition fixed and settled, usually for all time, or at least until *proven* uncertain, which is a tall order.

Perfection is not something that can be debated or is subject to change or modification. What is perfect must therefore be immutable; it is the best that can possibly be; nothing could even theoretically excel in quality or exactitude what is already perfect. Like perfection, certainty cannot be subject to debate or personal opinion.

The most obvious example of The Perfect is the religious conception of a Supreme Being and the pure and precise standards of morality and conduct associated with that Being. A Supreme Being in the great monotheistic tradition of Judaism-Christianity-Islam is One without flaw, correct by definition, and who is total and complete, omniscient and omnipotent. Perfection therefore equates with the Supreme Being and is absolute, not relative, qualified or conditional. No religious system posits a flawed, limited or impure Deity. Nor is that Being subject to doubt. Religious zealots thereby can come to equate their belief systems, which derive from their conception of the Deity, as being perfect in all respects.

Examples of The Perfect may also be found in political ideologies. Since the nineteenth century secular political thinkers have put forward visions of the perfect state or society. Marx's ideal of a perfect communist society or Hitler's conception of the perfect master race are two examples of extremist thinking focused upon their respective visions of The Ideal. Each model sets out its version of perfection in human affairs. Marx, Hitler, and their respective followers were absolutely certain that these visions were completely correct, neither subject to negotiation nor open to question.

In a mental concept of The Perfect or The Ideal, flaws are simply intolerable. A flaw in an otherwise perfect diamond greatly reduces its value. But unlike a flaw in a diamond, a flaw in a theoretically perfect society (à la Marx) or in an infallible Supreme Being is simply unthinkable. What is perfect is incapable of being incomplete or flawed.

By contrast, imperfection is the condition of being not finished or complete, lacking in something; having a defect, fault or error. An imperfection is, after all, a defect or flaw of some kind. Even a slight blemish or mar reduces The Perfect to imperfection. Put another way, imperfection may be 99% perfect, but must still be imperfect. Perfection *always* must be nothing less than 100 percent. Imperfection's companion is Doubt. What is not known with 100 percent certainty is open to investigation or speculation.

The American political ideal, as expressed in the Preamble to the Constitution, is to form "a more perfect union." Understood to the Framers was the fact that the newly formed United States was far from being united, that it was, in fact, an *imperfect* union, but nonetheless a union capable of considerable improvement. Whether the Framers believed it possible for their new political creation to attain perfection is open to speculation, their language suggests *striving* for perfection, not necessarily reaching perfection. It is most likely that the Framers in 1787, like most Americans today, see the political structure of the United States as subject to constant change and evolution in order to meet the needs of a dynamic society. Thus the Framers' unspoken goal became "steady improvement" over time, and change as the need arose, rather than the immediate or even eventual attainment of some theoretical perfection, final for all time.

By contrast, the two dominant "isms" of the twentielth century, fascism and communism, set out as their ideals views of theoretically perfect states or societies. Ideologists then used these theoretical models as their benchmarks for measuring human beings and their stages of social development. To the extent that the human beings (Jews, gypsies, capitalists, etc.) or stages of social development (feudal, capitalist, bourgeois democratic, etc.) fell short of The Ideal, they were condemned . . . and often liquidated.

Religion has a special claim on the concepts of perfection and certainty. Political conceptions of perfection rely for their justification on so-called "scientific" principles of historical development or upon racial theories codified into ideologies. Religion, however, bases its claims to perfection on nothing less than the revealed Word of God. If God is perfect, then it follows that His Word must also be perfect and complete. If His Word has been made known to Man, there can be no room left for doubt or speculation, much less for public debate and political consensus.

Religions establish conceptions of The Ideal, The Perfect. And they do so by claiming a monopoly on truth. What is within the belief system, and accepted by its leaders and the followers as true, *is* true. However, what lies outside that belief system can only be either irrelevant . . .or false. Something that is irrelevant to a belief system can be ignored. But a *challenge* to a belief system—a heresy—is a contradiction that must be suppressed because, by definition, it must be false. If a heresy is allowed to survive, it has the potential for misleading the believers and steering them away from revealed truth, which is perfect. A heresy is not merely another way of understanding truth, but is disturbing to true believers because it cleverly misrepresents falsehood as truth.

It might be observed that the danger of heresy threatens political ideologies as much as religions. Although lacking a Supreme Being to provide perfect Truth as in religions, rigid ideologies like communism and fascism cannot abide revisionists or anti-Party elements. If communism represents the highest possible ideal society, then those who advocate deviations from The Ideal are in fact moving society away from perfection, moving it backwards, in fact. Thus, these deviationists or revisionists must by definition be enemies of the people.

In the case of Religion, revisionists are called heretics. Throughout history, religious leaders have dealt harshly with heretics, much as the leaders of extremist political parties in the twentieth century dealt with revisionists. Differences of opinion, even very slight differences, were the cause of extensive examinations of purported heretics, as in the case of the Holy Inquisition. The heretic was usually given an unpleasant choice: recant or be burned at stake.

It may be that the leaders and rank-and-file regard heretics (or revisionists) as being more dangerous than persons completely outside the belief system. Those who hold other views—judged as *wrong* or *misguided* by the orthodox—are more to be pitied, placing them at a social disadvantage, than to be feared. Good examples of this are Jews in thirteenth century Europe, Christians in Islamic lands, the lumpenproletariat in Bolshevik Russia, and monarchists in Nazi Germany. These *misguided* elements were to be converted to the True Faith, but were seldom considered threats to orthodoxy. However, *those members of a belief system,* of whatever stripe, who advocated some change or perhaps a new interpretation of Scripture or Ideology were threats to the orthodox.

A good example of this quest for ideological purity is given in Wolfgang Leonhard's *Child of the Revolution* in which he reports that during World War II he and fellow Marxist students of German heritage living in Moscow could have the full, unabridged text of any Nazi speech or document they desired. But the students were strictly forbidden to have the texts of any speeches or documents by or about Leon Trotsky, who was viewed as a renegade and apostate by the ruling Communist hierarchy in Moscow. Possession of even a fragment of Trotsky's works was punishable not merely by expulsion from the Communist Party of the Soviet Union, viewed in itself as a terrible disgrace, but by a prison term.

The best example of this quest for orthodoxy in European history is the ideological struggle between sixteenth century Catholicism and its Protestant challengers. Viewed as heretical by the Catholic Church and its hierarchy, Protestant beliefs and those who held them were condemned. Protestants who fell into the hands of the Inquisition or other similar bodies were ordered to recant and confess the True Faith or be tortured and executed. It may be observed that the Catholics turned upon their former coreligionists, who had now fallen away from The Faith, with a ferocity well in excess of what was directed against either Jews or Muslims in Spain.

Extremism manifests itself as well in contemporary Islam. A Muslim believes that Allah is perfect and therefore His Word is perfect. Thus, the Qur'an—revealed to Muhammad by Allah—is by definition complete, correct and perfect. Therefore, if one follows the Qur'an word for word, without the least deviation, one is following Allah. The Qur'an provides the assurance of Certainty and lays out a vision of The Ideal life and society.

The great schism within Islam, the division of the faith into Sunni and Shi'a, is easily as great a divide as between sixteenth-century Protestants and Catholics. But like the ideological struggle between the European Christians of years past, Sunnis and Shi'ites sharply divide on which interpretation of Islam is true and correct. To a true believer, there cannot be more than one true and correct path; surely then, the other path must be a false one.

For true believers, both Sunni and Shi'a, the issue is vital. Indeed, Sunnis who consider themselves Salafists or Wahhabis view Shi'ite Muslims as apostates—worse than Unbelievers. The Salafist considers that the only valid model of the Islamic life is that practiced by Muhammad and his *ansar* (helpers) in the time of the Hejira [622 CE] and that any deviation constitutes apostasy. Since the Salafists believe that Shi'ites and other fallen-away Muslims, such as those who have accepted Western styles of life and thought, are guilty of spurning God's Revealed Word, they deserve punishment by death as prescribed in the Qur'an. Indeed, *not* to carry out such divinely ordained punishment is a sin. A Sunni extremist therefore believes that he has been commanded by God to execute apostates—God's enemies—who have deviated from the true path.

Perhaps it is in the context of The Perfect and The Certain that the concept of evil presents itself. For that which falls short of The Ideal, even a tiny blemish must not only be imperfect, but *anti*-perfect. To the extent that the blemish mars The Perfect or challenges established Truth, it must be evil for it is *anti*-Truth and *anti*-Ideal.

For religious true believers, evil is to be found in those practices, institutions, or *persons* who do not conform to The Ideal. Deviation from the true path, from what is thought to be perfect, is not only wrong, but provocative. A heretic is one who makes an effort to tinker with perfection either in his thoughts or his practices. This activity introduces flaws, doubts, and errors into what would otherwise be correct and complete. The heretic must therefore be evil, not merely misguided. As Ramsey Clark noted, "evil has no rights . . . [and] has to be destroyed." The heretic must be destroyed.

A search for the sources of blemishes or imperfections, as perceived by true believers, leads to affixing blame on those persons or institutions thought responsible. If, to a Nazi theorist, Germany's society suffers from failures or faults—deviations from The Ideal—it must be that some group stabbed Germany in the back. To a Marxist, if there is poverty and exploitation, it is obvious that someone else got rich at the expense of others. And if, to a devout Salafist, the Islamic world is being humiliated and Islam itself is under threat, there must be a traitor or apostate responsible.

Evil is not identical with accountability, but neither is it far removed. Usually the group or person held accountable for some fault or flaw in what would otherwise be a perfect social system is held to be evil. This makes Evil a byproduct of the extremists' concept of what is ideal; it is a deviation from what they believe, an assault on their certainty. Evil is necessary to extremists because their condemnation of evil serves to define the extremist as good. Extremists do not validate themselves by considering the relative merits of something, or by admitting their doubts or ignorance, but by boldly asserting their certainty and lack of toleration for others' perceived shortcomings.

Things that are imperfect offer the possibility of improvement. However, the mentality best suited to dealing forthrightly with imperfection is what might be called realism, pragmatism, innovation, and even opportunism, not true belief. Innovators are likely to be persons capable of dealing with imperfection for the reason that they seek practical improvements and inventions that lead to attainment of The Better. But, unlike true believers, innovators do not necessarily seek to attain The Perfect.

Innovators probably also are better at dealing with uncertainty, and especially with the concept of Possibility. The idea of Possibility cannot exist in an ideal world ruled by Certainty. Where all things are certain, possibility disappears. Things either are or they are not. There is no room for speculation, investigation or analysis. One accepts what *is* and rules out the possibility that there could be any Possibility to be explored.

A mind trained to accept a given concept as ultimate and complete truth, be it religious or political, cannot deal with the suggestion that alternatives or especially choices exist. All extremist believers hold that Truth is absolute and immutable. There is no alternative to be considered, hence there can be no individual choice other than full acceptance—or rejection—of established doctrine. This belief encourages rote copying of what has already been established as Truth, while discouraging the search for new possibilities, alternatives, and especially new truths.

But it is precisely the search for new truths, new possibilities, that gives rise not merely to scientific methods, but to what we call rational thought. It is the exercise of reason, judgment, and experience on things observed or intellectually conceived. Philosophers and scientists are trained to test ideas based upon their merits, not to accept ideas on the basis of tradition or dogma. To a Western mind the old saw "We've always done it this way" is a joke; but to a true believer, it is central to his belief. One cannot deviate from Perfection. And since Perfection has already been revealed in dogma, the very best that one can hope for is to copy that dogma faithfully from generation to generation. Such a philosophy strives to preserve the status quo, the faded glory of some past Ideal.

A good example of this traditionalist way of thinking, based upon adherence to an established Ideal, is the education of young Muslims in British India. Author Jason Burke in *Al-Qaeda* states that the Deobandi (a fundamentalist group) "believed that Indian Muslims could preserve their separate identity by carefully following the exact ritual and personal behaviour prescribed in the Qur'an and the hadith . . . " Burke goes on to say, "The huge volume of young men educated in the medressas had a rapid and obvious impact, playing an important part in creating and propagating the narrow, dogmatic worldview that is a mark of the modern militant."[1]

One final thought about extremism is that like attracts like. Conformity with others of like mind is not merely the norm for persons given to extremist thinking, but the means of perpetuating their established belief system. As noted, heretics and revisionists are not welcome in groups wedded to rigid views. Most such groups seek fellow believers and then mold them carefully so that their views, at least overtly, completely conform with their fellows. Exclusivity of membership and conformity of views tend to reinforce the group's view, often negative, of outsiders and those with different perspectives. The strength and cohesiveness of the group's values encourages a boldness of action that would otherwise be lacking were the members acting only as individuals, that is to say, a certain excessive and unreasonable zeal which is the hallmark of fanaticism.

Extremists and the groups that they form have remarkable strengths that should not be taken lightly. Perhaps their greatest strength is precisely that of certitude: the absolute, unshakable belief that their views are true and correct. This certainty gives extremists enormous self-assurance and confidence in the inevitable triumph of their particular belief system. Down through history true believers have been able to face persecution, physical torture, and even death due to the strength of their deeply held beliefs. That these beliefs focused upon visions of The Perfect and The Ideal helped them in no small measure to propound their visions to the masses, and to tenaciously defend their views when called upon to do so. No doubts or uncertainties clouded their minds, and they felt no need for

---

[1] Burke, p. 87.

discussion, much less a need for negotiation and compromise with their foes.

But it may be that the very strength of a true believer's beliefs is his Achilles heel. The extremist cannot conceive of any other truth but his own. He is so certain of his views that he cannot accept the merits of an opposing view, the possibility that an alternative might also be correct. Given his mindset, it is impossible for an extremist to conceive that doubt and uncertainty might lead ultimately to greater wisdom. Most paralyzing to an extremist is the fragility of his belief system: if it shows even the slightest crack or flaw, The Perfect has been destroyed. And with its collapse, the true believer's reason for being—indeed, his very identity and self-image as *good* in an *evil* world—vanishes.

ANNEX D

VIET CONG POLITICAL MOBILIZATION IN PHU YEN PROVINCE

The following material is reprinted verbatim from an article written by George McArthur of the *Los Angeles Times* that appeared in April 1970 in the *Pacific Stars and Stripes*. The author, then an Army captain stationed in Binh Dinh Province immediately north of Phu Yen, had been grasping for some understanding of the reasons for Communist success in insurgency despite overwhelming American military power. McArthur's article gave insight into Viet Cong methods, especially as they relate to building political power through careful indoctrination at the grassroots level.

The article describes what happened in Phu Yen in late 1969 and early 1970 that seemed to reverse what the U.S. command in Saigon had believed was pacification of that province. The program of the Viet Cong in this province at that time stands as a model against which other insurgent efforts at indoctrination and political mobilization may be compared.

George McArthur, "Phu Yen—Province That 'Went to Sleep'" *Los Angeles Times,* reprinted in *Pacific Stars and Stripes*, 10 April 1970

TUY HOA, Vietnam—In recent weeks, a rejuvenated Communist guerrilla force in Phu Yen Province has been slipping down by night from the foothills overlooking the verdant coastal plain and abducting—with little or no resistance—about 400 men.

In the official language of this war they were "abducted," but the word is not entirely accurate. All of them may or may not have been taken by force. Some have come back not at all displeased at having been given Communist indoctrination.

And although the more or less official number is 400, it may well have been higher. Such things frequently do not get reported in South Vietnam.

The precise number is hardly significant. It is significant that the abductions met with little resistance, if any, and that they were done on such a scale right under the noses of militia forces well enough armed and supposedly strong enough to curb such things.

In short, the abductions indicate that the war is going badly in Phu Yen Province, a test area for the "Vietnamization" process where the confrontation is largely between old-fashioned Communist guerrilla forces and militia of the Saigon government.

This is not to say that Phu Yen Province is going down the drain or that the reversal has been total. It is evident, however, that Saigon's forces have suffered one of those setbacks which Secretary of Defense Melvin R. Laird warned were inevitable. And although U.S. and top South Vietnamese officials in Saigon are well aware of the erosion in Phu Yen, measures to restore the situation are not in sight.

The difficulties of accurately judging what is happening in Vietnam are indicated by the situation in Phu Yen. Recently it was 14th from the top of South Vietnam's 45 provinces on the Saigon pacification scale. Nowadays, one expert said, it is one of the three or four worst.

Midway up the coast between the Mekong Delta and the 17th Parallel, Phu Yen's white-sand beaches, ocean breezes and languid palms arouse visions of South Sea delights. Fat cows and chubby youngsters wander through seemingly placid villages. There is enough rice and fish for the 300,000 population.

Although the province was an old-time Viet Cong stronghold, it seemed until late last year to be approaching surprising pacification. All the statistical indicators pointed in the right direction.

Then, one official recalled, "The rains came and everyone went to sleep." There was 21 inches of rain on one night alone last October [1969]. Nobody wanted to fight. By the end of the year the Communist force in the hills had quietly changed its tactics, however, adapting to the political warfare and small-unit maneuvers now called for.

The abductions began in earnest during early February. With evident ease, small guerrilla bands slipped through militia outposts and areas where ambushes were supposedly set up.

Of the 400 men and boys abducted, about half or more have come back. They told South Vietnamese interrogators they were held four or five days for indoctrination by the Viet Cong. Many have reportedly totally accepted the Communist version of the war and the accusation that the Saigon government is a puppet.

Several explanations for the abductions were offered. But the most significant is that the Communist command is seeking out soft spots in South Vietnam to win "defectors" and then leave them to influence future political developments.

BIBLIOGRAPHY

Barnett, A. Doak. *China on the Eve of Communist Takeover*. New York: Frederick A. Praeger, 1963.

Brown, Deneen. "At Anacostia museum, roots are found in translation." *Washington Post*. 6 Aug 2010. < http://www.washingtonpost.com/wp-dyn/content/article/2010/08/05/AR2010080506709.html>.

Buckley, Tom. *Violent Neighbors: El Salvador, Central America, and United States*. New York: Times Books, New York Times Book Co., Inc, 1984.

Burke, Jason. *Al-Qaeda: The True Story of Radical Islam*. London: Penguin Books Ltd., 2004.

Buttinger, Joseph. *Vietnam: A Political History*. New York: Frederick A. Praeger, 1968.

Christian, Shirley. *Nicaragua: Revolution in the Family*. New York: Vintage Books, Random House, 1986.

Cicero, Marcus Tullius. *De Officiis*. Trans. Walter Miller. Cambridge: Harvard University Press, 1913.

Clausewitz, Karl von. *Vom Kriege (On War)*. Ed. and trans. Michael Howard and Peter Paret, Princeton, NJ: Princeton University Press, 1976.

Clubb, O. Edmund; *Twentieth Century China*. New York: Columbia University Press, 1966.

Connable, Ben and Martin C. Libicki. *How Insurgencies End*. RAND, National Defense Research Institute; Santa Monica, CA, and Arlington, VA, 2010.

Cray, Ed. *General of the Army George C. Marshall, Soldier and Statesman*.

New York: Cooper Square Press, 2000.

Crouch, Elisa. "Colleges find area freshmen unready." *St. Louis Post-Dispatch.* 2 January 2011. <http://www.stltoday.com/news/local/education/article_868835a6-c104-5a33-a37b-42c733c6dcab.html>.

Dostoevsky, Fvodor. *The Brothers Karamazov.* Trans. Richard Pevear and Larissa Volokhonsky. New York:Farrar, The New American Library, Inc., 1957.

DuPuy, Ernest and Trevor N. DuPuy. *Encyclopedia of Military History.* New York: Harper and Row Publishers, 1977.

Ebner, Gregory R., Major. "Scientific Optimism: Jomini and the U.S. Army." The U.S. Army Professional Writing Collection. Combat Studies Institute Command and General Staff College (July 2004).

Ellul, Jacques. *Propaganda: The Formation of Men's Attitudes.* Trans. Konrad Kellen and Jean Lerner. New York: Knopf, 1965.

Fall, Bernard B. *Street Without Joy.* New York: Schocken Books, 1964.

Fehrenbach, T.R. *Fire and Blood: A History of Mexico.* New York: Da Capo Press, 1995.

Fremantle, Anne. *Mao Tse-tung: An Anthology of his Writings.* New York: Mentor Books, The New American Library, 1962.

Friedman, Lawrence. King's College London, in "Patience as well as power is the key to Coalition victory" in *The Times*, 28 March 2003. <http://www.timesonline.co.uk/tol/life_and_style/article1123879.ece>.

Garfield, James A. *The Works of James Abram Garfield.* Ed: Burke Hinsdale. Boston: James R. Osgood and Company, 1883, Vol. II, "A Century of Congress, 1987."

Gettleman, Marvin E., Ed. *Vietnam.* New York: Fawcett, 1965.

Greenberg, Lawrence M., Major; "The Hukbalahap Insurrection: A Case Study of a Successful Anti-Insurgency Operation in the Philippines, 1946–1955" Analysis Branch, U.S. Army Center of Military History; Washington, D.C., 1987.

Grivas, George. *General Grivas on Guerrilla Warfare.* New York: Praeger, 1965.

Hayek, Friedrich von. *The Counterrevolution of Science: Studies on the Abuse of Reason.* Indianapolis: Liberty Press, 1979.

Hammes, Thomas X. *The Sling and the Stone.* St. Paul, MN: Zenith Press, 2004.

Hubbard, Elbert. *The Book of Business.* New York: Roycrofters East Aurora, 1913.

Kaplan, Robert D. "The Coming Anarchy," *The Atlantic Monthly*, February 1994.

Katz, William. "The Ultimate Weapon." *Free Hudson New York.* 8 Oct. 2009. <http://www.hudson-ny.org/852/the-ultimate-weapon>.

Kilcullen, David. *The Accidental Guerrilla.* New York: Oxford University Press, 2009.

LeBeau, John J.; "The Renaissance of Insurgency and Counter-Insurgency: Examining Twenty-First Century Insurgencies and Government Responses," *The Quarterly Journal*, Spring 2008.

Lenin, Vladimir Ilyich. *Lenin Collected Works.* 4th English Edition. Trans. Dora Cox. Moscow: Progress Publishers, 1968.

Les, Christie. "America's Smartest Cities." *CNN Money.* 1 Oct. 2010. <http://finance.yahoo.com/career-work/article/110890/americas-smartest-cities?mod=career-worklife_balance>.

Liddell Hart, B.H. *Strategy.* New York: Frederick A. Praeger, 1967.

Lipset, Seymour Martin. *Political Man: The Social Bases of Politics.* Garden City, New York: Anchor Books, Doubleday and Company, 1963.

Mao Tse-tung. *Selected Military Writings.* Beijing: Peking Foreign Languages Press, 1963.

Mao Tse-tung, *On Guerrilla Warfare.* Trans. Brigadier General Samuel B. Griffith, USMC (Retired). Champaign, Illinois: University of Illinois Press, 1961,

McHenry, J. Patrick; *A Short History of Mexico*; Doubleday and Co.; Garden City, New York, 1962

Moore, Frank, *Diary of the Revolution 1775–1781*, Washington Square Press, Inc., New York, 1968

Nagl, John; *Learning to Eat Soup with a Knife. Counterinsurgency Lessons from Malaya and Vietnam.* Chicago: University of Chicago Press, 2005.

National Geographic. "Water—Our Thirsty World: A Special Issue" *National Geographic Magazine.* April 2010:1-184.

Nickols, Fred; "Strategy: Definitions and Meanings" occasional paper, Distance Consulting; 2003.

Nyozekan, Hasegawa. *Ushinawareta Nihon (The Lost Japan).* Tokyo: Keiyusha, 1952.

Paret, Peter. *French Revolutionary Warfare from Indochina to Algeria*. New York: Frederick A. Praeger, 1964.

Peter Paret, Ed. *Makers of Modern Strategy*. Princeton University Press, 1986.

Peterson, Houston, Ed. *A Treasury of the World's Great Speeches*. New York: Simon and Schuster, 1967.

Pottier, Philippe. GCMA/GMI: a French experience in counterinsurgency during the French Indochina war; Master's thesis, U.S. Marine Corps Command and Staff College; Quantico, Virginia; academic year 2003–2004

Pressfield, Steven. *Gates of Fire: An Epic Novel of the Battle of Thermopylae*. New York: Bantam Dell, 1998.

Rabelais, Francois and Charles Whibley. *Gargantua and Pantagruel*, Books 1-3. Trans. Sir T. Urquhart, March 2008.

SAR Magazine, The. "Back Where He Belongs: Returning George Washington to schools across America." Fall 2010: p. 11.

Sheehan, Neil. *A Bright Shining Lie: John Paul Vann and the American Experience in Vietnam*. New York: Vintage, 1988.

Sun Tzu. *The Art of War*. Trans. Samuel B. Griffith. New York: Oxford University Press, 1963.

Tuchman, Barbara W. *The March of Folly: From Troy to Vietnam*. New York: Alfred A. Knopf, 1984.

United States Department of State. Incoming Telegram (NOD 139), 1958.

United States Government Accountability Office: Report to Congressional Committees. *An Overview of Professional Development Activities Intended to Improve Interagency Collaboration (GAO-11-108)*. Washington, November 2010: 1–58.

Vo Nguyen Giap; *People's War People's Army: The Viet Cong Insurrection Manual for Underdeveloped Countries*. New York: Frederick A. Praeger, 1962.

Ward, Geoffrey C. and Ken Burns. *The War: An Intimate History*. New York: Alfred A. Knopf, 2010.

INDEX

D

T

W

Z